It has been 266 years since Robberd Hutchinson, defendant in one of the earliest cases on record, was whipped in the town of New Castle, and Delaware is still lashing her criminals! In fact, from 1900 to 1945 she whipped over sixteen hundred prisoners, and today her laws prescribe lashes for twenty-four different crimes.

Originally the "post" in southern Delaware was painted red, and when a prisoner was whipped the Negroes used to say that he had hugged Red Hannah. And Red Hannah, an anachronism in this day of scientific penology, remains the conspicuous symbol of the medieval jurisprudence that exists not only in Delaware but in varying degrees throughout the United States. However, since Delaware is the only state still to authorize and use whipping as a punishment for a number of crimes, she presents herself as the logical place for an urgently needed study of the value of this method of punishment.

This first serious survey of the centuries-old controversy raging around Delaware's continued use of the whipping post is told against a background of historical incident and sociological fact. A book for the general reader as well as for those interested in the special fields of history, sociology, law and penology.

A DELAWARE WHIPPING POST IN 1872

Red Hannah

DELAWARE'S WHIPPING POST

By

Robert Graham Caldwell

Philadelphia
UNIVERSITY OF PENNSYLVANIA PRESS
London: Geoffrey Cumberlege
Oxford University Press
1947

Copyright 1947
UNIVERSITY OF PENNSYLVANIA PRESS
Manufactured in the United States of America

To
LaMerle

FOREWORD

THE lash is probably the oldest of all punishments in the world. Its use rests on the belief that wrongdoing should be paid for by physical pain, "taken out of the culprit's hide"; that physical suffering is a correction that even the simplest mind can understand and try to avoid in the future; or that it is a kind of solvent cleansing the spirit and rendering an evil mind good. Thus the ingredients of vengeance, deterrence, and reformation have been blended, with a dash of expectation that the general public, knowing the threat of pain, would desist from violations of the law.

Whipping is still occasionally defined by the law of a few nations as a punishment for crime, but in modern times the tendency toward its abolition has been marked. Modern psychology has punctured the belief that physical violence practised on a person can render him a better man; indeed, it has proved that it usually makes him worse. And if man is not made better by a punishment, his future actions will hardly be governed by it. The deterrent power of the lash is therefore absent. Nor has any evidence been adduced to show that whipping frightens others into law obedience. Such an effect can hardly be postulated when one considers the nature of this penalty today. Finally, it has been alleged, and is probably true, that whipping has a brutalizing effect on those who inflict it. The beating of any defenseless person cannot but leave a mark on the executioner.

What then remains? Vengeance. If the whipping post neither deters nor reforms — and the author of this book has proved his case on these points — nor scares the prospective offender, its only purpose is to exact vengeance, a sordid motive for punishment which has no place in a democratic penal code. As if conscious of this, the legislator usually hides the whipping post inside the walls of the prison, safe from public gaze, like the family skeleton in the closet.

Enlightened democracies recognize today that penal legislation must protect society against crime by returning the offender to society better able to resist the pressures and temptations of the workaday world, and that if this cannot be done by any known methods of treatment he must be given prolonged care until he can be released without danger to his fellow men. In this scheme, sympathetic understanding and treatment must govern, not vengeance. The whipping post belongs to the trappings of a past age or to the tyrant's arsenal of weapons. Veneration for tradition and the cult of the antique have no place in modern penal law any more than in the workshop, the laboratory, or the farm. The law must keep abreast of the growth of scientific knowledge and the demand for efficiency and positive results that stamp our material culture.

Professor Caldwell has produced in this book the first real study of Delaware's most antiquated instrument of punishment. In so doing he has served all those interested in the history of punishment. We hope that he has also earned the gratitude of his fellow Delawareans for having taken the skeleton out of the family closet and proved that it is in need of speedy burial.

THORSTEN SELLIN

Stockholm
April 15, 1947

PREFACE

THE beginning of the nineteenth century may well be considered an important turning point in the history of crime and punishment, for not until then in Western civilization did punitive imprisonment succeed in generally displacing capital and corporal penalties for serious crimes. In America, where the Old World's primitive and sanguinary methods of inflicting pain upon criminals had been widely used during the colonial period, corporal punishment for crimes was subjected to severe criticism after the Revolution as the penal reform movement, emanating from its center in Philadelphia, spread throughout the country. State after state revised its criminal code until such punishment almost entirely disappeared from the nation's statute books. Delaware, alone among the forty-eight states, has continued to prescribe this type of punishment, in the form of public whippings, as a penalty for a large number of crimes,[1] and today in each of her three counties there stands a whipping post as a warning to those who are tempted to violate the law.

By continuing to lash her criminals, Delaware has attracted a great deal of unfavorable criticism and stirred up a widespread controversy over the value of the whipping post. In the "post's" favor it has been contended that it exerts a reformative influence upon hardened criminals, that it is a more efficacious deterrent than any other penalty, and that the humiliation involved destroys the criminal's prestige and solidifies public opinion behind law and order. On the other hand, whipping has been attacked as barbaric and revolting. Its opponents argue that it embitters the prisoner, making him a confirmed enemy of society, that it disrupts the constructive process of rehabilitation, and that it fails to deter others from committing crimes.

Actually, however, even though this controversy has swirled about the "post" for a number of years, there has been a lack of factual information regarding the value of whipping as a punishment for convicted criminals. A thorough study of the subject has been urgently needed, and since Delaware is the only state that continues to authorize and use whipping as a punishment for serious crimes, she presents herself as the logical place for such a study. It is the purpose of this book, therefore, to trace the development of the whipping post in Delaware, to evaluate its deterrent and reformative influence, and to analyze the arguments that have been advanced in favor of its retention.

Many years ago the "post" in southern Delaware was painted red, and

[1] Whipping is authorized in Maryland for wife-beaters, but is rarely used.

the negroes there used to call it "Red Hannah." Today its color is different and its structure has changed, but essentially it is still Red Hannah, a symbol of the medieval criminal jurisprudence that exists not only in Delaware but in varying degrees throughout the United States. Emphasizing the crime rather than the criminal, this jurisprudence is based upon the philosophy of punishment which, despite modification, still has as its chief aim the infliction of suffering upon the convicted criminal. Thus in whipping her criminals Delaware is not fundamentally different from other states; she has simply persisted in using a more spectacular method of punishment and has thereby received more publicity.

The words of this book, therefore, are not directed primarily at the "post," which after all has become largely nominal in Delaware's criminal jurisprudence, but rather at the philosophy of punishment of which the "post" is but an expression. What is needed is not the replacement of whipping with some other method of punishment, but the elimination of all methods of punishment not only in Delaware but everywhere in the United States, and the introduction of a system of scientific treatment that would focus attention upon the causes of crime as they appear in the individual, the rehabilitation of the individual in terms of such causes, and the modification of the conditions which produce criminality.

It has proved to be impracticable to include in this book all of the tables compiled during the study of the whipping post. However, a complete set of such tables has been placed on reference in the library of the College of William and Mary, and access may be had to them through the inter-library loan system.

This preface should not be concluded without some acknowledgment of my indebtedness to those whose assistance made the study of the whipping post possible. Accordingly I wish to express my appreciation to the many state, county, and city officials of Delaware for their invaluable help and coöperation. Specific acknowledgment should be given to the Social Science Research Council for its grant-in-aid, which assisted me considerably in the gathering of data, and to Mr. Leon deValinger, Delaware State Archivist, upon whose scholarly advice I frequently relied in matters pertaining to Delaware's history.

A great debt is owed to Dr. Thorsten Sellin, eminent criminologist and Professor of Sociology at the University of Pennsylvania. It was at his suggestion and under his guidance that the study of the whipping post was undertaken. Without his encouragement and counsel it might never have been completed.

I should also like to thank Mrs. Bertha Worth for her infinite patience and painstaking accuracy in the preparation of the manuscript, and Mr. William Bennett for his skill in reproducing the photographs and sketches.

To my wife, LaMerle Caldwell, who shared significantly in the making of this book, I am indebted for long, tedious hours of collecting data, for many conferences with public officials and interviews with prisoners, for valuable criticism and advice, and for much sympathetic understanding and encouragement. Together we worked in the hope that this study might contribute in some way to the progress of modern criminology.

R. G. C.

College of William and Mary
Williamsburg, Virginia
February 14, 1946

CONTENTS

Chapter		Page
	FOREWORD, by Thorsten Sellin	vii
	PREFACE	ix
	ILLUSTRATIONS	xv
I	LASHES WELL LAID ON	1
II	THE WHIPPING POST IN COLONIAL DELAWARE, 1638 to 1776	3
III	THE WHIPPING POST AND THE PENITENTIARY MOVEMENT, 1776 to 1829	10
IV	THE WHIPPING POST EMERGES AS A SEPARATE ISSUE, 1829 to 1900	16
V	THE MOVEMENT AGAINST THE WHIPPING POST, 1900 to 1945	32
VI	THE POST — RETROSPECT AND PROSPECT	59
VII	FORTY-THREE YEARS OF WHIPPINGS IN DELAWARE	69
VIII	THE POST IN THE FORUM	83
	NOTES	102
	APPENDIX A: TABLES SHOWING THE CRIMES PUNISHABLE WITH PUBLIC WHIPPINGS	118
	APPENDIX B: AN ENUMERATION OF CRIMES PUNISHABLE WITH PUBLIC WHIPPINGS	123
	APPENDIX C: TABLES ON WHIPPINGS IN DELAWARE	126
	BIBLIOGRAPHY	132
	INDEX	141

ILLUSTRATIONS

THE WHIPPING POST AND PILLORY AT
GEORGETOWN *End Papers*
From *Harper's Weekly*, November 18, 1876

A DELAWARE WHIPPING POST IN 1872 *Frontispiece*
From *Scribner's Monthly*, March 1872

THE WHIPPING POST AND PILLORY, *Facing Page*
NEW CASTLE COUNTY JAIL, 1897   24

A WHIPPING, NEW CASTLE COUNTY JAIL, 1897   40

AN EIGHTEEN-YEAR-OLD PRISONER RECEIVING THE
LAST OF TEN LASHES, NEW CASTLE COUNTY WORK-
HOUSE   56
From the *Philadelphia Record*, January 20, 1935

THE WHIPPING POST, KENT COUNTY JAIL, 1945   88

Chapter I

LASHES WELL LAID ON

ON June 3, 1679, at a court held in the Town of New Castle, Robberd Hutchinson, the defendant in one of the earliest cases on record in Delaware, stood indicted by the "high sheriff" for having feloniously broken open a chest belonging to Adam Wallis and stolen from it goods to the value of "three pounds sterling." To this charge Robberd Hutchinson pleaded guilty, and the court, after having "duly considered and maturely deliberated upon the matter," sentenced him to be taken to the fort gate and there, as an "example to others," be publicly whipped with thirty-nine lashes. The court further ordered that the prisoner "make good unto Adam Wallis" the remainder of the goods not yet found, and pay "all the charges and fees of the court action," and that he then be forever banished from the colony.[1]

It has been 266 years since Robberd Hutchinson was whipped in the Town of New Castle, and Delaware is still lashing her criminals. In fact, from 1900 to 1945, she whipped over sixteen hundred prisoners, and today her laws prescribe lashes for twenty-four different crimes. Red Hannah, the name given to the whipping post many years ago by the negroes in southern Delaware,[2] remains the conspicuous symbol of the state's retarded criminology.

On the morning of January 10, 1945, two more of Delaware's prisoners, Freddie L. Harris and Jack Palmer, who had pleaded guilty to charges of robbery and attempted robbery, were sentenced to be whipped. In pronouncing sentence in this case, Judge Rodney of the New Castle County Court of General Sessions in Wilmington declared:

The defendants shall pay the cost of this prosecution, as to each, and be imprisoned for a period of twelve years, as to each, commencing on the 10th day of January, 1945, and ending on the 9th day of January, 1957, as to each, and on Saturday, January 20th, 1945, between the hours of 10 A.M. and 2 P.M., they are to be whipped with ten lashes, as to each, and on Saturday, January 27th, 1945, between the hours of 10 A.M. and 2 P.M., they are to be whipped with ten more lashes, as to each. And they are to be committed to the custody of the Board of Trustees of the New Castle County Workhouse until their sentences are executed, as to each.[3]

In accordance with the order of the court, the prisoners were then returned to the Workhouse, where a routine medical examination, given to everyone upon admission, had already been made to ascertain their physical condition.

Ten days later, about thirty persons, including several women, gathered in the yard of the New Castle County Workhouse to witness the public flogging of Harris and Palmer. Before each prisoner was whipped, he was stripped to the waist, his hands were shackled to the "post," and the sentence of the court was read. Warden Wilson administered the whippings, and Deputy Warden Wheatley counted as each of the ten strokes was well laid on the bare backs of the prisoners. Although the Warden kept his arm stiff at the elbow while applying the lashes,[4] nevertheless great welts were raised on the bodies of the men, both of whom screamed and struggled during the whippings. The punishment was inflicted with the traditional cat-o'-nine-tails, which consists of nine leather cords, each a quarter of an inch wide and about two feet long, attached to a stick about eighteen inches in length. After the flogging the men were taken to the prison infirmary for examination and treatment.[5] On the following Saturday, January 27, with the temperature hovering around seventeen above zero, each of the prisoners, stripped to the waist, received ten more lashes.[6] In general, the procedure followed in the sentencing and whipping of Harris and Palmer is the one that is used in all three of Delaware's counties. However, the whippings are not always divided into two parts as they were in this case.

Why does Delaware still lash her prisoners? Why does the "post," which has been widely condemned as a "relic of barbarism" and a "monument of stupidity," still stand? Why do many citizens of the "tight little state" still believe in the efficacy of the lash? For the answer to these questions, one must turn to the history of the whipping post in Delaware.

Chapter II

THE WHIPPING POST
IN COLONIAL DELAWARE, 1638 to 1776

IF we could accept without reserve the genial chronicles of Diedrich Knickerbocker, we might state that the first public whipping of a criminal in Delaware, of which we have any record, took place in 1654. In that year, according to Knickerbocker, Johan Risingh, Governor of New Sweden, visited the Dutch at Fort Casimir (now New Castle), and Van Poffenburgh, the Dutch commander, in order to honor and impress his distinguished guest, staged a long and elaborate entertainment, the crowning feature of which was the flogging of three prisoners.[1]

Unfortunately, however, just when the state's first whipping was inflicted cannot be accurately determined since little is known of the administration of justice along the Delaware from 1638 to 1664, during which time the region was under the control of Sweden and Holland.[2] Still, corporal punishment was commonly inflicted upon criminals in these countries during this period, and therefore it seems safe to assume that violators of the law were whipped in the early Swedish and Dutch forts of Delaware, and that the roots of the whipping post thus reach back to the very beginnings of the state's history.[3]

At the time of the English conquest of the settlements in the Delaware Valley in 1664, there were two outstanding characteristics of English criminal jurisprudence. These were the extreme severity of the penalties imposed and the use of some kind of corporal punishment for almost all crimes.[4] Imprisonment had not as yet been established as the most widely accepted form of punishment, and many more crimes were then designated as capital than are today.[5]

In England, as well as on the Continent, some form of corporal punishment less than death was usually inflicted in the case of crimes that were not classified as capital. Whipping, branding, mutilating, confinement in the stocks or the pillory, and "ducking" were among the most popular types of such punishment.[6] The jails of the period were used principally for the detention of those who were awaiting trial, and the majority of persons confined in the prisons were debtors and political and religious offenders.[7] As a matter of fact, it was not until the beginning of the nineteenth century that imprisonment succeeded in generally displacing capital and corporal penalties in the punishment of serious crimes.[8]

The American Colonies inherited the Old World's sanguinary

methods of punishment, and eventually all of them put into effect, in varying degrees, the barbarous English criminal code.[9] Despite this, the colonial criminal laws were never so severe as those of the mother country, and even the notorious "Blue Laws" of Connecticut, adopted in 1642 and 1650, provided for only fourteen capital crimes.[10] Of course the comparatively humane and mild Quaker codes were notably progressive and went far beyond other American criminal jurisprudence,[11] but these did not remain in force very long. Nevertheless, it should be remembered that they initiated a movement that did much to liberalize and humanize the criminal codes of the United States, and that the influence of the Society of Friends was constantly directed toward not only the reduction of the number of crimes, but also the substitution of imprisonment at hard labor for corporal punishment.[12]

With the English conquest of the Delaware Valley in 1664 there were introduced fundamental culture patterns which, in their adapted form, constitute the foundations of Delaware's present social institutions.[13] However, the establishment of English laws and customs was by no means the work of a day, and a full decade was required to nurture the seeds of English jurisprudence into even a stunted growth.[14] Naturally, during the gradual process of change, Dutch and Swedish cultural influences, as well as those of the English, continued to operate in the lives of the colonists.[15]

Near the close of 1669, while these important adjustments were being made in the government of the colony, there occurred a disturbance which was caused by the seditious utterances and acts of Marcus Jacobson, better known as the Long Finn, who claimed to be the son of Konigsmark, a Swedish general. Long Finn was tried and convicted of attempted rebellion, and was sentenced to be publicly and severely whipped, branded with the letter "R," and sold to the planters of Barbados or some other remote place.[16]

On September 25, 1676, Governor Andros by proclamation made the laws of the Duke of York applicable to the settlements along the Delaware. These laws had been first promulgated in March 1664, at Hempstead, Long Island, and their criminal code is therefore usually called the Hempstead Code.[17] This code classified eleven crimes as capital. Included in the classification were the various degrees of treason, murder, blasphemy, bestiality,[18] buggery, kidnapping, perjury to deprive another of his life, and the unprovoked attack on a parent by a child of more than sixteen years of age.[19]

Milder penalties, especially various forms of corporal punishment, were provided for other offenses. Fornication carried the penalty of "marriage, fine, or corporal punishment," or any of these at the discretion of the court. Those guilty of forgery were to be sentenced to the pillory for "three several court days," compelled to render double damages to the party wronged, and barred from testifying in future court proceedings. Arson was punishable with death or complete indemnification to the injured party. Any person kindling a fire in any woods or fields which resulted in damage to another's property was to pay for all damage caused, and in addition be punished by a fine equal to one-half of the amount of the damages. If he was unable to pay this, the court was to sentence him to twenty stripes, or to service to expiate the crime.[20] A servant or laborer convicted of assaulting his master or overseer was to be imprisoned until the next session of the court and then sentenced to whatever corporal punishment the court might adjudge, "saving life and member."[21] Excessive drinking brought punishment by fine or the stocks, or both, to the tippler.[22] Persons guilty of lying or publishing false news were to be fined, or placed in the stocks for a period not exceeding four hours, or be publicly whipped with not more than forty stripes. The amount of punishment inflicted in such cases depended upon the nature of the offense and the number of times the person involved had been convicted of this crime.[23] Any person who committed bigamy after swearing that he was not already married was to have his tongue pierced with a red-hot iron. Moreover, he was to be punished for having committed adultery,[24] which carried the penalty of corporal punishment, a fine, or imprisonment.[25]

It was also provided that any person who committed burglary or robbery should, for the first offense, be branded on the forehead, for the second offense be branded as before and severely whipped, and for the third offense be put to death.[26] Anyone convicted of the larceny of property valued at more than ten shillings was to be whipped or fined an amount sufficient to cover all damages and costs.[27] However, the theft of swine, boats, and canoes exposed the criminal to a fine and the loss of one of his ears for the first offense, and to more severe punishment, in accordance with the judgement of the court, for any subsequent offense.[28]

This summary of the provisions of the Duke of York's criminal code clearly indicates how, in expressing the spirit of the age, it emphasized the death penalty, whipping, and other forms of corporal punishment. Less severe punishments were included for such minor offenses as disturbing church meetings and disobeying parents; and the code was filled with strange and sometimes humorous stipulations which, to those of us now accustomed to the impersonal relationships of complex city life in the United States, seem like petty and intolerable intrusions into an individual's private life, exposing the unwary to many spiteful annoyances. Apparently, not long after the application of this criminal code to Delaware in 1676, there was a whipping post and a pillory in some public place in each of the towns of New Castle in New Castle County, Dover in Kent County, and Lewes in Sussex County. However, there is no record of what these instruments of punishment looked like or where in each town they were located.[29]

An examination of the few surviving court records of colonial Delaware throws some light upon the way in which the lash was being used to enforce the law in these early days. On September 26, 1677, Captain Christopher Billop, then in command of affairs along the Delaware, called the New Castle County Court into special session to hear the case of Francis Jackson. The evidence revealed that Jackson on the previous Monday, while employed at the fort in the Town of New Castle, had become drunk and disorderly and had caused considerable disturbance, and that when Captain Billop had remonstrated with the defendant the latter had used very abusive and scurrilous language, calling the Captain a "son of a whore and a son of a bitch." Confinement in the stocks had failed to quiet Jackson, and while he was being put into prison he had become involved in a fight with Captain Billop. The court, after duly considering the case, sentenced Jackson to be whipped with twenty-one lashes and to remain in prison until the sentence was executed.[30] Later the court remitted the corporal punishment and placed Jackson in custody of "his master, Mr. Abram Man," who was to be responsible for the prisoner's behavior until the next session of the court, or for a longer period of time if the court deemed this proper.[31]

In another case, tried in the Court of New Castle on April 3, 1679, Agnieta Hendriks, who had been convicted of having given birth to three bastard children, was sentenced to be publicly whipped with twenty-seven lashes and to pay all costs.[32] The whipping was administered on the same day at the gate of the fort in New Castle, but apparently it had little effect upon the character of Agnieta, since in November of the next year she was convicted of having another bastard child. This time the court ordered that Agnieta Hendriks be publicly whipped with thirty-seven lashes, pay all costs, and be banished from the county for five years.[33]

In disposing of the case of Joseph Moore, on February 13, 1680, the court of New Castle again saw fit to impose the penalty of whipping.[34] Moore was convicted of having run away from Virginia and of having taken with him several servants belonging to various masters, a boat, and other goods. For his crimes, and as "an example to others," he was sentenced to be publicly whipped with twenty-four lashes, returned to Virginia, and forever banished from the "precincts of the Delaware River."[35] In the same year, on September 22, the Kent County Court ordered John Car[aw]ay to receive twenty-one lashes for having stolen various articles from the servants of John Briggs.[36]

On March 4, 1681, Charles II, King of England, granted the region now Pennsylvania to William Penn in liquidation of a debt owed to the Quaker leader by the Crown. Penn, after he had received this grant, realized that it would be inadvisable to let someone else possess the territory which is now the State of Delaware, since his commerce and trade might thereby be endangered.[37] Command of Delaware Bay meant control of the entrance to his colony, which he hoped to make a haven for the Quakers. He therefore persuaded the Duke of York to deed him this territory.[38]

Within a few weeks after Penn arrived in America he issued a call for an assembly, and the first representative body of the Province of Pennsylvania and the territories (now Delaware) met at Upland (now Chester) on December 4, 1682. At this session of the Assembly, Penn's "Great Law" was adopted and Delaware was formally annexed to the Province of Pennsylvania.[39] Penn's body of laws superseded the laws of the Duke of York and introduced into America the original Quaker criminal code. The differences between the Quaker philosophy and practices and those of the other colonies and of England are clearly reflected in this code.

Even a casual examination of the original Quaker code reveals a startling departure in criminal jurisprudence. One is immediately impressed with the wide reliance upon imprisonment as a mode of punishment and the extent to which it was used as a substitute for whipping and other forms of corporal punishment.

However, despite the fact that imprisonment at hard labor was prescribed as a punishment for a majority of the acts which were branded as crimes by the community, the penalty of whipping was retained for some offenses. Thus it was declared that arson was to carry the penalty of rendering double satisfaction to the injured party, imprisonment for one year in the house of correction, and such corporal punishment as the court should deem it proper to impose.[40] A married person who "defiled the marriage bed" was to be punished for the first offense with a public whipping and at least one year's imprisonment at hard labor, and for the second offense was to be imprisoned for life.[41] A person convicted of sodomy or bestiality was to be sentenced for the first offense to a public whipping, forfeiture of one-third of his estate, and six months' imprisonment at hard labor, and for the second offense was to be imprisoned for life.[42] A rapist was to be punished for the first offense with the forfeiture of one-third of his estate, a whipping, and one year's imprisonment at hard labor, and for the second offense was to be imprisoned for life.[43]

Although no punishment was provided for fornication and murder in the code of the "Great Law," the additions made in March 1683 did impose penalties for these crimes. Thereafter a person found guilty of fornication might be sentenced to marriage, a fine, or corporal punishment, or all or any of these, according to the discretion of the court,[44] while anyone convicted of murder was to suffer death.[45] Murder, therefore, became the only capital crime in the Quaker code of Pennsylvania and Delaware.

As the influence of the Quakers waned in America, their humane criminal laws were gradually weakened by additional acts which tended to increase the severity of the penalties and to reintroduce corporal punishment for various offenses.[46] Finally, Pennsylvania and Delaware in 1718–19 swept away the last vestiges of Penn's code.[47]

Although Delaware after 1704 had its own assembly and was joined to the rest of Penn's colony only through the executive branch of the government, it continued to enforce the same criminal laws that were being used in Pennsylvania.[48] Consequently, when the latter in 1718 enacted new criminal legislation which was applicable only to its own counties, it became imperative for the lawmakers of Delaware to take some action to clarify the situation for their constituents. This they did by the passage of the act of 1719,[49] in which the same offenses were declared to be capital that had been so designated by Pennsylvania in the law of 1718.

Delaware's act of 1719 prescribed the death penalty for treason, murder, manslaughter by stabbing, serious maiming, highway robbery, burglary, arson, sodomy, buggery, rape, concealing the death of a bastard child, advising another to kill such a child, and witchcraft. It also stated that any person convicted of any capital offense for which he might by the laws of Great Britain have the benefit of clergy was permitted to request that right.[50] He was not required to read to take advantage of this leniency, as had been necessary originally in Europe, but was immediately punished as a "clerk convict." In which case, if he had been convicted of murder, he was to be branded with an "M" on the brawn of the left thumb; and if for any other felony, with a "T" on the brawn of the left thumb. These marks were to be made by the gaoler in open court, and then, at the discretion of the court, male offenders might be imprisoned for not less than six months nor more than two years; and female offenders, for not more than one year. However, if any person who had once had the benefit of clergy was again convicted of a capital offense, he was to suffer the penalty of death without benefit of clergy. This law was used as the basis for the criminal jurisprudence of Delaware and, as the occasion required, it was added to independently of the action of Pennsylvania. In this way the criminal code of colonial Delaware was gradually brought to completion.

An examination of the criminal statutes passed in Delaware during the remainder of the colonial period immediately shows the increasing influence that the reactionary English criminal jurisprudence exerted upon the colony's legislators.[51] In some cases, the framers of legislation did not even take the trouble to be specific but merely stated that the crimes in question were to be punished according to the laws of Great Britain. Furthermore, not only were additional crimes made punishable with death, but the penalties of whipping, pillorying, branding, and mutilation were increasingly prescribed for lesser crimes. A few examples will suffice to illustrate these tendencies.

By a law passed either in the latter part of 1726 or early in 1727 it was stipulated that whoever committed adultery was liable to a fine of fifty pounds or a public whipping of twenty-one lashes, and that any person convicted of fornication was to receive twenty-one lashes on the bare back or pay a fine of three pounds. It was further provided by this law that if any white woman bore a bastard child by a negro, such child should be put out at servitude until he reached the age of thirty-one. The mother was to pay a fine of ten pounds, be publicly whipped with thirty-nine lashes on her bare back, and stand in the pillory for two hours. If she was a servant and unable to pay the fine, the woman, in lieu of the fine, was to serve her master for an additional period not to exceed five years. The negro father was to be publicly whipped with thirty-nine lashes on the bare back, placed in the pillory for two hours, "with one ear nailed thereunto," and upon release from the pillory was to have this one ear "cropped off." If any white man was convicted of fornication with a negress, he was to pay a fine of twenty pounds and be whipped with twenty-one lashes well laid on the bare back.[52]

An act for the punishment of petty larceny was passed in 1742, and according to its provisions, persons convicted of stealing any money or goods valued at less than five shillings were to be publicly whipped on the bare back with any number of lashes not exceeding fifteen, and in addition were to be compelled to return to the injured party the property stolen, pay as restitution an amount equal to the value of the stolen property, and pay the costs of the prosecution. In case the stolen property could not be found, the offender was to pay double the value of this property as restitution, and if the offender could not pay the restitution or the costs of prosecution, he was to be sentenced to servitude for not more than one year.[53]

Another act passed in 1742 provided for the punishment of persons convicted of stealing slaves or horses, breaking into houses in the daytime and stealing to the value of five pounds, entering a dwelling without breaking with the intent to commit a felony, or knowingly receiving stolen horses or slaves. Persons declared guilty of any of these crimes were to suffer the penalty of death without benefit of clergy. This law also stipulated that those who knowingly received stolen property were to be publicly whipped on the bare back with twenty-one lashes well laid on, branded on the forehead with the capital letter "R," and made to pay not only fourfold satisfaction to the injured party, but also the costs of prosecution. If offenders were not able to make the required restitution, they were to be placed in servitude for any term not exceeding seven years.[54]

Since it was not clear how the crimes of petty treason, misprision of treason, murder, manslaughter, homicide, bestiality, incest, and bigamy were to be punished, a law was enacted around 1742 which stated that persons found guilty of these crimes were to suffer the same penalties as those inflicted for like offenses in England.[55] The passage of this act indicates that the "patched-up" criminal jurisprudence of Delaware was causing confusion and foreshadowing the need of a complete and reorganized criminal code; but such a code was not to be provided for some years to come, and the conflicting interpretations continued to mount as successive laws were passed.

Thus, with the passage of the law of 1719, Delaware laid the foundation for the erection of a criminal code that rivaled that of the Duke of York in severity. The use of corporal punishment continued with general uniformity throughout the period, and the lash again became one of the most important instruments of punishment.

Chapter III

THE WHIPPING POST AND
THE PENITENTIARY MOVEMENT, 1776 to 1829

WHEN the American Revolution began, the Old World's severe methods of punishment were still being used in the settlements of the New World, but forces were already operating to produce a change in the treatment of criminals throughout Western civilization.[1] The sanguinary penal codes and the cruel treatment of prisoners were being scrutinized and condemned in the light of the theories of rationalism, which emphasized the belief that a better social order could be had through the use of reason, and penal reform was being vigorously advocated by eminent jurists and outstanding students of prison conditions. To their efforts was soon added the influence of a reviving religious idealism whose leaders looked upon imprisonment as a charitable kindness, a means whereby sinners might make earthly reparations for their misdeeds. America, where old ideas and methods were undergoing the test of new relationships, was well situated to feel the effect of the forces of change, and Philadelphia, with its traditions of humanitarianism, soon became the great center of penal reform. The Quakers again assumed a leading role in the penal reform movement, and many of them joined the Philadelphia Society for Alleviating the Miseries of Public Prisons.[2] Believing that the prevention of crime was the sole end of punishment, they contended that penal institutions should be penitentiaries,[3] that is, places where persons might reflect upon their crimes and become penitent. The purpose of prisons, therefore, was to produce better men and women, not to make them more vicious and perverted. Eventually the strong agitation that was directed against the existing penal system in Pennsylvania caused the barbarous criminal code of 1718 to be replaced in 1829 with one characterized by a justice, mildness, and humanity that were almost unique for that age.[4]

Delaware also, during the period 1776 to 1829, was the scene of many ambitious attempts at penal reform, but here such agitation met with determined resistance and ultimate failure. As in Pennsylvania, the attempt to abolish whipping and other forms of corporal punishment in Delaware was an integral part of a movement that had as its goal the establishment of a penitentiary system. Consequently, if one is to know why the use of the whipping post persisted in Delaware, one must understand the development and failure of Delaware's penitentiary movement.[5]

Even as early as February 1777, a legislative committee raised its voice against the severe nature of Delaware's criminal laws,[6] but it was not until January 1797 that a concerted effort was made to modify the methods of punishment in the state. At that time Governor Bedford advocated the abolition of corporal punishment and the introduction of the penitentiary system.[7] This attack was continued by a petition of the grand jury of Kent County, which condemned the conditions in their county's jail and asked for a general reformation of the criminal laws of Delaware.[8] However, these efforts seem to have been productive of little progress in the legislature, even though a legislative committee later in the session submitted a report in favor of the penitentiary system.[9]

That severe penalties actually were being imposed upon criminals is evidenced by the court records of the period. There was, for example, the case of William Berry, who was convicted of horse stealing in New Castle County in 1785. On November 6 of that year he was condemned to pay the costs of prosecution, make restitution in the amount of fifty pounds (double the value of the property stolen), be whipped with thirty-one lashes, stand in the pillory for one hour, and have the soft part of one ear cut off.[10] A few months later, in 1786, Berry was again convicted of the same crime, and again sentenced to pay costs and restitution (this time the restitution was forty pounds), be whipped with thirty-one lashes, stand in the pillory one hour, and have the soft part of his other ear cut off.[11] At the same term of the court, another prisoner, Samuel Glover, was found guilty of the same offense and was similarly sentenced.[12]

Then there was Negro Dick. He was convicted of assault with intent to ravish, and on August 11, 1789, he was sentenced to pay the costs of the prosecution, stand four hours in the pillory with both ears nailed thereto, and finally, before being taken down from the pillory, have both ears cut off close to his head.[13] Several years later, in November 1792, Negro Philip also received a severe sentence. He was found guilty of fornication and bastardy with Catharine Moore, a white woman, and the court ordered that he pay the costs, be whipped with thirty-nine lashes, stand two hours in the pillory with one ear nailed thereto, and then have the ear "cropped off."[14]

While unsuccessful efforts at penal reform were being made, a new edition of Delaware's laws was completed and published in 1797.[15] This compilation proved to be very disappointing to those who had been laboring for a revision of the state's criminal code. Not only did the number of capital crimes remain the same, but imprisonment was not introduced to any great extent as a mode of punishment and whipping was still prescribed for a large number of crimes.

According to the new compilation, treason, murder, manslaughter by stabbing, highway robbery, burglary, arson, sodomy, buggery, rape, advising the killing of bastard children in cases where such children were killed,[16] defacing of charters,[17] certain types of forgery and counterfeiting,[18] and serious maiming[19] were all offenses punishable with death.

The penalty for larceny[20] was the restoration of the stolen goods, and payment to the owner of an amount equal to double their value. If the goods could not be found, the offender was required to make fourfold restitution, along with the full costs of prosecution, suffer imprisonment until this was done, be publicly whipped with any number of lashes not exceeding twenty-one, and wear a Roman "T" on the upper left arm for six months as a badge of the crime. Persons convicted of such offense for the second time were to be placed in the pillory for two hours instead of having to wear the Roman "T," in addition to having to pay a fine and being whipped publicly. The penalty of death, without benefit of clergy, was to be inflicted on those convicted for the third time of larceny.[21]

Persons convicted of stealing a horse or slave, or knowingly receiving such stolen property,[22] were to restore the property and pay to the owner double its value. If the property could not be found, the offender was to forfeit fourfold its value to the injured party, pay the costs of prosecution, be publicly whipped on the bare back with thirty-nine lashes well laid on, be set in the pillory for one hour, and have the soft part of one of his ears cut off. If the offender could not pay the forfeiture imposed and the costs of prosecution, he was to be sold by the sheriff, for the amount involved, for any term not exceeding seven years.

Persons knowingly receiving stolen goods, wares, or merchandise (other than slaves or horses) were to be publicly whipped on the bare back with twenty-one lashes well laid on, be branded on the forehead with the capital letter "R," and in addition were to make "fourfold satisfaction" to the injured party and pay the costs of prosecution. If such offenders were unable to pay the forfeitures and the costs of prosecution, they were to be "assigned to servitude" for any term not exceeding seven years.[23]

Persons convicted of kidnapping and taking into another state any free negro, or free mulatto, or of aiding or abetting such practice, were to be publicly whipped on the bare back with thirty-nine lashes well laid on, stand in the pillory for one hour, with both ears nailed thereto, and at the expiration of the hour have the soft part of both ears cut off.[24]

Drunkenness was to be punished by a fine of five shillings or, upon refusal or inability to pay, by a sentence of two hours in the stocks; profanity and cursing by a fine of five shillings or, upon refusal or inability to pay, by a sentence of not more than three hours in the stocks. Blasphemy made the offender liable to two hours in the pillory, branding with the letter "B" on the forehead, and a public whipping of not more than thirty-nine lashes.[25]

A person convicted of a felony for which he might have the benefit of clergy was entitled to request that right. In which case, if he had been convicted of murder, he was to be branded with an "M" on the brawn of his left thumb; and if he had been convicted of any other felony,

THE POST AND THE PENITENTIARY MOVEMENT 13

with a "T" on the brawn of his left thumb. In addition, at the discretion of the court, male offenders might be sentenced to the county house of correction or workhouse for not less than six months or more than two years; and female offenders for not more than one year. However, if any person who had once had the benefit of clergy was again convicted of a capital offense, he or she was to suffer the penalty of death, without the benefit of clergy.[26]

Negro slaves convicted of attempting to commit rape on white women were to be publicly whipped on the bare back with thirty-nine lashes well laid on, be sentenced to the pillory for one hour, with both ears nailed thereto and, at the expiration of the hour, have the soft part of both ears cut off.[27]

Some idea of the extent to which divergence had taken place in the development of the criminal legislation of the two former parts of Penn's colony, Delaware and Pennsylvania, can be obtained by a comparison of the foregoing summary with the provisions of the act of April 22, 1794, passed by the Pennsylvania legislature.[28] By this act, benefit of clergy was abolished in Pennsylvania and imprisonment was introduced on a large scale as a method of punishment. Furthermore, there had disappeared from Pennsylvania's statute books the brutal and revolting phases of colonial criminal jurisprudence, and the death penalty was retained for only one crime, namely, first degree murder.

Not discouraged by the inertia of the legislators, the advocates of penal reform persisted in their efforts, with the Quakers contributing much of the leadership in the movement.[29] Governor Bassett in 1800 and again in 1801,[30] and Governor Hall in 1805[31] both urged the state legislature to revise the criminal laws and to establish the penitentiary system, but their advice went unheeded despite the fact that they were supported by petitions and resolutions in the legislature.[32] In 1810, however, a legislative commission submitted an enthusiastic report recommending the revision of the criminal code and the construction of a penitentiary.[33] That public opinion was rising in favor of such a move is indicated by the fact that a large number of petitions which urged the substitution of imprisonment for corporal punishment were introduced into the legislature during this session.[34] As a result of this pressure, the first bill for the erection of a penitentiary ever to come before a Delaware legislature was passed by the Senate,[35] but it was blocked in the House by the votes of the conservative representatives from Kent and Sussex counties.[36]

The penitentiary system found a staunch supporter in Governor Haslet, who vigorously advocated its establishment in his messages to the legislators in 1812 and 1813.[37] Bills for this purpose were presented at both these sessions, and although they were again defeated, largely through the efforts of legislators from Kent and Sussex, the one introduced in 1812 was kept from becoming a law by only one vote.[38] This proved to be the closest to a penitentiary system that Delaware came during the entire period from 1776 to 1829. After these defeats, little was done to revive the issue until 1818 when a legislative committee, which had been appointed to study the question, submitted a report condemning the sanguinary criminal code and recommending the establishment of the penitentiary system.[39] Upon this committee's recommendation another penitentiary bill was introduced into the legislature, but the measure was killed in the House by a tie vote when seven representatives from Sussex and three from Kent cast their ballots against it.[40]

In 1819 a number of petitions addressed to the legislature from New Castle and Kent counties called upon the lawmakers to repeal the cruel criminal laws which degraded the citizens of the state and offended reason, justice, and mercy. Pointing to the use of the penitentiary system in Pennsylvania as proof of the efficacy of that type of punishment, the petitioners asked for an appropriation to introduce such a system into Delaware.[41] Such a strong expression of public opinion helped to make possible the introduction of a fifth bill for the construction of a penitentiary. The bill passed the Senate but was irretrievably lost in the House through the efforts of representatives from Kent and Sussex counties.[42] The opposition had certainly solidified its ranks. So vigorous, in fact, had it become that not another penitentiary bill was introduced into the legislature, and even a resolution for the revision of the criminal code could not get through the Senate in 1822, being defeated there by the combined votes of senators from Kent and Sussex.[43]

Those in favor of penal reform changed their tactics in 1823 and attempted to introduce penitentiary methods into each of the existing county jails. It was hoped by this approach to win over some of those who opposed the centralization of Delaware's prison system, but this move too, even when reduced to a mere plan to erect a treadmill in New Castle County only, was frustrated in the Senate, where all senators from both Kent and Sussex counties voted against it.[44] Although Governor Thomas again raised the issue in 1824 with a strong recommendation of the penitentiary system,[45] the opponents of reform had been victorious, and the criminal code of 1829 contained no fundamental changes in the methods of punishing criminals.

The new code[46] prescribed death[47] by hanging for persons convicted of treason, murder, rape, burglary, arson, and the second offense of kidnapping a free negro, and a public whipping, in addition to other penalties, for those found guilty of willful and malicious poisoning, mayhem by lying in wait, assault with intent to rape, breaking and entering with felonious intent, the first offense of kidnapping a free negro, robbery, larceny, knowingly receiving stolen goods, sodomy, and witchcraft.[48] Mutilation, branding, and sentences to the stocks had been eliminated from the criminal laws; but badges indicating the crimes committed were substituted in some cases for the old penalty of branding, and pillorying was still prescribed for many offenses.

THE POST AND THE PENITENTIARY MOVEMENT 15

Delaware's court records for the first few decades of the nineteenth century show that during the state's penitentiary movement many prisoners were sent to the whipping post. Reference to several cases will make it clear that judges were applying the harsh laws to both men and women. The General Sessions Court of Kent County on November 28, 1804, sentenced Araminta Caldwell, who had been convicted of larceny, to be whipped with eleven lashes and to pay Walter Reed nine shillings, double the value of the property stolen.[49] In Sussex County, in 1811, Henry Brereton stole a negro slave valued at $150, and the court in Georgetown[50] decreed that he forfeit to the owner twice the value of the property stolen, pay the costs of prosecution, and on December 4, 1811, be whipped with thirty-nine lashes, stand in the pillory for one hour, and have the soft part of one of his ears cut off.[51] A colored woman named Sarah Ann Morris, who had been convicted of larceny, was sentenced on December 16, 1829, by the New Castle County Court of General Sessions to pay the costs of prosecution, forfeit $93.31 as restitution to the owner of the property (the property, some of which was recovered, was valued at $33.15), be publicly whipped with twenty-one lashes well laid on the bare back, and if necessary, in order to pay the costs and restitution, be disposed of as a servant for any term not in excess of seven years to the highest bidder residing in the state. The sentence was executed to the letter, and on January 1, 1830, Sarah was sold to Henry Till for fifty cents.[52] Apparently the bidding was not very spirited.

The history of penology in Delaware during the years 1776 to 1829 is, by contrast with the remarkable progress made in Pennsylvania, a depressing record of stagnation and blasted hopes. Marked by many ambitious attempts to abolish corporal punishment and to establish the penitentiary system, the period closed in Delaware with the complete rout of the advocates of reform. Consequently, in 1829, the same year in which Pennsylvania's Eastern Penitentiary was opened at Cherry Hill, near Philadelphia, and when other states were embarking, or had already embarked, on programs of expanding their penitentiary systems, Delaware lost her fight for penal reform, adopted a criminal code that possessed many of the characteristics of the old sanguinary law of 1797, and established a county jail system, much of which has lasted until the present day.

Chapter IV

THE WHIPPING POST EMERGES AS A SEPARATE ISSUE, 1829 to 1900

AFTER the publication of the code of 1829, little was done to revive the fight against corporal punishment until January 1835,[1] when Governor Bennett reopened the question in his message to the legislature.[2] He asked the lawmakers to revise the criminal code, some of which, in his opinion, was "abhorrent to humanized feelings," and to introduce the penitentiary system. Although Governor Bennett's efforts bore no fruit,[3] this did not deter Governor Comegys, who during the legislative sessions of 1837, 1839, and 1841, vigorously condemned the pillory and the whipping post, and recommended the adoption of the penitentiary system. Again the lawmakers remained adamant. Not only did they refuse to be moved by the Governor's earnest appeals, but some, in 1841, sternly criticized him for the manner in which he was exercising his pardoning powers. This brought an energetic reply from Governor Comegys in which he explained that since public opinion was not in favor of the severe criminal code, he was under constant pressure to show leniency to convicted criminals. He contended that the solution was to be found in the elimination of the "taint of cruelty and barbarism" from the laws so that they would be more expressive of the views of the people.[4]

Despite the fact that no progress was being made in the legislature, those in favor of penal reform in Delaware were not idle, and public opinion was rallying to their support. As a result, in 1841 many citizens in New Castle and Kent counties petitioned the legislature to revise the criminal code and create a penitentiary system.[5]

Other evidence of the opposition to the severity of the criminal code appeared in the form of protests in the newspapers of the day. One of these, published as an editorial in the *Delaware Gazette* on November 26, 1841, asserted:

> A young girl, who pleaded guilty on ten different indictments for larceny, was sentenced to pay double the value of the goods stolen to the owners, to wear ten "T's" on her outer garment, and to receive 21 lashes on the bare back, well laid on, in each case, making 210 in all. And this on a woman, a very genteel looking young girl! tied up to a post, her naked body exposed to the gaze of a crowd — striped and scored! But enough, the theme is shocking. The barbarous law must be repealed — it is a crying disgrace to the State. We are glad, however, . . . that this shocking cruelty will not be inflicted in this in-

stance, as we understand the Governor has interposed his clemency, and pardoned her as to the corporal punishment. . . .[6]

Nevertheless, the renewed agitation for a penitentiary met with strong opposition upon the inauguration of Governor Cooper in 1841, for this marked the accession to office of the first chief executive of Delaware who publicly attacked the penitentiary system in an address to the legislature. His expression of disapprobation and distrust in January 1843[7] came at a time when this system was experiencing a recession in the states into which it had been introduced.[8]

The legislature adjourned in 1843 without having taken any steps to modify the state's criminal code, but during this session an attempt was made to abolish the whipping of white women. On February 14 the House passed a bill for this purpose, but after the Senate by an amendment made it applicable to all women, both white and negro, the House permitted the measure to die in committee.[9]

The pardoning power continued to be the subject of much controversy, and the state's governors felt called upon to devote a large part of their messages to the legislature to this aspect of the executive's duties. There is no doubt that much of this controversy resulted from the growing agitation by the people of Delaware for the reformation of the criminal code.[10] Unable to obtain relief through legislation, the leaders of the reform movement, as well as those whose relatives and friends had been convicted of crimes, were bringing increased pressure to bear on the governors for the greater use of executive clemency.

Nothing was accomplished by those interested in penal reform during the next few meetings of the legislature, and when the revised code of 1852 appeared, it was found to have virtually all the objectionable penal features of its predecessor, the code of 1829.[11] The punishments of whipping, pillorying, and servitude[12] still remained, and in no case was imprisonment the only penalty provided for a crime.[13] Prior to the issuance of the code of 1852, Delaware's criminal law had not specified how many lashes might be included in the combined sentences of an individual who had been convicted on more than one charge. The new code made such a provision by stating that when a prisoner was convicted on several indictments for crimes punishable with whipping, or pillorying, the court was to graduate the sentences in such a way that the person would not be whipped with more than sixty lashes, nor be made to stand in the pillory for more than one hour, under all such sentences combined.[14] It was also stipulated in the provisions of the code of 1852 that whippings were to be publicly inflicted with strokes well laid on the bare back by the sheriff, his deputy, or by a constable, and that the whipping post and the pillory were to be in or near the jail yard of each county.[15]

The publication of the code of 1852 was followed by a prolonged lull in the legislative fight for penal reform,[16] but during these years one law was enacted which did reduce somewhat the severity of Delaware's criminal code. This law, passed on January 27, 1855, abolished whipping and the wearing of a convict's jacket for white women convicted of larceny.[17]

Although the penal reform issue was not being pressed in the legislature, the controversy remained alive and often found expression in the newspapers of the state. For example, the following vigorous defense of Delaware's criminal code was published in the *Delaware Gazette* on November 11, 1853:

> There frequently appear in the papers of Philadelphia and other places, articles strongly condemnatory of our mode of punishing crime by pillory and whipping. For this we are pronounced cruel, barbarous, and behind the age in our criminal code. We shall, therefore, say something in defense of our system, which we believe better adapted to our location and situation, than the highly vaunted, and as we believe, greatly overrated Penitentiary mode of punishment, which prevails in the larger States of the Union. Our State is entirely too small to bear the expense of a Penitentiary; for with it would necessarily have to be created a new set of officers to be supported at the public charge. And owing to the very small number of criminals who would become its inmates, theirs would be merely sinecure offices. Situated as we are, between two states, of speedy and easy access, were it not for fear of our pillory and whipping post, we should be troubled much more than we now are with incursions from their numerous thieves, robbers and burglars. . . .
>
> The Penitentiary punishment scarcely ever reforms the criminal, and we believe that it is much less efficient than our old fashioned mode of whipping and pillory. . . . There is at the present day, in our opinion, far too much sensibility manifested toward criminals. . . .[18]

Those opposed to the whipping post and the pillory also voiced their views in the press of the day by such statements as the following:

> The Dover Reporter states that on Saturday, the 29th inst., in accordance with the sentence of the Court, Daniel Morgan was, by the Sheriff, placed in the pillory for one hour, at the expiration of which time twenty lashes were inflicted on his bare back with a willow switch, the Sheriff declaring positively that he would not use a cowhide on any white man. Whilst the prisoner was standing in the pillory, the blood became so stagnated in his face and hands that they became almost black. After the sentence of the law had been completed, the prisoner was remanded to the County Prison, there to stay until he shall have paid the costs, $75.00 restitution money and a fine of $100.00. Being a man of no means whatever, this fine and restitution it will be impossible for him ever to raise; for, there being no facilities in the prison, he cannot, as he could in a penitentiary, work it out. This infliction of whipping, and the barbarities of the pillory torture, are degrading to the State. Why cannot we have them abolished, and a penitentiary erected instead?[19]

Almost all the early spokesmen for penal reform in Delaware had advocated not only the establishment of the penitentiary, but also the abolition or mitigation of the severe punishments contained in the criminal code. Gradually, however, increased stress was placed upon the employment of prisoners, which originally had been considered as just one part of the penitentiary system, preferably as a technique in effecting the reformation of the individual.[20] The speeches of Governor Causey, in 1859,[21] of Governor Burton in 1861,[22] and of Governor Saulsbury, in 1866, 1867, 1869, and 1871,[23] as well as discussions and reports in the legislature and in the newspapers of the day, clearly reflect this shift in emphasis.[24] In fact, during the last few decades of the nineteenth century the construction of an institution where a large number of prisoners could be kept employed, commonly referred to as a workhouse,[25] became the primary object of the penal reform movement in Delaware. Agitation against the severity of the criminal code continued, but it was not as an integral part of the campaign for such an institution; and thus the abolition of the whipping post and the pillory gradually emerged as a separate issue.

While Governor Saulsbury was appealing to the legislators to take action on the question of penal reform, the state's use of corporal punishment was being discussed in the newspapers of Delaware and neighboring states. Whipping especially attracted much attention, and it was bitterly attacked as barbaric and revolting. The following, an article from the *New York Times* reprinted in the *Wilmington Daily Commercial* on April 13, 1867, gives some impression of the type of criticism that was being directed against Delaware by other states:

> The effect of scourging a man in public and of exposing him fastened in a pillory, is to utterly degrade him. If he had previously existing in his bosom a spark of self-respect, this exposure to public shame utterly extinguishes it. Yet without the hope that springs eternal in the human breast, without some desire to reform and become a good citizen, and the feeling that such a thing is possible, no criminal can ever return to honorable courses. The boy of eighteen who is whipped at New Castle for larceny, is in nine cases out of ten ruined. With his self-respect destroyed, and the taunt and sneer of public disgrace branded upon his forehead, he feels himself lost and abandoned by his fellows. . . . Such a boy will return to the courts again and again for new offences, and every repetition of his degradation will but harden and confirm his wickedness.
>
> If flogging be wise and proper, then why not branding in the hand or forehead, cropping the ears, or slitting the nose? Why abandon the rack, the wheel, the thumbscrews, the iron-boots, or any other of the diabolical and horrible means which men have invented to maim and torture? . . .
>
> No reasonable man dare longer attempt to defend the lash and the pillory. No just, humane or Christian man can do it. The time surely cannot be far distant when the precepts of decency, civilization and Christianity will prevail over the relics of barbarism, even in Delaware, and remove the stain forever.[26]

This same newspaper later in the year sought to convince its readers of the horrible futility of the post by publishing the following detailed description of a whipping:

> The whipping of Thomas Oliver, the negro who pleaded guilty to assault on two white women, was entrusted to the hands of Jim Wingate . . . well known for his fiendish hatred of the black people. The punishment was 60

lashes. Thirty of these were inflicted in the morning. The instrument employed was a cowhide, which was used with such fury that the blood flowed at every cut, causing the fellow to utter the most piteous screams. . . . The man was again brought out in the afternoon, and the lashes were reversed across his back, making cross bars. The wounds were afterwards washed with brine. . . . There is no doubt that Oliver will additionally be convicted, at another Court, of rape, for which, it being a capital offense, he will be hanged. This torture is, therefore, a mere preliminary to his execution.[27]

The attack on the "post" had caused many to rally to its defense as an efficacious preventive of crime. Newspapers and men in public places argued in its favor and excoriated its enemies. The following excerpts from an article printed in the *Delawarean* on January 4, 1868, were typical of a point of view often expressed during this period:

People of Delaware believe theft and burglary, and assault upon the chastity of their women to be crimes, and seek to deter people within their borders from committing them. For this they have enacted laws, not for vengeance upon the criminal, but for mercy to the community, that honest men and women may be safe in property and person, and that felons may not be safe or comfortable here at any rate. Therefore, we whip thieves and other felons and make them wear a convict's jacket as a badge of crime. We are not educated up to the Massachusetts standard and do not deal in "moral ideas" . . . as a stock in trade to lecture our neighbors with. . . .

We do not lock them up in jail to meditate fresh crimes and fatten in idleness at public cost, but they are whipped and turned out to work as they ought to be, as they can be, and as we intend they shall be.

In "Frank Leslie's Illustrated Paper" of December 21, is a large picture representing what the editor is pleased to call "Legal Barbarities in Delaware" confirmed by a descriptive article. The true history of the picture is as follows: A negro is tied to a post and a stout man of the well-known, conventional "slave-driving type" flourishes a cat-o'-nine-tails over him. A white man nearby awaits the same punishment. This negro waylaid a poor little white mistress on her way to a county school, dragged her into a thicket and by brutal force overcame her desperate resistance, and regardless of her supplications, was in the act of ravishing her when the crack of a passing teamster's whip frightened the editor's black pet, and the poor child, nearly sacrificed to his brutal lust, was just able to drag her bruised and wounded body to safety. It is the criminal justice of the state of Delaware that placed the black ravisher at the whipping post to be punished for the crime. What father or mother would bid the officer spare the lash?

It is the *crime* which degrades not the *punishment*. And when punishment prevents crime, surely its chief end has been gained.

When Frank Leslie says a crowd of both sexes witnessed the whipping, he disregards the truth. The scene never took place. The sentences are executed inside the county prison walls. It is the execution of a law instituted for public policy to prevent and punish crime, and it does it. The men who profess to shudder when a black or white scoundrel is soundly thrashed, looked on smilingly for five years whilst men were butchered by the tens of thousands in a fratricidal war, and widows and orphans sat starving amid the ruins of once happy homes.

Away, then, with such false and spurious lamentations. Our legal punishment is just and has nothing in it revolting to sound-hearted and sensible men and women. Hollow-hearted and crack-brained fanatics oppose it, as they do everything that does not chime in with their confused and oven-heated ideas.

Delaware, it seems, is unpopular with felons and their sympathizers, and we are proud of the fact.

Long may it be before self-righteousness and Puritanism blind us to the real nature of crime and the proper mode for its prevention and punishment.[28]

The *Wilmington Daily Commercial* persisted in its attacks on the whipping post and frequently described the whippings in strong words of condemnation. On November 21, 1868, an article in this newspaper referred to the lashing of seven prisoners at New Castle as "the regular semi-annual exhibition of barbarism," and stated that the large crowd present had contained many children, some of whom were not five years old, and that they had been brought to see the "show."[29] According to the article, Sheriff Richardson, with the cat-o'-nine-tails in hand, had made his appearance at eleven o'clock in the morning, and immediately afterwards a small colored boy, who had been convicted of stealing some pig iron valued at seventy-five cents, was led out into the yard. He had to stand on a soap box to get his hands into the manacles on the "post" and received twenty lashes on his bare back. The next person whipped was a mulatto boy of about sixteen, who had pleaded guilty to having stolen a pair of shoes and five cents. He too was given twenty lashes. Five other prisoners were whipped, each receiving twenty lashes. They included a young white man, convicted of stealing a bundle of clothing, an old, infirm, gray-haired man who had stolen a shirt, a young white man convicted of stealing a pair of boots, a prisoner who had stolen a valise, and another who had been found guilty of having stolen "store goods," and had been confined in the pillory for one hour before the whippings had begun. The "exhibition" was concluded amid a "shout of triumph from the delighted children."

The *Evening Bulletin* of Philadelphia also published a "full and graphic description" of these whippings at New Castle, and its reporter observed that public opinion in Delaware appeared to be strongly in favor of this mode of punishment.[30] He caustically criticized the whippings, declaring:

Fallen angels in Delaware never rise again. Law clips their wings and stamps upon them with its heel, and society shakes off the dust of its feet upon them, and curses them in their degradation. . . . They know that they will not be allowed to reform. . . . They come out of their prisons, confused, hopeless criminals. . . . The press must lead in [the attack on the whipping post]. But one newspaper in Delaware has had the courage to do this. The *Wilmington Daily Commercial* has been the sturdy and able advocate of reform.

On December 7, 1872, the *Delawarean,* of Dover, which along with other of the state's newspapers was attempting to justify the whipping post in the face of increasing opposition, published, with the editor's comments, the following quotation from an article originally printed in the Philadelphia *Day*:

> Another of Delaware's periodical public whipping performances occurred a few days ago. Some one half dozen persons convicted of theft and other crimes received a certain number of lashes, each well laid on their bare backs, the whipping being witnessed by all who desired to enjoy the exhibition. The newspapers in other states, and one or two in Delaware, that opposed this mode of punishing criminals, have set up their usual howl over this latest public whipping, denouncing the practice as "barbarous," a "relic of feudal times," "disgraceful to the present age," and so forth. But none of these papers seem to recognize the criminality of the men thus punished nor the necessity for protecting society against the depredations and lawless doings of such persons.
>
> Far advanced in enlightenment, as we are, there never was a period in the barbarous past when crime was more rife or society more in need of the strong hand of the law to protect it against thieves, robbers, and murderers, than it is in this boasted age of civilization. In the states and cities whose newspapers cry out against the "barbarism" of the Delaware Code, crime is far more prevalent and frequent than in that state of "post and pillory." . . . While professional criminals in our large cities, and in many cities that are not large, go unwhipt . . . and crime therefore flourishes therein, Delaware is blessed with comparative freedom from thieves, robbers, and kindred villains. . . . If any of this class are resolved to continue in criminal courses, they go elsewhere after one flagellation, and it is the fault of the other states if their laws offer inducements for such immigrants. Property is safe in Delaware; door locks find dull sale in that state. Her whipping post compels general observance of honesty. . . . If they are relics of barbarism, they are better than Pennsylvania's civilization.
>
> *Editor's Comment:* We publish the above from the Philadelphia *Day* to show that there are two sides to the whipping post and the pillory, and that the weight of good counsel is on the side of its retention as a means of punishment. We find that the public opinion, as expressed through the press, is far from being unanimous in its opposition to the post and the pillory. The public character of the punishment is its chief merit, however. The rascals who endure it care little for the pain, but they do not like to be seen.[31]

A source of much of the agitation against whipping was the infliction of this type of punishment upon women and youthful offenders. Cases like the ones commented on in the following newspaper articles caused many intelligent men and women to enlist in the movement for the abolition of corporal punishment in Delaware:

> A large number of persons, much larger than usual . . . collected about the New Castle County jail this morning at 10 o'clock . . . to witness the whippings. . . .
>
> The most touching sight was the suffering of the two lads, aged about thirteen, whose contortions and cries while they were being whipped were very pitiful to see.[32]

WHIPPING A WOMAN

> What is called "justice" in Delaware is a species of barbaric cruelty which would be disgraceful to a tribe of savages. . . . On Thursday last, a colored

woman was brought to trial on the charge of having murdered her illegitimate child. . . . The Attorney General requested the jury to render a verdict of murder in the second degree. . . . On Wednesday the woman was brought before the court and sentenced "to pay a fine of $5,000 and costs, to stand in the pillory for one hour, to receive on the same day sixty lashes upon her bare back, and to be imprisoned for life." It seems hardly credible that in the nineteenth century in a civilized and professedly Christian land, and in a State which forms a part of a free republic, so barbarous a sentence as this should be pronounced upon a criminal. . . .[33]

The colored woman referred to in this article was Mary E. Meeter, who had been convicted of murder in the second degree. Although the court records[34] show that she was to be punished in the way that the *Philadelphia Press* reported, the governor remitted the penalty of whipping and Mary Meeter was not lashed.[35] If she had been whipped, she would have been the last woman to be so punished in Delaware. Since she was not, and since some of the court records of Kent County for the years 1860 to 1870 are missing, it is uncertain when the last woman was lashed in Delaware. However, according to the court records that do exist, another colored woman, Sarah E. Robinson, was the last female prisoner not only sentenced to receive lashes but actually whipped in Delaware. She was convicted of larceny in the New Castle County Court of General Sessions, and sentenced on November 20, 1865, to pay the costs of prosecution, forfeit $35.25 as restitution to Charlotte E. Mack, be whipped with twenty lashes, and be sold as a servant for a term not to exceed seven years to anyone residing in Delaware. The lashes were inflicted on November 25, 1865, and on December 16 of the same year she was sold to John B. Vining for five cents for a term of seven years.[36]

The last woman whipped in Kent County, according to the existing court records of that county, was Phoebe Jane Brinkloe, a colored woman, who was convicted on two charges of larceny and sentenced on October 7, 1861, to pay the costs of prosecution, forfeit $13.45 as restitution, be whipped with twenty-four lashes, and be sold as a servant for a term of not more than fourteen years to anyone residing in Delaware. The lashes were inflicted on October 12, 1861, and on the same day she was sold to Thomas Jones for $17.21 for a term of ten years.[37] In Sussex County the last woman whipped was Maria Swain, a negress, who was convicted on two charges of larceny and sentenced on October 12, 1865, to pay the costs of prosecution, forfeit $48.00 as restitution, be whipped with twenty-four lashes, and be sold as a servant for a term of no more than fourteen years to anyone residing in Delaware. The lashes were inflicted on October 21, 1865, and on October 31 of the same year, she was sold to Charles K. Warrington for $60.50 for a term of fourteen years.[38]

The regularity with which detailed tabulations of whippings appeared in the state's leading newspapers during the latter part of the nineteenth century seems to indicate the importance attached to such punishments. These digests, such as the ones shown below, also convey some idea of the number of lashes that were being inflicted for various crimes:

NEW CASTLE WHIPPINGS

The second exhibition this season of Delaware's manner of administering justice to her criminals took place at New Castle on Saturday. The following are the names of those whipped, and the number of lashes each received, together with the time spent in the pillory:

        Enoch Rash ...... 1 hour in pillory, 30 lashes.
        James Brady ...... 1 hour in pillory, 30 lashes.
        James Darrah .... 20 lashes.
        Charles Harrison (negro) .... 10 lashes.
        Thomas F. Hyde .... 20 lashes.
        Isaac Hayden .... 20 lashes.
        Thomas Davis .... 20 lashes.
        Samuel Bush .... 20 lashes.
        Wm. L. Cooper (negro) .... 20 lashes.
        David Reed (negro) .... 20 lashes.

Of these, Rash and Davis have been whipped before. Rash and Hayden squirmed considerably during the performance, and their backs were well scarred. The rest bore it well.[39]

THE WHIPPING AT NEW CASTLE

The semiannual whipping and pillorying of criminals convicted at the present term of the court, of theft and other crimes, took place on Saturday. The attendance was small, probably not exceeding one hundred people, most of whom were boys. The following are the names of the "candidates," and the offenses for which they were sentenced:

Joseph Derias, colored, horse stealing, 20 lashes, one hour in pillory.
Scott Wilson, larceny of clothing, 20 lashes.
John Carpenter, colored, four cases of larceny (ice cream freezers, a cow, carriage reins, and a cow).
  He received 10 lashes in each case.
John Conner, larceny of tomatoes, 5 lashes.
John Smith, colored, house breaking, 20 lashes.
John Brown, horse stealing, 20 lashes and one hour in the pillory.[40]

As the controversy over the whipping post was becoming more intense, an event occurred in the city of Wilmington that has had persistent repercussions in the history of penology in Delaware. On the evening of November 7, 1873, a group of men made a daring attempt to rob the National Bank of Delaware, located at Sixth and Market streets in Wilmington, and within a short distance of the city's police headquarters. The *Daily Commercial* of Wilmington the next day described the attempt as "without parallel in the criminal records of our city."[41]

The cashier of the bank, Mr. Samuel Floyd, resided with his family in the rear part of the bank building; and while they were at tea, about

THE WHIPPING POST AND PILLORY, NEW CASTLE COUNTY JAIL, IN 1897

half-past six on the evening of the crime, a gentle rap was heard on the outer door of the basement where the table was spread. There were present around the table, Mr. Floyd and his wife, along with Mrs. Floyd's two nieces, Miss Irene Chardon and Miss Jennie F. Kates, the latter of whom was about sixteen years of age. At first, when the rapping was heard, all thought that it was caused by the wind. However, as it continued, Mr. Floyd went to the door to investigate. As he opened it, several masked men pushed their way into the room and quickly overpowered him. The women were thrown into a panic, and Miss Kates, seemingly in a swoon, sank down to the floor and crawled under the table. The robbers assured them that no one would be hurt if they all kept quiet.

In the meantime a colored maid had tried to hide herself under a side table. As several of the men were trying to drag the woman from her hiding place, Miss Kates ran out into the street. Although she was pursued by one of the men, she safely eluded him and sought safety in Mrs. Gordon's trimming store. The man who had chased her returned to the bank and notified his confederates that the alarm had been sounded. They immediately rushed out of the house, but were quickly followed by the colored woman, who screamed for the police.

Policeman Carbury, who chanced to be near-by, gave chase and caught up with the bandits on Eighth Street, between French and Walnut. They attacked him, striking him a blow on the head that knocked him to the ground. Chief Brady and Officer Hettrick, who had heard the servant's shouts, now came to Carbury's assistance, but the robbers escaped, although in their wild retreat they had abandoned tools and handcuffs.

On Saturday morning, the day after the attempted robbery, information was communicated to the chief of police that suspicious characters had been seen moving about the neighborhood of Ninth and Poplar streets. These men, according to neighbors, had been occupying a house at the southwest corner of that intersection for about four weeks.[42] It was said that men had been going in and out of this house for some time, and that although a trunk, a stove and some coal had been put into the house, no furniture had been seen.[43]

Upon hearing of this, officers went to the house and, finding it deserted, carefully searched its interior. They found the trunk, which contained jimmies, gags, powder, handcuffs, and a general assortment of burglars' tools. Later the police, after a general search of the neighborhood, discovered the robbers in an untenanted house at Ninth and Kirkwood. They were identified as Francis H. Carter (also known as "Big Frank" and Francis McDonald), Edward Hurlbert, James Thomas, alias James Hope, and Joseph Lawler, all of whom were residents of other states. They were quickly brought to trial, prosecuted by Attorney General Charles B. Lore, convicted, and each was sentenced to pay the costs of prosecution and a fine of $500, stand one hour in the pillory, be publicly whipped with forty lashes well laid on the bare back, and be imprisoned for ten years.[44]

The attempted robbery and ensuing trial had caused great excitement not only in Wilmington but also throughout the state. When it was rumored that certain parties were trying to persuade the governor to remit the part of the sentence which prescribed pillorying and whipping, there were strong expressions of indignation and anger on all sides.[45] These were intensified when it was reported that the sheriff had been informed of plans to rescue the prisoners. In order to thwart any such move, seventy-five armed men were kept on guard at the county jail during the night preceding the whipping, but the threatened rescue failed to materialize.

On December 10, 1873, the day set for the whipping, feeling was at a high pitch in the Town of New Castle, where the whipping was to be inflicted. An immense crowd had gathered, including many from near-by cities.

The *Wilmington Daily Commercial,* in describing the scenes preceding the whipping, had this to say:

Bright and early this morning, Sheriff Armstrong began his preparations for the carrying out of the sentence of the Court. A high board fence was stretched across the prison yard to keep back the crowd, and a space of about thirty-six by forty feet, at the entrance to the prison, was set apart for the spectators. The remainder of the yard was devoted to press reporters from Philadelphia, New York, and Baltimore, and those to whom the Sheriff had granted passes of admission. The number thus admitted would reach, probably, two or three hundred. . . .

At 10:30, when the gates were thrown open, an immense concourse of people, who had been standing outside of the jail, rushed in pell-mell and filled up the space allotted to them.

Shortly after ten o'clock, everything being in readiness, Carter and Hope were led out to the pillory. Just before their appearance in the prison yard, twelve men, armed with Springfield rifles, with bayonets affixed . . . were stationed along the fence and "dressed up" by ex-Councilman Quinn. Policemen, also, took up their stations in the intervals between the guards. When Carter and Hope were led out to the pillory, they walked firmly, but there was an unusual pallor upon the face of the former. Hope manifested none of this, but beneath the outward calm exterior, it was evident he was suffering mental anguish within. . . .

When Hurlbert and Lawler were led out, the former looked contemplatively upon the object of punishment before him. Lawler evidently felt that the disgrace was far more a matter of concern than the bodily pain which he would be called upon to endure, and his eyes were downcast. . . . While Lawler's neck was being fitted, Hurlbert laughingly contemplated the scene, which provoked much comment from the crowd outside.

When the first prisoners were put into the stocks, the whole street in front of the folding gates was completely filled with people. There were more persons standing there than could get into the yard, but still the crowd grew, and men and boys climbed into trees or on housetops so that they might get a better view. No trains had arrived at this time, the Court train, which leaves at 9:22, having been withdrawn. A special train of seven cars, however, was put upon the Delaware road just preceding the regular train, and when both had arrived and emptied their living freight, the whole space on the east side of the prison was filled up completely. Many persons, however, did not remain long, but finding themselves unable to gain admission put out on foot for Wilmington. . . .

When the whippings were to begin, Sheriff Armstrong told the crowd that any comments or disturbance would lead to imprisonment. This quieted the crowd that was surging about in the yard. . . .

The first of the prisoners led to the whipping post was "Big Frank." He wore his dress coat . . . which was removed as soon as he was ready to be fastened to the post, and a physique of only ordinary mould was revealed. He bowed his head between his arms and took the castigation without shrinking or flinching under the stings of the thongs. His back was considerably reddened and slight welts were raised but no blood was drawn.

Hope, Lawler and Hurlbert followed Carter to the post in the order named and no blood was drawn on any of them. Those who went to see blood were disappointed, and this was shown by suppressed remarks which were expressed by large numbers. Many were heard to say that the punishment was a farce, but the more humane were satisfied and glad that the whipping had not been more severe.[46]

After the whipping had been inflicted, the Town of New Castle was the scene of the wildest confusion. Street fights broke out in a surging mass of drunken men as they sought other means of satisfying their desire for more excitement.

The next day the *Wilmington Daily Commercial*, in reporting these disorders, pointed out that:

Drunken fights and rows followed in rapid succession. In many portions of the town, men in a beastly state of intoxication could be seen clinging to trees, lamp posts, and fences, or else perambulating in curious tracks down the streets, making altogether and at once the most comical and sickening sight to be imagined. . . .

At 2:30 P.M., the extra train of eight packed cars started for Philadelphia, taking away the most disorderly parties of the crowd to the great relief of the town's citizens, but enough were left to make the appearance of the town very noticeable.[47]

An editorial appearing in the same newspaper on December 10, 1873, contended that if the state had a penitentiary, the robbers could be put to work.[48] It added that although the New Castle jail was well arranged and kept, it was always crowded, and that the prisoners could not be properly employed and detained in solitary confinement. The editor, in concluding, declared that since the state had just paid several thousand dollars for Kent County's share of the State House Building and had contracted to pay about fifteen or twenty thousand more for its repair and alteration, the argument that Delaware was too poor to construct a penitentiary was completely refuted.

For several days after the whipping of the bank robbers there was a great deal of criticism in Delaware and her neighboring states regarding the mildness with which the punishment had been administered. There were even rumors that Sheriff Armstrong had been bribed to "let up" on the criminals.[49] Striking out against this criticism, the *Every Evening,* of Wilmington, denounced the insinuations that were being made against Sheriff Armstrong and asserted that if the sheriff had yielded to the popular passion and made every stroke draw blood, he would have exposed the "post" to further condemnation.[50]

The description of the attempted bank robbery, together with the subsequent events, has been presented in some detail because the lashing of these criminals has been used as the classic argument in favor of the retention of the whipping post in Delaware. Since then it has been persistently contended that the state owes the absence of any large bank robberies to the example made of Carter, Hope, Lawler, and Hurlbert in 1873.

While the discussion of the whipping of the bank robbers was still being reflected in the newspapers of the state, the following poem on the "post" was printed in the *Every Evening,* and it is reproduced here because it throws further light upon the feeling which the controversy had stirred up:

THE GOOD OLD WHIPPING POST

All hail to thee, O relic fine!
  Of grand and ancient times
When rogues and rascals, great and small,
  Were punished for their crimes,
The terror of the base and vile,
  And all the thieving host,
Reformer of dishonesty,
  The good old whipping post.

The most ingenious instrument
  That ever was designed
To teach the whole light-fingered mob
  Their duty to mankind.
Not one of all the scheming throng,
  Who thy acquaintance boast,
Forgets the lesson given at
  The good old whipping post.

Thy mark upon society
  May easily be traced,
Although thy form by honest hands
  Has never been embraced.
And few reluctant worshippers,
  Of all thy hardened host,
Embraces thee a second time,
  The good old whipping post.

No preacher ever could convert
    A criminal like thee,
Or leave so deep a mark upon
    The back of knavery.
To every rogue thy form appears
    As grim as Banquo's ghost,
But honest men can smile upon
    The good old whipping post.

The thief may howl and scream at thee
    And gnash his teeth in rage,
Denounce thee as a relic of
    A by-gone, cruel age.
But when reform can be achieved
    By milk and buttered toast,
We may give up and throw aside
    The good old whipping post.[51]

Another code of Delaware's laws appeared in 1874, and its pages furnished additional evidence of the retardation of the state's penology.[52] However, even though the new code did not differ fundamentally from that of 1852, the advocate of reform could find some comfort in knowing that all discriminatory provisions concerning negro criminals had been eliminated,[53] and that the whipping of women convicted of larceny had been abolished.[54]

The legislative sessions of 1875 and 1877 were marked by strong moves to establish a state workhouse, but bills for this purpose were defeated each time in the Senate.[55] This legislative campaign provides further evidence of the extent to which agitation for a state penal system had separated from that which aimed at the abolition of corporal punishment. A state workhouse was a much less extreme innovation than the penitentiary system which the early reform movement in Delaware had tried to establish. The introduction of the latter would have carried with it far-reaching implications regarding the revision of the state's criminal laws, founded as it was upon imprisonment as the only important mode of punishment. The establishment of a state workhouse, however, required no such modification, for the idea involved only the erection of a place where prisoners could be employed for their own and the community's benefit, and not the abolition of corporal punishment.

During the next few decades, questions of executive clemency and the punishment of youthful offenders received much attention. The earnest appeals for remissions and pardons, provoked largely because of the severity of the criminal laws,[56] impelled Governor Hall in 1881 to ask for the creation of an advisory board to aid him in the exercise of his pardoning powers, but his request did not meet with a favorable response in the legislature.[57]

The lawmakers, however, did try to close up some of the gap that had opened between Delaware and other states[58] in the field of juvenile delinquency by passing a series of acts relating to children.⁵⁹ Among the first of these was one enacted on February 15, 1883, which declared that in cases of conviction of larceny, when the prisoner was of tender years, or charged with crime for the first time and had been of good character prior to his offense, the court might in its discretion omit the penalty of whipping from the sentence. This law further stated that in cases where corporal punishment by whipping and the pillory, or either, was part of the sentence to be inflicted on a convicted person, the court might, if it seemed proper to do so, and if the jury recommended mercy, omit such corporal punishment, or either part of it, from the sentence.⁶⁰ By thus increasing the discretionary powers of the judge, the legislators indirectly reduced the severity of Delaware's criminal code. Two years later, in 1885, Delaware's first reformatory, the Ferris Industrial School for Boys, was founded, but it was not until April 1893 that the state acquired such an institution for girls,⁶¹ and even then provision was made for only white girls.⁶²

While these events were taking place, Delaware's whipping post continued to be the target of much caustic criticism throughout the country. A particularly informative article, appearing in the *Lippincott Magazine* of March 1879, condemned the use of the whipping post in these scornful words:

> In such a system there is no place for the spirit of reform. Absolutism, indeed, has neither time nor inclination to reform men. Concerned for nothing but to compel and maintain their subserviency, it requires the fetter for their limbs and the lash for their backs.⁶³

Opponents of the "post" had been especially severe in their criticism of that part of Delaware's criminal code which provided for the whipping and pillorying of women. Despite this, the approach of the twentieth century found these penalties for female prisoners still upon the state's statute books, although only a few women had been whipped or confined in the pillory in Delaware since the close of the Civil War. Finally, however, the legislators responded to the pressure of public opinion and, by a law enacted on February 26, 1889, abolished the whipping and pillorying of women convicted of crimes in Delaware.⁶⁴ Thus another milestone was passed in the long struggle to eliminate corporal punishment from the state's criminal code.⁶⁵

At the time when this important step was taken, a whipping post and a pillory were located in or near the yard of each of Delaware's three county jails in accordance with the state's criminal code.⁶⁶ The whipping post in the Town of New Castle was in the jail yard, but the whippings were public, as the law required, since the gates were opened so that all who chose could enter. At the Kent County jail in Dover, and at the Sussex County jail in Georgetown, the whippings were administered with an instrument which resembled the stock of a carriage whip, but in the New Castle County jail a "cat-o'-nine-tails" was used. The stock of this was twenty inches long, and its nine lashes measured twenty inches.[67]

The whipping post at the New Castle County jail was about one foot square, and together with the pillory, which was above it, about fifteen feet high. On each side of the "post," and about five feet from the ground, there were iron clasps, fitting over staples, in which the wrists of the prisoner were placed. The pillory was on a platform above the whipping post and was a part of it. This platform was supported by numerous stays underneath, and the part of the "post" above the platform had a cross-beam about five feet from the floor. The arms of this beam on each side of the "post" consisted of two pieces, the upper ones being movable, and fastened with a hinge, so that they could be raised. Each of these arms had three openings, one for the prisoner's head and the other two for his wrists, so that two persons could be placed in the pillory at one time. When a prisoner was to be placed in the pillory, the upper part of it was raised and his head and arms were placed in the openings. The movable piece was then shut down and secured with a clasp at the end, the criminal thus being as securely held as if he were in a vise.[68]

Within a few years after Delaware had abolished corporal punishment for women, the code of 1893 was published, but except for the above-mentioned changes and the elimination of the convict's jacket as a badge of crime,[69] it contained no fundamental revision of the state's criminal laws.[70] In fact, three crimes, namely, embezzlement by carrier or porter,[71] unlawfully and feloniously obstructing a railroad track,[72] and altering, defacing, or destroying any legislative bill or act,[73] had been added to the list of offenses punishable with whipping since the publication of the code of 1874.

During the remainder of the nineteenth century, most of the efforts of those who were interested in penal reform in Delaware were concentrated upon the establishment of a workhouse. Convinced that they could not obtain the necessary support for a state institution, the advocates of penal reform labored for the creation of a county workhouse. In this they were successful, and the New Castle County Workhouse, established by a law approved on March 16, 1899, emerged as a compromise between an urban North and a politically stronger rural South.[74]

Chapter V

THE MOVEMENT AGAINST THE WHIPPING POST, 1900 to 1945

WITH the enactment of the law to establish the New Castle County Workhouse, many progressive and enlightened citizens who had been laboring for its passage turned their attention to the pillory and the whipping post. The campaign against corporal punishment was now intensified in the hope that the public indignation which had been aroused against the idleness of convicts might also sweep away these "relics of barbarism."

The controversy over corporal punishment was reflected in the prominence given to articles on the subject in the state's newspapers. That many Delawareans were deeply conscious of the retention of the post and the pillory and were seeking to defend their use is clearly revealed by such newspaper sarcasm as the following:

> Delaware's whipping post has from time immemorial furnished a fruitful theme for song and story. Paragraphers the country over have reaped rich harvest from the swish of the cat-o'-nine-tails, and space writers have curdled the blood of sensitive readers with lurid descriptions of its "awful terrors." So stereotyped has all this long ago become that Delawareans pay no attention to it, and the swish of the lash on the backs of the offenders goes on with undisturbed regularity whenever the wrongdoers under our laws deserve it.
>
> There is a little grain of satisfaction, nevertheless, in the fact that despite all the harangue and literary hash in reference to it, the efficiency of the whipping post as a salutary corrective is being recognized in other states. Maryland and Virginia have adopted it as a punishment for certain offenses, and the other day in staid old Boston, the very center of erudition and wisdom, a learned Judge in disposing of a wife beater said: "If I have any influence with the other magistrates of this county and state, I will go to the legislature and ask that a law be passed to allow corporal punishment for wife beaters. I hope to live to see the day when I can order the lash to be applied to the naked back of the man who assaults his wife."
>
> There are circumstances where the "cat," well applied, seems to be the only thing that fits in.[1]

This tendency to seize upon expressions of opinion in other states and to use them as a justification of Delaware's use of corporal punishment is well illustrated by the following editorial, which was published originally in the Philadelphia *Inquirer* and later reprinted in the *Delawarean* on May 19, 1900:

THE MOVEMENT AGAINST THE POST

OPPONENTS OF POST AND PILLORY NOW SEE GOOD IN IT

There are multiplying and impressive indications that students of penology in the United States are being led by observation, study, and experience to the conclusion that the total abandonment [of corporal punishment as a penalty for crime in this country] . . . is a mistake. Several of our own judges have lately expressed the opinion that for a certain class of crimes and for certain criminals and offenders the whipping post ought to be reëstablished. In the British House of Lords a few weeks ago, no less a person than Lord Salisbury declared that in many instances no kind of punishment is more salutary and effective than the cat-o'-nine-tails or the birch, and in England magistrates have authority to order the whipping of a juvenile or brutal offender. His Lordship ridiculed the idea that there was anything degrading in this kind of punishment, and reminded his hearers that they had often been flogged at school without suffering any loss of self-respect.

In this country the impression has prevailed that corporal punishment is in some way incompatible with an advanced system of civilization and, with the exception of Delaware, we know of no state in which it is now legally practiced. . . .

In this connection, it may be noted as a significant circumstance that at a recent meeting in New Haven of the Connecticut Congregational Association, an organization which includes both lay and clerical members, a resolution was adopted in which the re-institution of the whipping post as a punishment for petty crimes and for youthful offenders was strenuously urged.[2]

Chief Justice Lore, who had played a leading part in the agitation for the Workhouse, now began to participate in the controversy that was being waged over corporal punishment in Delaware. At a meeting held in Wilmington on January 20, 1901, under the auspices of the Society of Friends, the Chief Justice said: "The pillory ought to go. It is a relic of barbarity."[3]

Even so, he was just as firmly convinced that the whipping post should be retained, and in the discussion which took place on this occasion he opposed Alfred H. Love, of Philadelphia, and David Ferris, of Wilmington, both of whom argued for the abolition of all forms of corporal punishment in Delaware. Justice Lore, in declaring that he would have all wife-beaters whipped, stated, "I'd have the wife whip him if I could get her to do so, and would like to stand beside her at the time."

He also referred to the bank robbers, who had been sentenced to forty lashes in 1873, and said that although these men had returned to their criminal ways in other states, they had kept "religiously away from Delaware." Wilmington, according to Justice Lore, since it was situated on principal railroads, would become the dumping ground for criminal classes if the whipping post were abolished. He stressed the fact that he had never heard of a whipped criminal returning to Delaware.

David Ferris, a Quaker of Wilmington, arguing in favor of the abolition of both the "post" and the pillory, expressed the belief that the Workhouse would be an efficacious substitute for the whip. He said that Justice Lore had built the Workhouse with one hand and would tear it down with the other because the whip increased the number of criminals.

A few days after this discussion, the following very interesting letter was written to Justice Lore by David Ferris:

No. 301 West St.
January 25th, 1901

Dear Friend Chas. B. Lore,

I want to thank thee for attending our meeting at 4th and West and for thy frank yet kind remarks, even more complimentary to Friends than they deserve, perhaps. If Delaware's penal laws could be made to accord to thy expressed convictions to abolish the pillory and exclude girls, boys and women from the whippings, and limit the attendance of men, say to 8 or 10, it would be a distinct step gained for humanity. But to enact any law to whip wife-beaters would, in my view, be a deplorable relapse toward barbarism. I hope and pray it will not be done. I realize that there is a strong feeling in favor of continuing the lashing even among my own society. The community needs more Christian education on this point, but to enact a law to whip for a crime that has not so far been punished in that way, would be very discouraging to many of us who think the lash should be discontinued. I do hope if we move at all, it will be to advance, not retreat, in morality. I think thee knows that four-fifths of the wife-beatings are from husbands demonized by alcohol. I feel from thy kind spirit that thee will not be offended by my frank expression of dissent from thy opinion. I don't believe Chas. B. Lore would feel quite comfortable standing in public by an enraged woman, encouraging her to lay the lash unsparingly on her cruel drunken husband, and I feel sure he could not get one woman in ten to do it. They would vote by an overwhelming majority against husband-whipping. There is a better way, and a more effectual one. Put them in the Workhouse, set them to remunerative work, and let them devote their earnings to the support of their injured wives and families, and don't let them leave as intoxicants.

> My brother man, Beware!
> With that deep voice which from the skies
>   Forbade the Patriarch's sacrifice,
> God's angel cries, Forbear!

Sincerely and Truly Thy Friend,
DAVID FERRIS[4]

Finally, as a result of the movement to eliminate corporal punishment from the state's laws, a bill to abolish the pillory came before the Senate for pasage on January 29, 1901.[5] So far as the author can discover, no bill for the abolition of the pillory or the whipping post had ever before advanced this far in either branch of the legislature. A bill to abolish the whipping post and the pillory, introduced by Senator Alrichs of New Castle County, was read twice in the Senate during its 1897 session but was killed in committee.[6] The House, in 1899, was notified that a bill to abolish the pillory would be introduced, but the Journal of the House makes no further mention of this bill.[7] At the 1901 session, however, the Senate passed the bill for the abolition of the pillory by a vote of eleven to six, three senators from Sussex, two from Kent, and six from New Castle County voting for the bill, and two senators from Sussex, three from Kent, and one from New Castle County voting against it.[8]

Although there seemed to be no consolidated opposition in the two lower counties, yet, as the foregoing analysis indicates, this bill received its strongest support from New Castle County, the old stronghold of penal reform in Delaware. In the legislature of 1901, the Republicans had nine senators and twenty representatives; the Democrats, eight senators and fifteen representatives.[9] Since in the Senate seven Republicans and four Democrats favored the measure, while two Republicans and four Democrats opposed it, it is apparent that the balloting did not follow party lines.[10] In the House, the committee to which the bill was referred submitted an unfavorable report on February 11, 1901, and no further action on it was taken at that session.[11]

Despite the movement against corporal punishment, two bills that proposed its specific extension were presented to the legislature in 1901. One of these, the Clements bill, was for the prevention of wife-beating; the other, the Ewing bill, perhaps satirically, provided for the punishment of husband-beaters.[12] The Clements bill was passed by the legislature and became a law on February 22, 1901.[13] By its provisions, husbands convicted of beating their wives were to be guilty of a misdemeanor and sentenced, at the discretion of the court, to be whipped with not less than five nor more than thirty lashes, and fined and imprisoned.

The Ewing bill, the only measure calling for the whipping of female offenders that had been introduced into the legislature in many years,[14] was sponsored by Representative Frank P. Ewing of New Castle County. It declared that any wife who by physical violence abused, maltreated, or beat her husband was, upon conviction, to be adjudged guilty of a misdemeanor and be punished with not less than five nor more than thirty lashes, which were to be inflicted by the sheriff or by the husband, if he so desired.[15]

Representative William Chandler, of New Castle County, chairman of the crimes and punishments committee, was asked, on January 31, what he thought of the bill. He replied: "We shall call the committee together and consider the measure, if the member introducing it insists upon it, and we may even refer it to the floor of the House, without recommendation for argument, but I don't think we want any such bill as that on our statute books."[16]

Representative Shadrack Short, of Sussex County, a member of the same committee, in referring to the Ewing bill, said: "I thought that bill had gone as far as it was intended. I don't think we can afford to send women to the whipping post. It is bad enough to send them to jail."[17]

Such public statements as these were made by other members of the legislature, and the Ewing bill,[18] which was probably introduced to cast discredit and ridicule upon the Clements wife-beating bill, did not receive any serious consideration by the lawmakers, never coming before them for a vote.

When the New Castle County Workhouse was constructed, the county's whipping post and pillory, in accordance with the law, were set up at the new institution. They were located in a small yard which was connected with the main building by a tunnel. The pillory was covered with a shed so as to protect the prisoners from the weather, and the "post," separated from the pillory, was built against a stone column in the wall.[19] The whipping post is still located in this small yard at the Workhouse.

The first corporal punishment to be inflicted at the recently completed New Castle County Workhouse was administered on Saturday, November 23, 1901, when Warden Meserve, in the presence of about one hundred persons, discharged his duties in accordance with the orders of the court.[20] The prisoners punished were: William Walker, a white man who had been convicted of housebreaking and sentenced to pay a fine of $500, stand one hour in the pillory, be whipped with twenty lashes, and serve ten years in prison; John King, another white man who had been convicted of assault with intent to commit murder and sentenced to stand one hour in the pillory, pay the costs of the prosecution and a fine of $1,000, and serve five years in prison; and Walter Thomas and Richard Coverdale, two colored men who had been convicted of housebreaking and each of whom had been sentenced to pay $27 as restitution money, stand in the pillory for one hour, be whipped with twenty lashes, and serve one year in prison.[21]

Warden Meserve began to administer the corporal punishment at ten o'clock in the morning, when the two white men, John King and William Walker, were placed in the pillory. At the expiration of their hour, they were succeeded in the pillory by Walter Thomas and Richard Coverdale, the two colored youths, who also stood there for one hour. None of the men had anything to say, but all acted as if the punishment was a terrible ordeal for them. A misty rain was falling during part of the time while they were in the pillory, but the men were protected there by the roof which covered the corner of the yard where the punishment was being inflicted.

At 12:35, just five minutes after the last man had been released from the pillory, William Walker, the only white man whipped on that day, was brought out. While the men had been in the pillory they had worn coats, but when they were shackled to the "post" their backs were bare. After Walker had been fastened, Warden Meserve began to apply the lashes and every one left its mark. Several times, while being whipped, Walker moaned and squirmed and said that he could not stand the punishment, but the warden ignored his pleas and the twenty lashes were well laid on.

The next prisoner to be whipped was Richard Coverdale, a colored man, who also received twenty lashes. He squirmed and twisted but did not say much. His back was marked with welts, and when the last stroke fell he dropped to his knees as if exhausted. The last prisoner lashed was Walter Thomas, the other colored man, who appeared to suffer the most. He cried and moaned, wriggled and bent his body and arms, twisted about and tried to protect his back with his feet, but all to no avail.[22]

The legislative session of 1903 was unproductive of any laws regarding corporal punishment, but this did not deter those who were seeking to abolish the whipping post and the pillory. On the contrary, advocates of penal reform laid plans for another legislative campaign, and in December 1903, the New Century Club of Wilmington held a meeting to discuss the desirability of eliminating corporal punishment from the criminal code of Delaware. Professor Frederic H. Wines, President of the Prisoners' Aid Association of New Jersey, gave an address at this meeting, and during his speech, in which he opposed the use of the lash, he said: "Whipping is bad for the man whipped, bad for the man who does the whipping, and bad for those who witness the whipping."[23]

Such efforts as these laid the foundation for an important victory by the forces of penal reform during the next meeting of the legislature in 1905. At this session, a bill to abolish the pillory was introduced into the Senate and there passed on March 8, 1905, by a vote of fourteen to two. The measure was supported by six senators from New Castle County, four from Kent, and four from Sussex, whose combined strength overwhelmed the two opposing votes cast by one senator from New Castle County and one from Sussex.[24]

This abolition bill lay dormant in the House for a week because some of the representatives claimed that they did not understand why "humanitarians and reformers," who desired to abolish the pillory, wished to keep the whipping post.[25] On March 16, prominent citizens, eager to have the bill enacted into law, appeared on its behalf in the House. Horace G. Knowles, representing the bench and the bar of Delaware, eloquently pleaded for its passage and presented an appeal in the form of a letter from Chief Justice Lore, in which the latter stated, "I am deeply impressed with the propriety, indeed, the necessity for the abolition of the pillory." At the same time, however, he again stressed his belief that Delaware should retain the whipping post since without its deterrent influence the state might become a haven for criminals from several large cities located near-by.[26] When the bill was put to a vote in the House, only Representative Prettyman of Kent County registered his dissent, and it passed by a vote of thirty-one to one.[27] Thus, in impressive fashion, by the act of March 20, 1905, an ancient form of corporal punishment was at last removed from Delaware's criminal laws.[28]

Apparently the pillory, on this occasion at least, did not constitute a source of contention among the counties, nor in fact was it an issue that divided the two political parties in the state. The legislature of 1905 was composed of thirty-one Republicans and twenty-one Democrats.[29] It will be noted, by reference to the foregoing vote, that the great majority of the members of both parties favored the abolition of the pillory.

This victory by the advocates of penal reform meant more than the mere removal of a nominal threat from the statute books of the state, for the pillory was in use until almost the last minute of its legal existence in Delaware. In 1905 two men were placed in the pillory in New Castle County,[30] and although neither of the other two counties pilloried prisoners during this year, in 1904 one man in Kent[31] and six others in Sussex were so punished.[32] The last men to be pilloried in Delaware were William Ryans and Alonzo Green, negroes, who received this penalty at the New Castle County Workhouse on February 11, 1905. Ryans, convicted of highway robbery, had been sentenced to pay a fine of $300 and costs, stand one hour in the pillory, be whipped with forty lashes, and serve five years in prison. Green, found guilty of breaking and entering, had been ordered to pay a fine of $500 and costs, stand one hour in the pillory, be whipped with twenty lashes, and be imprisoned for six years.[33]

Since the race of the prisoner was not always shown in the court records, and since the prison records of Kent and Sussex counties for the early part of the twentieth century are missing, there is no way of ascertaining when the last white man was pilloried in Delaware. However, the last man pilloried whose race was indicated as white in the state's records was Charles Lewis, age thirty-six, a carpet salesman of Wilmington, who received this punishment on May 28, 1904. Lewis had been convicted of breaking and entering, and sentenced to pay the costs of prosecution, forfeit $17 as restitution, stand one hour in the pillory, receive twenty lashes, and be imprisoned for eighteen months.[34]

In Kent County the last man pilloried was Alfred Josephs (race unknown), who received this punishment on October 29, 1904. Josephs had been convicted of breaking and entering, and sentenced to pay the costs of prosecution, stand one hour in the pillory, receive twenty lashes, and be imprisoned for one year.[35]

Sussex County pilloried its last man on November 5, 1904. The prisoner was Lawrence M. Durham (race unknown), who had been convicted of pretending to exercise the art of witchcraft and sentenced to pay a fine of $100 and costs, stand one hour in the pillory, and be imprisoned for one year.[36]

A few weeks after the pillory had been abolished, Justice Lore received the following letter from David Ferris, with whom, it will be recalled, the Justice several years before had discussed the question of corporal punishment at a meeting held under the auspices of the Society of Friends:

THE MOVEMENT AGAINST THE POST

No. 301 West Street
4-6-05

Dear Friend Chas. B. Lore,

I ought to have thanked thee before this for thy message to the legislature, saying "it would be doing the state a great service by abolishing the pillory." I do thank thee. I was so anxious that the whole thing should go that perhaps I did not enough appreciate this first step. I am so desirous to see Delaware rid of the whole instrument of torture that I pray to live two years longer to see the end. I enclose a card from A. H. Love with a message to thee.

Truly,
D. Ferris[37]

Before it adjourned in 1905, the legislature enacted another law which affected the administration of corporal punishment in Delaware. By an act approved on April 3, Kent and Sussex were given access to the New Castle County Workhouse.[38] This law not only provided that all prisoners with unexpired terms of six months or more were to be transferred in April 1907 from the jails of these counties to the New Castle County Workhouse, but also declared that during April 1907 and thereafter, the courts of Kent and Sussex might, at their discretion, send all prisoners to the latter institution. As a result of the passage of this law, it became customary for these courts to commit prisoners with sentences of six months or more to the New Castle County Workhouse, and therefore virtually all corporal punishment in Delaware, from 1907 to 1931, inclusive, was administered by that institution's officials.[39]

The abolition of the pillory heartened those who were opposed to the whipping post, and they once more carried their fight to the legislature in 1907, the Quakers of Delaware assuming a leading part in the movement. On January 23 of that year, the House received the following communication concerning the whipping post from a group of Wilmington Friends:

To the House of Representatives of the State of Delaware.

The Committee of Philanthropic Labor of the Wilmington Monthly Meeting of Friends (held at Fourth and West streets), believing that the whipping post is of no value in preventing crimes, or reforming the criminal, but is brutal and degrading in its effect on both the culprit and the on-looking public, and that its use is opposed in the enlightened spirit of the times and is a disgrace to the state, respectfully ask that the Legislature pass a law abolishing its use as a means of punishment for criminals in Delaware.

Signed on behalf of the Committee,
Chairman, D. I. K. Evans
Secretary, Mary K. Evans

Wilmington, Delaware
January 22, 1907[40]

As a result of the increased pressure for the abolition of the whipping post, a bill for that purpose came before the Senate on January 29, 1907.

On the basis of the available evidence, this appears to be the first bill of this kind ever to advance in the legislature as far as a vote for passage. The measure had been unfavorably reported upon by a Senate committee, and its defeat was made final when fifteen senators, without opposition, voted against it.[41]

On July 17, 1907, Warden A. S. Meserve, the first warden of the New Castle County Workhouse, presented his resignation and that of Mrs. Meserve, who had been employed as matron of the institution,[42] and explained that one of the reasons for his resignation was his opposition to the whipping post. In explaining his position on this question, he said:

> I have made a very careful and unbiased study of the effect of the whipping post on men of the criminal class and have come to the conclusion, beyond a doubt, that it is all bad. I cannot recall a single case in which it was not bad. It brings out in a man all that is revengeful and hurtful and he arrays himself against law, order and society.[43]

The *Every Evening,* of Wilmington, Delaware, in commenting editorially on this statement of Warden Meserve regarding the "post," emphatically asserted: "The whipping post . . . is retained in Delaware's penal code and without apology. As we have before remarked, it has proved itself a deterrent to crime and a protection to the community."[44]

When the legislature convened in 1909, the lawmakers were again petitioned to abolish the whipping post. A counter-campaign was soon organized, however, and one of its leaders on January 2, 1909, declared through the pages of the *Delawarean*:

> A man who does not hesitate to beat a man and rob him on the highway, another who is daily beating his wife, a man who does not hesitate to apply the iron of torture to folks whom he surprises in the privacy of their rooms, stealing their valuables and treasures of a lifetime, is not to be given punishment to fit the crime? Why not? It is not the post that the criminals fear, it is the public and the press at the post.[45]

In the face of such determined opposition, the efforts of those who were seeking the removal of the "post" proved fruitless, and the legislatures of 1909[46] and 1911 adjourned without taking any action on the question. Before the state's representatives were again called upon to consider it, a storm of national indignation broke over Delaware because of its persistent use of corporal punishment. For years in many other states there had been deep resentment, punctuated by bitter attacks, against the whipping of Delaware's criminals, but 1912 was to see this antagonism burst into a fulmination, the echoes of which the following year reached the floor of Congress. The incident that caused this furious outburst was the sentencing in Kent County of Dick Wright, a white man who was a notorious burglar and horse thief, to seventy lashes. Forty of these were to be applied on March 2, 1912; and thirty, the following Saturday, March 9.[47]

A WHIPPING, NEW CASTLE COUNTY JAIL, 1897

THE MOVEMENT AGAINST THE POST

Seventy-five persons saw Wright whipped the first time in the open enclosure of the New Castle County Workhouse on an intensely cold day. While Warden Crawford lashed Wright and four negroes, the temperature stood at twenty-six degrees. The Wilmington *Sunday Star,* on March 3, in describing the whipping, declared: "While Wright was being lashed, the four negroes were covered with blankets and their hands were shielded with gloves. Prior to the laying on of the lash, the men showed their feelings plainly."[48]

On the same day the *Sunday Star* reprinted the following criticism of Delaware's whipping post, which had appeared in the *Gazette,* of York, Pennsylvania:

Commenting on a recent case of whipping in Delaware, the San Francisco *Star,* moved to pity for Delaware's ancient custom, had this to say: "The other day they whipped two men into insensibility in a Delaware prison. Cut, gashed and bleeding, the two unfortunate men endured until human fortitude could endure no more, and then they sank into blessed unconsciousness. And sometimes it has been supposed that Delaware is a civilized commonwealth. Merely to record the foregoing truths is to indict Delaware as lagging far behind in the procession of States. In a cruelty that is of the past, she stands alone, and is ashamed in her loneliness. She should awake, rub her eyes open, and move forward among those who happily have discarded the ways of savagery. As it is, she earns not only startled wonder, but contempt as well."

This has touched to the quick the *Every Evening,* of Wilmington, Delaware, which denies brutality. . . .

If the whippings are not brutal, why do the criminals fear them as they would a deathly scourge? Perhaps the San Francisco *Star* was in possession of a false report when it said that two men who had been punished at the Delaware whipping post were cut and gashed until they were bloody from the beatings inflicted, but as to the savagery of the Delaware law, the *Star* is right. It is a shame and disgrace to Delaware as well as to civilization.[49]

The protests against the severe sentence given to Wright assumed such serious proportions in both Delaware and elsewhere that Governor Pennewill remitted the remaining thirty lashes. The Wilmington *Sunday Star* assured its readers on March 17, 1912, in the following article, that the action of Governor Pennewill should not be considered as an expression of sympathy for Wright, but as a move to prevent the abolition of the state's whipping post:

REMIT LASHES TO SAVE WHIPPING POST

That the board of pardons of Delaware should be petitioned to show mercy to a young white convict, who committed a chain of crimes throughout the state and ended up by the midnight torture of a woman, living alone in her bed chamber, which he burglarized, carrying off her savings, seemed almost inconceivable to persons not in touch with Dick Wright's case, but such is the situation.

Governor Pennewill has remitted the remaining thirty lashes at the whipping post, to which he [Wright] was sentenced. He got forty lashes the day he arrived at the Greenbank Workhouse. It is not sympathy for Wright that has prompted the movement before the board of pardons, where the matter now goes after Governor Pennewill's reprieve of the corporal punishment part of the sentence for sixty days.

The nation-wide attack on Delaware because of the whipping post this winter has caused advocates of the post to join in the Wright remission movement. Wright does not figure at all except that he is a man who has already been recently severely whipped with forty lashes, suffering humiliation and great pain. . . . Advocates of maintaining the whipping post in Delaware feel that if Wright is punished with the additional thirty lashes, to which the court has sentenced him on his plea of guilty, and if there should be any physical breakdown as a result, the whipping post would be doomed and "Little Delaware" would be at the mercy of midnight cutthroats and thieves from Baltimore and Philadelphia, as a distinguished Chief Justice once said.[50]

When the state's legislature convened in January 1913, Governor Pennewill, in his address to the general assembly on the seventh of that month, felt called upon to defend the whipping post against its enemies. At that time the state's chief executive declared:

Much has been said during the past year by the press, and particularly by the press outside of the state, concerning this mode of punishment which is still adhered to in Delaware. I am convinced that an investigation at the New Castle County Workhouse, where this punishment is now inflicted, will convince any reasonable person that it is not done in a barbarous manner, as the articles appearing in the press would lead one to think, but that those who receive this punishment are shown as much consideration as the circumstances will warrant.

The fact that the English Parliament has recently passed a bill providing for this method of punishment for certain offenses, and that other states in this country, also, are considering its adoption, should be sufficient proof that we have made no mistake by continuing it.[51]

Despite the seething agitation against the whipping post, the legislature during its 1913 session did nothing to appease those who were clamoring for the abolition of corporal punishment in Delaware. This complete indifference to widespread criticism merely served to throw more fuel upon the fires of public indignation, and national feeling over the issue drove the controversy into the United States House of Representatives. On November 11, 1913, a resolution to compel Delaware to abolish her whipping post was placed before that body by Representative Evans of Montana, who a few days later, in a speech before the House, denounced the whipping of prisoners as futile and degrading. The resolution stated that such punishment was a violation of the eighth amendment to the Constitution, which provides that "cruel and unusual punishments" shall not be inflicted, and it therefore asked that the President of the United States and the Attorney General be authorized and directed to cause an injunction against Delaware to be brought into the Federal Courts to prevent that state's officials from using the whipping post in the punishment of criminals.[52]

The House of Representatives adjourned without action and, on November 14, Representative Brockson of Delaware answered the resolution of Representative Evans, and tried to prove that the Federal Courts had no jurisdiction in the matter. During the course of his speech, Brockson said he conceded that other states had the right to their own opinion about corporal punishment, but that they had no right to tell another state how to treat its criminals.

After quoting the Bible in defense of corporal punishment, he concluded his speech amid much applause, with the following words:

> The practice of making martyrs of criminals is a modern curse of society. I have but little patience with any man who permits his sympathy to run with a felon so far as to forget the rights of law-abiding citizens of the State. The State of Delaware, being satisfied with the justice of her laws, is willing to demonstrate the principle, if need be, that it is better to stand alone for that which is right than to stand with the multitude for that which is wrong.[53]

The United States Attorney General upheld Delaware in its contention that the Federal Courts had no authority to issue the injunction demanded by Representative Evans, and that it was free to apply the lash without interference from the Federal Government.[54] Although this decision stilled the controversy in Congress,[55] the opponents of the "post" in Delaware persisted in their agitation for its abolition. The Quakers of the state continued as leaders in this movement, and on January 18, 1914, at a meeting held under their auspices in Wilmington, Professor Louis N. Robinson, of Swarthmore College, delivered an address in which he severely criticized the whipping post. During this speech, while carefully analyzing many aspects of the subject, Professor Robinson declared:

> In the first place, I expect to be told that I, as a citizen of Pennsylvania, am a rank outsider, who has no business to meddle with the affairs of Delaware. This argument, as you know, is not new and has been invoked on many a similar occasion. It represents the attitude of a type of man who fails to realize that, in matters of right and wrong, state lines cannot act as barriers to the natural impulses of man. . . .
>
> Secondly, I have noticed in your newspapers that it is rather common for the advocates of the whipping post to resort to that form of argument which consists of calling names. Weak, hysterical, sentimental, and even worse adjectives are applied to those who denounce this form of punishment. This is, of course, no argument, and it will be found, I think, that men do not turn to it unless all their other arguments have been proven false and useless. . . .
>
> I have found in examining the literature on the subject, but four real arguments in favor of a flogging as a punishment for crime. They are: (1) the argument of retaliation; (2) the argument of economy; (3) the argument of prevention of crime; and (4) the argument of reform of the offender. . . .
>
> The argument based on retaliation is simple. Its theory is approximately the Old Testament notion of an "eye for an eye, a tooth for a tooth." . . . Flogging is thus defended as a means of making the criminal pay back what he owes to society.

There is no denying that this desire to get even with the offender is found in nearly every one of us. But the question is not whether such a feeling exists, but whether it is wise to give expression to it, whether it is wise to let it dominate our actions. . . .

Secondly, flogging is the cheapest form of punishment. . . . The question for society must always be, which is cheaper in the long run? Nor is money cost the only cost which society must consider. The whipping post, as I shall point out later, lays a burden on society, through its brutalizing influence, which cannot be estimated in money. . . .

Without doubt, the third argument which I have mentioned, the argument of prevention, is the most potent one yet adduced in favor of the whipping post. It is claimed that it prevents crime. . . .

An eminent American jurist, in discussing the means necessary to prevent crime, has said: "Society must make the evil heavy enough and distasteful enough to outweigh the element of uncertainty and distance." . . . You will notice that this idea of balance is based on a pleasure and pain theory of conduct — a theory of ethics which, by the way, is largely discredited at the present time. . . . It is a well-known fact that criminals are notoriously short-sighted. . . . If men who commit crimes were so far-seeing as to calculate with exactness the pleasure to be obtained from their contemplated crimes and to balance over against it the possibility of detection, conviction, and the pain of a flogging, they would be men of sufficient sense and acumen to choose another career than that of crime, and they would do so. . . .

Fourthly, the whipping post is defended on the ground that it reforms the offender. . . . I cannot see what element of reform there is in taking away from a man what little self-respect he has, and in beating him down to the level of a brute. . . . "Treat a man like a dog and he will be a dog," should be written in every prison and criminal court in this land.[56]

Soon after arrangements for this meeting had been made, a circular letter asking for an expression of opinion on the whipping post was sent to many persons throughout the country. The answers to this circular letter were almost unanimous in their opposition to any use of the whipping post and, coming as many of them did from prominent persons who had had much experience in dealing with criminals, they constitute an impressive mass of testimony against corporal punishment.[57]

Encouraged by this display of opposition, the Society of Friends in Wilmington prepared a bill for the abolition of the whipping post and sent it, together with a pamphlet containing Professor Robinson's address and the letters referred to above, to Representative Downward, of New Castle County, who was to sponsor it in the legislature. In an accompanying letter Mr. George B. Miller, of the Society of Friends, expressed the hope that the measure would be passed and that a blot would thus be wiped from "the state's escutcheon."[58]

On March 2, 1915, Representative Downward, who in the meantime had presented the bill for the abolition of the whipping post to the legislature, delivered a well-prepared speech in which he called the "post" a cruel and inhuman instrument, and said that Delaware was the only state that still used it for such crimes as larceny.[59] Representative Hall, of Kent County, complimented Downward on his eloquent address, and also the House committee that had submitted an unfavorable report on the bill. He said that he hoped that the House would defeat the bill, and then asked Representative Downward what he had meant by saying in his address, "We can't get the people here we want because of the whipping post."

Representative Elliott, of New Castle County, interrupted by declaring, "I hardly think we want the criminals who are afraid of being whipped."

Representative Downward then explained that a president of a Wilmington bank had originally made that remark. Representative Saulsbury, of Sussex County, retorted with, "Prisoners who are whipped don't come back to Delaware."

The bill was soon thereafter put to a vote and overwhelmingly defeated by a vote of thirty to four, only Representatives Davis, of Sussex, Downward and Grantland, of New Castle County, and Jones, of Kent, voting for its passage.

The *Every Evening*, of Wilmington, the next day editorially acclaimed the crushing defeat of the Downward bill as "representative of public sentiment in the state."[60] The editorial asserted that the whipping post was a potent protection against attacks on property by dangerous burglars from the large cities, and pointed out that "the professionals of the burglarious fraternity" had avoided Delaware as a place of pestilence ever since the whipping of the notorious bank robbers in 1873. Arguing that none of the "big fellows" wanted the "disgrace of the post," the editor declared that they robbed post offices in Delaware because the federal law did not provide a punishment of whipping. In conclusion, the editor said, "Let us hope the agitation for a change will be abandoned, at least until there shall be ample evidence of a strong public sentiment to this end."[61]

In the spring of 1915, a meeting of public-spirited citizens was held in Wilmington to create an organization which became known as "The General Service Board of Delaware Civic and Social Welfare." The object of this board was to study social problems and to work for the passage of laws in order to advance public welfare in Delaware. An organizing committee was appointed and in its report expressed itself on the subject of the whipping post in the following manner:

> It is kept on the statute books not by the "unenlightened" members of the community, but by the influence of opinion expressed by some lawyers and members of the courts who contend that fear of the pain and public shame of whipping is the only thing which keeps marauding negroes in subjection. The contention has still the status of an opinion as no figures or data are available for proof. Whether the desired effect is secured or not the predominance of opinion, both within and outside of the state, seems to be that the brutalizing effect of maintaining this form of punishment offsets any reduction there might be in the number of cases of petty theft or marauding.

The law requires that the punishment of whipping shall be inflicted publicly by strokes well laid on the bare back, but not many members of the community care to attend, and those who do endorse the penalty do not attend in sufficient numbers to really carry out the value of the law as they interpret it.[62]

Although the year 1915 produced no real progress in the campaign to abolish Delaware's whipping post, it did witness the publication of another code.[63] The pillory had been abolished, it is true, but the new code revealed that more crimes had been added to the list of offenses punishable with whipping since the codification of 1893. These crimes, providing convincing evidence of the reactionary nature of the state's criminal laws, were burglary at night with explosives,[64] wife-beating,[65] perjury, and subornation of perjury.[66]

Those who had been directing the attack against the whipping post were undaunted by the strength of their opponents and courageously continued their agitation for its abolition. The Society of Friends was still a leader in this movement, and on January 21, 1917, sponsored a public meeting in Wilmington to arouse public interest in the question. Captain Richard F. Cross, warden of the New Castle County Workhouse, was among those who spoke at this meeting, and he vigorously opposed the use of the whipping post. In his opinion, whipping did not reform criminals but merely made them sullen. During the course of his remarks, he made this very interesting statement:

> To get some more definite information about . . . the whipping post . . . I walked into the dining room yesterday and said, "Boys, there is a movement on foot to abolish the whipping post. Now I want all of you who have been whipped more than once to raise your hands." I found that eleven had been whipped twice, three had been whipped three times and one had been at the whipping post four times. I also heard that there was a man out of prison who had been whipped seven or eight times.[67]

Another speaker at the meeting was Professor Louis N. Robinson, of Swarthmore College, who, it will be recalled, had addressed a similar meeting in Wilmington several years before. He argued that physical pain was of no use in reforming a criminal, and said that the abolition of the "post" would be an act of scientific reformation and not of maudlin sympathy.[68]

The *Every Evening*, of Wilmington, was quick to respond to this attack and on January 23, 1917, editorially defended the whipping post, advancing the old argument that it had protected the state from the depredations of the professional criminals of near-by large cities. The whipping of the bank burglars of 1873 was again held up as the "horrible example," and it was once more contended that the professional burglars who did come to the state confined their attention to post offices since there was no federal law for the imposition of corporal punishment.[69]

A few days later, George B. Miller, of the Society of Friends, in a

THE MOVEMENT AGAINST THE POST 47

letter addressed to the editor of the *Every Evening*, criticized that newspaper's stand on the whipping post issue, and said that if the other forty-seven states had believed in the deterrent value of the "post" they would certainly have used it against bank robbers. He declared that another bill to abolish the "post" would be presented to the legislature at its 1917 session, and then served notice that, in case of its defeat, still another such measure would be introduced at the 1919 meeting of the lawmakers.[70]

On January 20, 1917, the bill to which Mr. Miller had referred was presented to the House by Representative Downward, of New Castle County.[71] Later, an unfavorable report on the bill, signed by all members of the committee that had been studying its contents, was presented to the House, and this action was hailed by the *Every Evening* as a "straw" which indicated a trend away from the sentiment of condoning crime and coddling criminals. "Apparently," declared this newspaper, "our people are not yet ready to say that crime should be condoned, and that punishment should not be of a kind that the offender will feel plainly. . . ."[72] On February 27, 1917, Representative Downward, foreseeing the overwhelming defeat of his bill, requested its withdrawal from the list of bills to be considered by the House.[73] His request was granted and thus expired another legislative move against the "post."

Despite this insurmountable opposition in the legislature, another bill for the abolition of the whipping post was presented to the lawmakers in 1919. Once more, however, on February 28, the measure was peremptorily rejected, this time in the Senate, by a vote of fifteen to two.[74] It was quite evident that the overwhelming majority of the senators from all parts of the state, and regardless of party, were in favor of retaining the "post." The following week, the *Every Evening*, a persistent foe of the movement to abolish the "post," editorially pointed to the action of the Senate and called it representative of the people's sentiment on the question. Again repeating the old claim that the whipping of the bank robbers in 1873 had protected the state from professional criminals, the editor asserted that the citizens of Delaware considered it better to endure reproach than to eliminate so efficacious a punishment.[75]

The *Every Evening* continued to publish articles on the "post," and on May 23, 1921, in discussing the subject, it declared that the most significant argument that had been advanced against the whipping of criminals was contained in a statement issued several years before by the warden of the New Castle County Workhouse. This statement showed that of the 461 prisoners lashed during the previous thirteen years, fifty-four had been whipped twice; fourteen, three times; four, four times; and one, five times.[76]

In the meantime, on April 13, 1920, Mordecai S. Plummer had succeeded Captain Richard F. Cross as warden of the New Castle County Workhouse. Like his predecessor he was opposed to the whipping post, and when Dr. O. F. Lewis, General Secretary of the American Prison Association, visited the Workhouse on April 16, 1921, Warden Plummer, in discussing the use of the lash, said:

> This whole whipping business is wrong. The whipping post does no good, only harm. It humiliates. The board of trustees of the Workhouse is against it, but the board can't abolish it. That has to be done by law. And the people of the state want the whipping post. . . . You must understand that the law gives to the warden no discretion . . . but the law doesn't tell me how hard to whip![77] Here's the way I whip. . . .

Then, according to Lewis, the warden showed how he used the lash. "Slowly, gently, almost doubtfully, the warden's right arm swung back and forth, like the pendulum of a clock deciding to cease work," wrote Lewis, in describing the warden's demonstration.[78]

Thus, of the first four wardens of the New Castle County Workhouse, only one, Warden Crawford, is reported to have favored the lashing of prisoners. The latter is quoted as having said on one occasion: "The lashes make men think. They have a good effect upon their minds. Criminals must be punished. Delaware would have more than her share of crime but for the whipping post."[79] The other three, Wardens Meserve, Cross, and Plummer, publicly opposed the whipping post. It is apparent, therefore, that the movement against the lash was not composed of just "theorists" but included "practical men" who had had much experience in dealing with prisoners.

During the controversy over the whipping post, one of the accusations that had often been hurled at Delaware was that the laws of the state were deliberately framed to protect the rich, the well-to-do, and the so-called better classes of society from the "post," and to send the negro and the poor and friendless white to be lashed. This charge was energetically expressed in an article which appeared in the *Sunday Star,* of Wilmington, on February 18, 1923.[80] In this the author, William H. Conner, severely attacked the injustice of the "post" and declared:

> It has been said that the usual crime for which lashes are ordered is larceny. But when the greater criminal steals it is called embezzlement. The writer is fully aware of the legal distinction between larceny and embezzlement, but submits that after all, the distinction is a legal one. There is a physical difference between the burglar and robber as compared with the one guilty of larceny — the probability of assault on the victim, but larceny and embezzlement are closely akin.
>
> The criminal of better family, or having more influential friends, may steal, or embezzle, if you will, as high as two hundred thousand dollars and never get a lash. There are in the New Castle County Workhouse several men who have embezzled amounts ranging from $25,000 to $200,000 and who have never been lashed, while there are others there who have stolen a chicken or a pair of shoes and have received their full quota of lashes.
>
> But we will say that the small thief deserves what he gets for not embezzling instead of committing larceny. Then let us peep into the Revised Code.

Under embezzlement, we find that embezzlement by a carrier or porter, presumably one of the lower stratum of society, is a felony punishable by twenty lashes, but we find also that embezzlement by a cashier or clerk (note the social level) is merely a misdemeanor, and is punishable by a prison term without lashes. And if the treasurer of the state, city, or municipality chooses to embezzle, it is a misdemeanor, and punishable with a prison term but no lashes.

To go further, forging a bank note, a nice genteel occupation, is a felony but without lashes, but to have in one's possession a counterfeit plate or die is a felony with thirty lashes as punishment. Strange to say, however, to counterfeit the Great Seal of Delaware, or to forge a court record, is punished merely with fine and imprisonment. . . .

When the 1923 session of the legislature opened, the opponents of the "post" were still very active, and Senator Simonton, of New Castle County, introduced another bill to abolish the whipping of prisoners. This, like several previous ones, had been prepared by George B. Miller of the Society of Friends, which for a number of years had been the leader in the movement against the "post."[81] Reported out of committee "on its merits," the measure came before the Senate for passage on March 28, 1923. Its fate, however, was no better than that of its predecessors, and it went down to defeat, as party lines were broken, by a vote of eleven to five. Two senators from New Castle County and three from Sussex supported the bill, but they were overwhelmed by the opposition of five senators from New Castle County, five from Kent, and one from Sussex.[82]

Despite repeated failures, the movement against the whipping post remained alive, and its leaders again introduced a bill to abolish it at the 1925 session of the legislature. This time Representative Downward, of New Castle County, then speaker of the House, presented the bill to the lawmakers, who quickly manifested their opposition to the measure. Once more it was handicapped by an unfavorable committee report,[83] and when it came before the House for final consideration on March 26, Speaker Downward was the only representative to take the floor in its support. After reading a letter from George B. Miller of the Wilmington Society of Friends, who had requested him to introduce the bill, he began a vigorous attack against the "post." During his speech he explained that the army and the navy had found whippings to be useless in disciplining men, and contended that in Delaware the "post" was a symbol of class legislation directed against the poor, who, he said, were the only ones lashed.[84]

Warden Leach, of the New Castle County Workhouse, also spoke on behalf of the bill and said that after every whipping he received a flood of letters in protest from all parts of the country. At this point he was interrupted by Representative Virden, of New Castle County, who asserted that if the "post" created so much talk outside of the state, "it must be doing some good." Warden Leach continued his speech and explained that his experience indicated that whippings did not protect society and failed to reform prisoners. Furthermore, he asserted that corporal punishment clashed with the policy of reform which he was trying to introduce at the Workhouse. Representative Virden again interposed a remark and asked Warden Leach what percentage of prisoners were whipped more than once. The warden said that his records showed that out of every hundred men whipped, at least forty had been lashed once before; twelve, two or more times before.

At the conclusion of this discussion, the bill was voted upon and decisively defeated, thirty-one to one, only Speaker Downward voting in its favor.[85] Newspapers in many large cities in other states commented on this repulse of the reform movement in Delaware, the *Boston Evening Transcript* satirically remarking: "It is said of the daughter of a prominent Delaware jurist that while she was in England some years ago, she was taken to see an ancient whipping post . . . and when the guide said to her, 'Lady, I fear the sight of this will make your blood run cold,' she replied, 'Oh, that's nothing! I live just across the street from one!' "[86]

The *New York Times* merely observed, "Delaware legislators, endorsing the efficacy of the whipping post for certain classes of crimes, now as in former years, today voted almost unanimously in favor of retaining the post."[87]

The *Every Evening*, of Wilmington, however, insisted that there were two sides to the question and that Delaware had good reasons for using the "post." An article in that paper, in referring to the increase of crime in Delaware, stated:

> How far this noticeable increase in crime, instead of the notable decrease that was promised as a result of prohibition, is due to the leniency of the so-called corporal punishment and the coddling of the inmates of our workhouse may be an interesting and pertinent question. So finally it would seem that the real question for discussion is not: "Should the whipping post be abolished?" but: "Should not the whipping post be properly and judiciously administered, or abolished altogether?"[88]

Apparently the *Every Evening* reflected the opinion of many influential citizens, for those advocating the abolition of the "post" have never again been able to push the issue as far as a vote in the state legislature. However, opposition to the whipping post during the 1925 legislative session did seem to exert some influence upon the lawmakers, because before adjourning they passed several laws that were significantly related to the use of the lash. The first of these, approved April 7, 1925, provided that in all cases of conviction of crime where whipping was made part of the punishment to be inflicted, the court might, in its discretion, if the prisoner was of "tender years," or charged for the first time, or if other circumstances were shown, deemed by the court sufficient, omit such corporal punishment from the sentence.[89] Thus the provisions of the act of February 15, 1883, which had declared that corporal punishment in certain cases might be remitted,[90] were repealed, and the sentencing of a prisoner to a public whipping was placed entirely within the discretionary powers of the court.

Within a few days after the enactment of this law, several acts were passed which apparently were intended to be an answer to the charge that whipping was a "poor man's punishment" in Delaware. One of these made embezzlement by a cashier, servant, or clerk punishable with a public whipping, with not more than twenty lashes, and imprisonment for not more than ten years.[91] The other provided that fraudulent misapplication or conversion of funds by executors, administrators, guardians, justices, constables, or attorneys-at-law was to be punished with a public whipping, with not more than ten lashes, and imprisonment for from one to five years.[92]

A few years later, at the 1931 session, the legislature attempted to create an exception to the law that had placed the sentencing of a prisoner to a public whipping entirely within the discretionary powers of the court. Both the Senate and the House passed a bill which provided that any person over sixteen years of age, convicted of stealing chickens, was to be publicly whipped with not less than ten lashes, in addition to being fined and imprisoned.[93] Whipping for this type of offense was thereby made mandatory.[94]

To this, Governor C. D. Buck objected and refused to sign the bill, declaring in his veto message to the legislature:

> To take away from the Courts the discretion of imposing lashes for this felony is, in my judgment, a mistake, as a law of this kind could prove most embarrassing to the State. Particularly would this be true if a culprit was a girl or woman, an imbecile or physical derelict.
>
> Delaware believes the post is a deterrent to crime or the law legalizing it would not remain on the statute books. It has withstood years of criticism and is likely to withstand many more, provided its use when authorized is left to the judgment of the courts.[95]

Articles about the whipping post continued to appear in the newspapers of Delaware and other states, and occasionally some prominent person would advocate that his state should whip its criminals. Among such persons were Judge Brown and Judge McDevitt of Philadelphia. The former, in sentencing a group of youths to the penitentiary, said, "It would be a good thing if we had a whipping post, as they have in Delaware, for these young bandits."[96] The latter several times recommended the public whipping of criminals as a "deterrent against lawlessness," declaring that he knew of no other form of punishment that would prove "so effective in halting the increasing flood of lawlessness" that was sweeping Philadelphia.[97]

Other prominent persons, however, persisted in condemning the lash and urging its abolishment. George Bernard Shaw, for example, in an article appearing in the *New York Times,* said, "In France the horrors of Cayenne and Devil's Island, and in America the frightfully long periods of solitary confinement and Delaware's flogging suggest the civilization of fiends rather than of human beings."[98]

At the next meeting of the general assembly in 1933, a legislative campaign was begun to have all Kent and Sussex prisoners incarcerated in their own jails. This move was partly successful, and by a law approved June 1, 1933, it was provided that all persons convicted in Kent and Sussex, and sentenced to terms of imprisonment of ten years or less, were to be committed to the jails of those counties. The courts of Kent and Sussex might, at their discretion, still commit all prisoners sentenced for terms of more than ten years to the New Castle County Workhouse.[99] The passage of this law meant that from this time on corporal punishments were once more to be administered in the Kent and Sussex County jails as well as in the New Castle County Workhouse.

The series of shattering blows which the opponents of corporal punishment had received during the legislative sessions from 1915 to 1925 deprived the reform movement of much of its vigor, and organized agitation against the "post" rapidly dwindled throughout the state. From time to time, however, outstanding citizens of Delaware made public statements in which they criticized the whipping of criminals and branded the practice as futile. Warden Leach of the New Castle County Workhouse was one of these persistent critics, and in January 1935, a short time before his retirement as warden, he let it be known in no uncertain terms that he was still absolutely opposed to the use of the whipping post. Describing the "post" as a "barbaric relic of the past," he declared:

Unless an honest attempt has been made to redeem a man during his period of confinement, a prison has no more right to exist than a hospital that turns its patients out no better than when they were admitted with no attempt to cure.

When a man who presumably is to be turned from the wrong course and reestablished in society is taken out into the yard, stripped to his waist, shackled to a post and lashed on his bare back in view of the public, that man certainly does not leave the whipping post with as good a feeling towards society as when he went there, but with bitterness and humiliation in his heart which oftentimes is hard to overcome.

The belief that the whipping post keeps away professional criminals is not to be considered, as no man who commits a crime, whether it is petty larceny or a notorious robbery, ever goes into that deed until he feels that his plans are such that he will never be caught, otherwise he would not attempt it. It is a popular remark, accepted without a qualification by the unthinking, that criminals fear the Delaware lash. So would every murderer fear the chair or the noose if he expected to encounter it.

The whipping post . . . is the one thing that interferes with the effort made to rebuild the men that come to the Workhouse, and send them out better fitted to take their place among the world's workers. . . . With many prisoners the difficult task of rehabilitation must begin with a punishment that degrades and embitters and does nothing else.[100]

THE MOVEMENT AGAINST THE POST

A few days after he had thus condemned the whipping post, Warden Leach was again called upon to use the lash, this time upon three young white men, John Lightcap, Walter Bedwell, and Hazel Donovan, each of whom had been sentenced to ten lashes and three years in the Workhouse for robbery.[101] It was during these whippings that Mac Parker, a reporter for the *Philadelphia Record,* surreptitiously took a candid camera photograph of the lashing of one of these prisoners, who was only eighteen years old at the time of his punishment. This photograph, facing page 56, appeared in the newspapers of the larger cities of other states, and in an accompanying story Mac Parker ridiculed the whippings and sarcastically observed:

> Delaware's whipping post isn't all it's lashed up to be.
> By reputation, it's pretty terrible. But in actual practice, — well, I saw Warden Elmer J. Leach "lay it on" three youths this morning at the New Castle County Workhouse, at Greenbank, with all the enthusiasm of a gentleman brushing dust off his coat.
> The average American boy takes a harder "spanking" when the average American "Pop" gets out the shingle. . . .
> In the hands of a sadist, it could be a punishing instrument. But Warden Leach doesn't use it that way. The punch behind his blows was just sufficient to overcome the force of gravity in raising the whip to drop it across the back of his prisoners.
> You could almost imagine him whispering to the youth as he whipped him: "Son, this hurts me more than it does you."
> The three prisoners were smiling when they reached the infirmary after the "floggings."[102]

This publicity apparently struck many Delawareans in a sensitive spot, because a short time later at the legislative session of 1935, an attempt was made to limit to twelve the number of persons who might be permitted to witness a whipping.[103] This attempt failed, but the legislators were spurred on to enact a law on April 12, 1935, which made it a misdemeanor for any person to have a camera or a picture-taking device at or near the whipping post in any county in Delaware. Persons found guilty of violating this law were liable to a fine of not less than $500 or more than $1,000, at the discretion of the court, and upon failure to pay the fine and costs such persons might be imprisoned for not less than three or more than six months, at the discretion of the court.[104]

A week after the whipping of Lightcap, Bedwell, and Donovan, Warden Leach lashed two more prisoners, one of whom was a negro. The *Journal Every Evening,* in describing this whipping, said:

> Forty men, including four trustees of the Workhouse, witnessed the two whippings, standing in ankle-deep snow. Thirty-five lashes were applied.
> The two men whipped were Bernardo "Rock" Farne, also known as Bernardo Fiorentino, of Third Street near French, and Harry Ward, a negro. The former had been sentenced to 20 lashes and three years' imprisonment for breaking and

entering and the latter had been sentenced to 15 lashes and one year's imprisonment for larceny.

When he imposed sentence on Farne about ten days ago in General Sessions Court, Chief Justice Daniel J. Layton directed that the attention of the Workhouse trustees be called to the provision of the whipping statute which provided that the lashes shall be "well laid on the bare back." Chief Justice Layton also sentenced Ward, but in imposing sentence on him, did not make the statement he made in Farne's case.

The lashes, however, were laid on both men with the same force, considerably heavier than in the past whippings. A number of the spectators, however, admitted they were disappointed, having been under the impression that the flesh-breaking and blood-letting whippings of 40 and more years ago would be repeated.

Welts heavier than those raised on the backs of three white youths who were whipped last Saturday were raised on the backs of Farne and Ward and the blood blisters on Farne's back were more noticeable. Farne took the lashes with remarkable self-control but the negro winced and moaned after the fourth lash.

The lashes left no cuts. The welts on Farne were particularly noticeable where several of the leather thongs on the "cat" struck the tender flesh on each side of the abdomen.

After the whippings, nearly a score of other persons arrived at the Workhouse but were informed they were too late. They had been delayed by the treacherous roads, chiefly the one leading from Newport to the powerhouse of the Workhouse. A number of cars were stalled on this road.

The temperature in the Workhouse yard was about 28 degrees, as compared with 25 degrees last Saturday.

When the three youths were whipped last week, they were stripped to the waist in the Workhouse, marched down the cold tunnel into the yard, shackled without any covering on their backs, and then whipped.

Today a different procedure was followed to guard against the two prisoners' contracting pneumonia. The two were stripped in the Workhouse, and then a blanket was wrapped around each of them. They were taken through the tunnel to the yard and shackled to the whipping post, the blankets still remaining on their backs. Their backs remained covered while Warden Elmer J. Leach, who applied the lashes, read the court commitments. After the commitments had been read, the guard removed the blanket and the whipping followed.

After the last lash fell, the blanket was replaced and the two men taken to the Workhouse hospital where medication was applied to their bare backs. . . .

This was the second time both Farne and Ward have been whipped. . . .[105]

The most recent codification of Delaware's laws appeared in 1935, and by its provisions,[106] five crimes, namely, treason, murder of the first degree, rape, kidnapping, and burglary, are made punishable with death by hanging. Twenty-four other offenses are to be punished, in part, at the discretion of the court, with public whippings. Three of these, assault with intent to rob,[107] embezzlement by cashier, servant, or clerk,[108] and fraudulent misapplication of funds by administrators, etc.,[109] had been added to the list of crimes punishable with whipping after the publication of the code of 1915. Therefore, although the use of the "post" had been placed entirely within the discretionary powers of the court,[110] there had been no tendency to reduce the number of different kinds of crimes for which lashes might be inflicted.

The penalty of whipping must be inflicted publicly with strokes well laid on the bare back. Contrary to popular opinion, the law does not specify that the person who inflicts the lashes must keep his elbow stiff during the whipping, although this practice has been followed for a number of years in Delaware. In New Castle County, the whippings must be administered by the board of trustees of the New Castle County Workhouse through their keepers, officers, agents, and servants. In Kent and Sussex counties the lashes must be applied by the warden of the jail. The law requires that the whipping post be located in or near the yard of the jail or of the workhouse of each of the three counties.[111]

Whenever corporal punishment is a part of the sentence, the day of its execution must be fixed by the court. If a person is convicted at the same term of the court on several indictments for crimes punishable with whipping, the court must so graduate the sentences of such a person that he will not be whipped with more than a combined total of sixty lashes under all sentences.[112]

Since the publication of the code of 1935, there has been no concerted drive to abolish the whipping post. Its opponents have not as yet recovered from the series of crushing defeats suffered in the legislature during the period 1915 to 1925, and no organization in Delaware has been active in preparing public opinion for another legislative campaign.

Those who had been working for the abolition of corporal punishment were deeply dismayed when in April 1937, Elwood H. Wilson, the new warden of the New Castle County Workhouse, in an address to the Knights of the Round Table, described the "post" as a deterrent of crime. He declared that it was "paying dividends" despite the fact that it drew criticism from other sections of the country, and that he was convinced, as a result of his experiences as a warden and as a captain of detectives for the city of Wilmington, that it was keeping the state free of the pickpockets, hold-up men, gangsters, and crooks who plagued other states.[113] Warden Wilson, in thus aligning himself with Warden Crawford, became the second warden of the Workhouse to make a public statement in favor of the whipping post. The other four wardens of this institution (Meserve, Cross, Plummer, and Leach) had emphatically and publicly condemned the lashing of prisoners.

The *Journal Every Evening*, of Wilmington, Delaware, in commenting editorially upon Warden Wilson's statement, observed:

He said that of the 347 prisoners whipped at the Workhouse since 1923, only 18 were repeaters.

This does look significant, but it must be admitted that there is a humane side to the matter. Some persons consider the post a relic of barbarism. They feel it has no place in modern civilization.

Yet, if the post is giving the people of the state the protection it seems to give, it does not seem advisable to dispense with it. That is the view that has been taken by many Legislatures which have rejected proposals to abolish the whipping post just as the pillory has been scrapped.[114]

On August 2, 1938, the following interesting historical note on Kent County's whipping post was published in Wilmington's *Journal Every Evening*:

Here is a little penological history which may be of interest to Delawareans and others who are cursed with pilfering fingers and who live in constant danger of being punished at our much discussed and much abused whipping post. In days gone by, the whipping post down in Kent County stood out brazenly in the open courtyard of the county jail not far from the old state house. It looked like an old-time octagonal pump without a handle. It had a slit near the top of it in which the equally old-time pillory boards might be inserted when needed for punitive use. There also were iron shackles for holding the prisoners while they were being whipped. That whipping post was painted red from top to bottom. Negro residents bestowed upon it the name of "Red Hannah." Of any prisoner who had been whipped at the post it was said, "He has hugged Red Hannah!"

Since those days the pillory has gone out of use in Delaware and for several years all the whipping was done at the New Castle County Workhouse at Greenbank. Those old days are recalled by the fact that on last Friday each of four prisoners who had pleaded guilty in the Court of General Sessions here [Wilmington, New Castle County] was sentenced to imprisonment and also to receive 10 lashes. It is safe to assert that none of the four prisoners whipped under the sentences imposed will care to pass through the ordeal again.[115]

During its session of 1939, the legislature modified the law which prescribed whipping for certain crimes of breaking and entering. By an act approved on April 7,[116] the wording of this law, in general, was modified to read "with intent to commit any crime or misdemeanor" instead of "with intent to commit any felony."[117] The basis of prosecution was thus broadened, and breaking and entering offenses that previously had not carried the penalty of whipping were now made to do so.

Another law relating to the penalty of whipping was enacted at the 1941 session of the legislature, but the effect this time was to reduce the use of the whipping post. By this law, which was passed on February 14, 1941, larceny was divided into grand larceny (the theft of goods valued at twenty-five dollars or upwards), which was made a felony, and petty larceny (the theft of goods valued at less than twenty-five dollars), which now became a misdemeanor, and the latter was no longer to be punishable with whipping.[118]

Thus another step was taken in the long process which has gradually reduced the role that the whipping post has played in the criminal jurisprudence of Delaware. An important stage in this process was

AN EIGHTEEN-YEAR-OLD PRISONER RECEIVING TEN LASHES AT GREENBANK. THIS PHOTOGRAPH, APPEARING IN THE PHILADELPHIA RECORD, JANUARY 20, 1935, LED TO PASSAGE OF A LAW PROHIBITING PHOTOGRAPHING OF WHIPPING

THE MOVEMENT AGAINST THE POST

passed in 1883 when the court was empowered in certain cases of juveniles and others deserving of leniency to omit corporal punishment from the sentence. Then, in 1889, came the abolition of the whipping of women prisoners; in 1925, the placing of the use of the whipping post entirely within the discretionary powers of the court; in 1935, the prohibiting of the taking of pictures of whippings; and finally, in 1941, the removal of petty larceny from the list of crimes punishable with whipping. This last step was a far more important one than it appeared to be at first glance since a large percentage of the whippings in Delaware had been inflicted for crimes of petty larceny. It is therefore destined to have an important effect upon the future use of the "post."

In July 1941, at a meeting of the Prisoners' Aid Society of Delaware, an organization that has been active for many years in the state's penal reform movements, a committee was appointed with instructions to study the use of the whipping post and to submit a report of its findings. It was hoped that such information could be utilized in preparing the citizens of Delaware for another campaign to abolish the "post"; but unfortunately these plans were soon interrupted by the declaration of war, and the committee abandoned its work.

Partly as a result of the abolition of whipping for petty larceny, only eight prisoners were whipped in Delaware during 1942. Two of these received their lashes in Kent County, and in its report on their punishment, the *Journal Every Evening,* on December 4, 1942, said:

> With backs bared, and the thermometer registering 33 degrees, Leroy Gibson, 29, and Clarence Jackson, Jr., 26, negroes, stood in the Kent County jail at Dover today and received 20 lashes each. Sheriff Norris C. Adams administered the whippings.
>
> The pair had been convicted at the October General Sessions Court on charges of robbing a truck driver while they were supposedly at work outside the jail. Gibson was convicted on two charges and Jackson on one charge.
>
> The lashes given the men today were only half their sentence. Twenty more lashes will be administered on January 8th.
>
> The two men, their backs bared, were manacled to the whipping post. They did not wince under the blows and after the punishment their backs showed no marks of the lash.
>
> About 100 spectators were gathered outside the jail yard. [Whippings in Kent County can be seen through the iron fence that surrounds the yard of the jail.]
>
> Twenty-five official witnesses and police were in the jail yard at the time of the whipping.[119]

The annual number of whippings in Delaware has continued to be small. In 1943 only five prisoners received lashes; and in 1944 only six, all of these eleven prisoners except one being negroes.[120] This, however, did not prevent Representative Samuel B. Bird from introducing a bill for the abolishment of the whipping post into the legislature in February 1945. In explanation of this move, Representative Bird, Republican floor leader in the House, declared that he considered the whipping post a "relic of barbarism," and that he did not place much reliance upon the argument that it was keeping crime and criminals away from Delaware.[121] A short time later, the board of directors of the Prisoners' Aid Society of Delaware passed a resolution endorsing this bill and distributed a circular which advanced cogent reasons for its enactment.[122] Nevertheless, Delaware's legislators were not impressed, and the measure never even emerged from the committee to which it had been referred. Once more, as on many previous occasions, the "post" had successfully withstood an attack, and today the criminal laws of Delaware, as shown in Appendix B, still list twenty-four different crimes for which public whippings may be administered.

Chapter VI

THE POST – RETROSPECT AND PROSPECT

THE persistent use of the whipping post in Delaware clearly demonstrates how an archaic culture pattern, because of inertia, ignorance, and fear, can stubbornly resist widespread social change even after such use has become largely nominal. Introduced early in the colonial period, whipping, in accordance with the criminal jurisprudence of the Old World, was prescribed for most crimes down to the time when the colony came under the control of the Quakers. During their rule the legal basis of the whipping post was greatly reduced; but as the power of the Quakers waned, corporal punishment was reintroduced for many offenses, and both Pennsylvania and Delaware gradually erected criminal codes that were almost as severe as that of the Duke of York.

After the Revolution the penitentiary movement, which had its origin in Pennsylvania, produced large-scale penal reforms throughout America and Europe. However, although it resulted in the establishment of the penitentiary system and the abolition of corporal punishment in Pennsylvania, it failed in Delaware. This collapse of the penal reform movement left Delaware's whipping post undisturbed and insured its perpetuation as an important instrument of punishment in the state's criminal jurisprudence.

An analysis of the social, political, economic, and geographical factors operating in Delaware reveals why the penitentiary movement was defeated and why, in defeat, it received its greatest support in New Castle County.[1] Of Delaware's three counties, New Castle had the greatest cultural heterogeneity, the strongest tendency toward urbanization, the largest amount of the state's business and commerce, the closest contact with Philadelphia, America's center of penal reform, and the highest percentage of the state's Quakers. All these were conditions that favored the penal reform movement and, as a matter of fact, social change in general. In Kent and Sussex counties, on the other hand, life was carried on in small, scattered communities, sealed off by peninsular isolation. Non-Quaker, British traditions and customs became strongly established in these communities of southern Delaware, and rural simplicity prevailed in a slowly changing culture. These were conditions that provided an atmosphere hostile to penal reform and one that finally stifled the penitentiary movement.

The opposition to penal reform expressed itself effectually in the legislature through the political superiority of Kent and Sussex counties. According to the provisions of the state constitutions of 1776 and 1792, all counties had equal representation in both branches of the legislature. This made it possible for conservative members from the two southern counties to combine their votes in the legislative campaigns in order to thwart the efforts at reform exerted by the more progressive elements in the northern part of the state. During this controversy, the tendency for legislators to disregard their affiliations with state political parties in voting on penitentiary bills and resolutions caused the pattern of conflict between the northern and southern sections of Delaware to stand out in bold relief.

Unlike Pennsylvania, Delaware had no great body of citizens who were motivated by a reforming zeal, no politically powerful group like the Quakers whose traditions were steeped in a philosophy of penal reform, no rapidly growing urban centers where increasing cultural complexity facilitated social change and made a revision in penal methods imperative, no crusading society like the Philadelphia Society for Alleviating the Miseries of Public Prisons, to lead its socially conscious citizens to victory. Delaware had none of these, and so her penitentiary movement died in the ensuing conflict among her counties. Eventually every other state abolished corporal punishment, and Delaware, ensconced in provincialism, stood alone with her pillory and whipping post.[2]

The year 1830 found Delaware committed to a system of county jails and a criminal code still characterized by sanguinary punishments. During the next few decades attempts were made to revive the penitentiary movement, but the same forces that had previously defeated it were still operating, and these attempts were quickly blocked.

Almost all the early spokesmen for penal reform in Delaware, as well as elsewhere in the United States, had advocated not only the introduction of the penitentiary system, but also the abolition or mitigation of corporal punishments. Gradually, however, throughout America greater emphasis was being placed upon the employment of prisoners, which originally had been considered as just one part of the penitentiary system, preferably as a technique in effecting the reformation of the individual. This tendency was present in Delaware, and during the latter part of the nineteenth century the establishment of an institution where a large number of prisoners could be kept employed, commonly referred to as a workhouse, became the principal goal of the penal reform movement in Delaware. It is true that agitation against corporal punishment continued, but it was not an integral part of the campaign for such an institution. Consequently the abolition of the whipping post emerged as a separate issue, and when, in 1899, Delaware did finally secure the passage of a law for the creation of a county workhouse, which was a compromise between an urban North and a politically stronger rural South,[3] the state's criminal code still prescribed the penalties of whipping and pillorying for many crimes.

While the workhouse movement was meeting with some success, Delaware's persistence in the use of corporal punishment was stirring up a widespread controversy. In public meetings, magazines, and newspapers, the "post" and the pillory were condemned, and many appeals for remissions and pardons, addressed to the governors, were evoked by the severity of the criminal laws.

With the enactment of the law for the construction of the New Castle County Workhouse, the advocates of reform concentrated their attention upon corporal punishment and succeeded in having the pillory abolished in March 1905. Flushed with victory, they pressed their campaign against the whipping post, the Quakers contributing in an important way to this agitation. As a result, bills for the abolition of the "post" were introduced at the legislative sessions of 1907, 1915, 1917, 1919, 1923, and 1925, but each time the attack was decisively repelled. These were crushing blows, and the movement against the lash rapidly subsided in Delaware. An attempt was made to revive the fight in the legislature in 1945 when a bill for the abolition of the "post" was again introduced, but the move was quickly blocked and the measure never even came before the lawmakers for a vote.

Tendencies that had been apparent in Delaware prior to 1900 persisted during these legislative campaigns to eliminate corporal punishment from the criminal laws of Delaware. The state's population continued to concentrate in New Castle County, especially in the city of Wilmington. Table 1 shows this tendency in a particularly impressive way. The population of Delaware by 1900 had increased to 184,735 and was distributed among the counties as follows: New Castle County had 109,697; Kent County, 32,762; and Sussex County, 42,276. Thus by that year the population of the northern county was much greater than that of the other two counties combined. Moreover, this concentration of population tended to center in Wilmington, where by 1900 the population reached the total of 76,508, an increase of 62,529 since 1850. This meant that in 1900 well over one-half of the county's population lived in the one big city of the state, and that that city's population was larger than that of Kent and Sussex combined.

An examination of Delaware's population figures in the census of 1940 indicates the way in which the tendency to population concentration has continued. By that year the state's population had grown to 266,505, which was divided among the counties as follows: New Castle County had 179,562; Kent County, 34,441; and Sussex County, 52,502. In other words, New Castle County's population had increased until it was more than twice the size of that of the other two counties combined. In the meantime, the number of persons living in Wilmington had become 112,504 by 1940. This represents almost two-thirds of the total population of New Castle County, and was considerably greater than that of the combined totals of the other two counties.

TABLE 1

POPULATION OF DELAWARE*

1770 — Estimated Population in the State 25,000
1780 — Estimated Population in the State 37,000

	White	Negro Free	Negro Slave	State	New Castle County	City of Wilmington	Kent County	Sussex County
1790	46,310	3,899	8,887	59,096	19,688	2,335	18,920	20,488
1800	49,852	8,268	6,153	64,273	25,361	3,241	19,554	19,358
1810	55,361	13,136	4,177	72,674	24,429	4,416	20,495	27,750
1820	55,282	12,958	4,509	72,749	27,899	5,268	20,793	24,057
1830	57,601	15,855	3,292	76,748	29,720	6,628	19,913	27,115
1840	58,561	16,919	2,605	78,085	33,120	8,367	19,872	25,093
1850	71,169	18,073	2,290	91,532	42,780	13,979	22,816	25,936
1860	90,589	19,829	1,798	112,216	54,797	21,258	27,804	29,615
1870	102,221	22,794	....	125,015	63,515	30,841	29,804	31,696
1880	120,160	26,442	....	146,608	77,716	42,478	32,874	36,018
1890	140,066	28,386	....	168,493	97,182	61,431	32,664	38,647
1900	153,977	30,697	....	184,735	109,697	76,508	32,762	42,276
1910	171,102	31,181	....	202,322	123,188	87,411	32,721	46,413
1920	192,615	30,335	....	223,003	148,239	110,168	31,023	43,741
1930	205,694	32,602	....	238,380	161,032	106,597	31,841	45,507
1940	230,528	35,876	....	266,505	179,562	112,504	34,441	52,502

*The population estimates for 1770 and 1780 were taken from Walter A. Powell, *A History of Delaware*, Appendix A. The population figures for the City of Wilmington for the years 1790, 1800, 1810, 1820, and 1830 were obtained from J. Thomas Scharf, *History of Delaware*, Vol. 2, p. 643. The rest of the figures appearing in Table 1 are from the United States Census Reports.

RETROSPECT AND PROSPECT

In fact, the city of Wilmington is by far the largest city in Delaware. Dover, the capital and next in size, in 1940 had only 5,517 inhabitants. Newark, New Castle, and Milford in 1940 ranked next in the order named, having 4,502, 4,414, and 4,214 inhabitants respectively. The rural nature of the state, outside of Wilmington, is further evidenced by the fact that a total of only seventeen other towns, as shown in Table 2, had populations in excess of 1,000 at that time.

TABLE 2

INCORPORATED PLACES IN DELAWARE WITH POPULATIONS OVER 1,000 IN 1940

1.	Wilmington, New Castle County	112,504
2.	Dover, Kent County	5,517
3.	Newark, New Castle County	4,502
4.	New Castle, New Castle County	4,414
5.	Milford, Kent and Sussex Counties	4,214
6.	Laurel, Sussex County	2,884
7.	Seaford, Sussex County	2,804
8.	Bellefonte, New Castle County	2,593
9.	Lewes, Sussex County	2,246
10.	Harrington, Kent County	2,113
11.	Smyrna, Kent County	1,870
12.	Georgetown, Sussex County	1,820
13.	Elsmere, New Castle County	1,630
14.	Middletown, New Castle County	1,529
15.	Rehoboth, Sussex County	1,247
16.	Milton, Sussex County	1,198
17.	Bridgeville, Sussex County	1,180
18.	Delaware City, New Castle County	1,163

The tendency for the concentration of Delaware's population to center in its one big city can be effectively indicated by comparing its growth from 1850 to 1940 with that of the state for the same period. The population of Wilmington increased from 13,979 to 112,504, or a total of 98,525 during these years, while that of the state changed from 91,532 to 266,505, or a total of 174,973. Thus, over one-half of the state's total population increase took place in the city of Wilmington during this ninety-year period.

These pronounced population changes resulted from the growth of the northern part of the state, especially Wilmington, as the state's center of commerce, industry, and banking. The development of New Castle County and the retardation of Kent and Sussex can be largely explained by their different locations on the same peninsula. As New Castle County is at the top of this peninsula, Delaware's industries and commercial enterprises tended to cluster there so as to take advantage of trade routes that cut across the state, and through the city of Wilmington, to avoid Chesapeake Bay. Most of the traffic moving along the Atlantic seaboard did not penetrate into the southern part of the peninsula, and consequently its stimulating influence only indirectly affected the two lower counties.[4]

Other aspects of the state's geography do not tend to offset her disadvantageous location but, on the contrary, accentuate its influence. Delaware is only about one hundred miles long and has an average width of little more than twenty miles, being next to the smallest state in the Union. It possesses no important mineral resources and no great harbors that in themselves might have stimulated the growth of trade and industry. Then, too, the close proximity of the important industrial and commercial center of Philadelphia has contributed to the subordination of Delaware's only large city, Wilmington, to a minor position among the nation's municipalities. On the other hand, the fertility of the soil, an abundance of rainfall, and a temperate climate have made the state outstanding in agriculture.[5]

As such cities as Philadelphia and Baltimore increased in size and importance, traffic along the Atlantic coast grew in volume, and New Castle's expansion was thus accelerated. During the past few decades, Delaware's roads have been greatly improved, and a fine state highway system, running down through the center of the state, has been created. This has brought the lower part of Delaware into closer contact with New Castle County and its urban and industrial life, and has directed more traffic, with its invigorating effects, into Kent and Sussex. At present there are indications, such as the movement of some industries into the southern counties, that these changes are beginning to leave their mark upon the affairs of the state, and that the stage is being set for a more homogeneous and united Delaware.[6]

New Castle County, always more heterogeneous in population and culture than the rest of the state,[7] became increasingly so as its developing industries and commerce attracted immigrants, many of them from southern and eastern Europe. In 1940, of the total number of 14,833 white foreign-born persons in Delaware, 13,526, or about 91 per cent, were in New Castle County, and 10,481, or about 71 per cent, were in the city of Wilmington. The tendency that has existed in Delaware for immigrants to make the northern county, and especially Wilmington, their home, rather than Kent and Sussex, is very clearly shown by the distribution in the state in 1930[8] of the white native-born of foreign or mixed parentage. In that year there were 23,477 native-born white persons of foreign parentage in the state. Of these, 94 per cent lived in New Castle County; and 78 per cent, in Wilmington. New Castle County in the same year had 90 per cent of the total native white persons of mixed parentage in Delaware, while Wilmington had 66 per cent of the same total.

The heterogeneity of the population of New Castle County becomes more apparent when an examination is made of the following figures. Of that county's total population of 161,032 in 1930, 59 per cent were native whites of native parentage, 14 per cent were native whites of foreign parentage, 6 per cent were native whites of mixed parentage, 10 per cent were foreign-born whites, and 11 per cent were negroes. In other words, in 1930, of the 142,484 white persons in New Castle County, 33 per cent were either foreign-born or native-born of foreign or mixed parentage.

The figures of Wilmington are even more impressive. Of that city's total population of 106,597 in 1930, 53 per cent were native whites of native parentage, 17 per cent were native whites of foreign parentage, 7 per cent were native whites of mixed parentage, 12 per cent were foreign-born whites, and 11 per cent were negroes. Thus, of Wilmington's total white population of 94,459 in 1930, 40 per cent were either foreign-born, or native-born of foreign or mixed parentage. These percentages for Wilmington indicate how the concentration of immigrants in New Castle County tended to center in that city.

On the other hand, if attention is turned to the population totals of Kent and Sussex for the year 1930, it will be seen by contrast how homogeneous their populations were at that time. Of the 77,348 persons living in these two counties, 59,645, or 77 per cent, were native white of native parentage. This percentage, however, has been obtained by including in the computation the 14,131 negroes who represented 18 per cent of the population of the two counties. If they are removed from the calculation, it will be found that 94 per cent of the whites in the lower two counties were native-born of native parentage as compared with 67 per cent in New Castle County. This clearly indicates that the politically inarticulate negroes alone constitute the only intrusive element in a population otherwise decidedly homogeneous and largely of British descent, and reveals the difference between the composition of the population "down-state" and that of the people of New Castle County.

While New Castle County's industries and towns were expanding, life in the two lower counties changed but little. Their towns remained small and scattered, shut off as they were by peninsular isolation from the main travel routes in the northern part of the state. The largest town "down-state" is Dover, the capital, situated in Kent County. In 1940 it had but 5,517 inhabitants. Only ten other towns in Kent and Sussex at that time had populations of more than 1,000.

The life of the people in these counties continued to be chiefly rural. In 1940, of the 34,441 persons in Kent County, 26,974, or over 78 per cent, were classified by the United States Census Bureau as rural.[9] This condition existed to even a greater degree in Sussex, where at that time 44,550 persons,[10] or almost 85 per cent of its total population of 52,502, were designated as rural.[11] The inhabitants of these counties, confronted with neither startling changes nor intricate social problems, still cling to many of their old English customs and traditions, in which the roots of the whipping post are deeply embedded.

It can be seen from the foregoing analysis[12] that just a small part of

Delaware has as yet felt the impetus of modern social movements. Throughout most of the state there is still a pronounced provincialism that tends to obstruct the abolition of the whipping post and the creation of a satisfactory penal system. Only in the northern part of the peninsula, in the city of Wilmington and its environs, has there been any complex urban development. There one finds the greatest cultural heterogeneity, urbanization, industrialization, and geographical accessibility — all factors favoring intellectual stimulation and social change. Here, too, has been the home of most of Delaware's Quakers, a sect long opposed to the use of corporal punishment. As one would expect, therefore, the agitation against the "post" has received its greatest support in that section of the state. Nevertheless, in all parts of Delaware, many influential citizens have favored corporal punishment, and in contrast to the workhouse movement the movement to abolish the "post" has had no ready and striking argument for economy to win supporters and to provide a common ground where persons of divergent views on punishment have been able to meet for the purpose of waging a united campaign for penal reform. Indeed, those who have believed in corporal punishment have contended that it lowers the cost of maintaining prisoners because with its use, so they claim, shorter prison sentences can be imposed. In answer to this, of course, these questions have been raised: "Is corporal punishment a more effective deterrent than any other method of handling criminals and is it, therefore, cheaper in the long run? Does not corporal punishment brutalize the prisoner as well as the one who inflicts the penalty?" It is impossible, however, to translate these questions into dollars and cents, and consequently they have not been very impressive to those who wish to reduce the cost of operating Delaware's penal system.

Furthermore, even though the northern part of Delaware tends to be urban and the southern part rural, this difference has been bridged by the argument that corporal punishment protects the city against professional criminals and the country against marauding negroes and chicken thieves. As a matter of fact, since the whipping of the bank robbers in 1873, it has been persistently argued that the state has been protected against large bank robberies by the example made of these criminals. A unity of belief in favor of corporal punishment has been in this way made possible for many citizens in all sections of the state, even though such persons have lived under different conditions, and therefore on this question there has not been the legislative conflict between the urban North and the rural South which has characterized other penal reform movements in Delaware.[13]

Even in New Castle County there has not been a concerted movement against corporal punishment. Moreover, if a strong movement were initiated there, it would still be confronted with the concentration of political power in conservative, rural Kent and Sussex because, according to the provisions of the state constitution of 1897, the two southern counties by uniting their forces can still outvote the northern county in both branches of the legislature. This is so in spite of the fact that since 1900 the population of the city of Wilmington alone has been greater than the combined populations of Kent and Sussex counties.

Although the movement against corporal punishment has met with determined opposition, it has exerted considerable influence, and some important steps have been taken to modify the role that the "post" has played in the criminal jurisprudence of Delaware. In 1889 the whipping of women was abolished; in 1905 the pillory was eliminated; in 1925 the use of the "post" was placed entirely within the discretionary powers of the court; in 1935 the taking of pictures of whippings was prohibited; in 1941 petty larceny was removed from the list of crimes punishable with whipping. Undoubtedly this process of attrition has checked the amount of criticism that has been directed against the whipping post, and certainly the last few steps have been responsible to a large extent for the decline in agitation against it in Delaware since 1925. By rendering the "post" a much less spectacular instrument of punishment than it otherwise would have been, this series of changes has cut away much of the ground upon which the opposition can stand. Stripped of many of its dramatic aspects, the whipping post is only a shadow of its former self, and it has become, therefore, much more difficult to arouse public opinion against its use. In spite of this process of attrition, however, after the publication of the code of 1915 three more crimes were added to the list of those punishable with whippings, and today the criminal laws of Delaware still provide that lashes may be inflicted for twenty-four different crimes.

Although it is not known whether the majority of Delaware's citizens agree with their lawmakers' views on the whipping post, there are indications that many persons in all walks of life everywhere in the state favor the use of corporal punishment. They tenaciously hold to the belief that the "post" not only reforms those who are whipped but also deters others from committing crimes and, furthermore, performs these valuable services at a minimum cost to the state. A considerable number of the legal profession have shared in this belief and have not hesitated to speak in praise of corporal punishment as a deterrent of crime. Apparently the firm and unswerving advocacy of whipping by prominent persons in the past, such as Justice Lore, who as attorney general prosecuted the bank robbers in 1873, has been partly responsible for the strong support that has been given to the "post," and constitutes a precedent to which men in public life repeatedly refer in order to substantiate their own position on this question.

Over a long period of time many interesting stories have been woven about the "post" and these, too, have deeply affected the thinking of a large number of the state's citizens. Tales that attribute extraordinary powers to the lash are widely accepted, sometimes even by well-educated persons who very solemnly cite these stories as indisputable evidence in the defense of corporal punishment. The whipping post, therefore, is more than an instrument of punishment. Encrusted with tradition, it has become a legend. Nominal though it may be in the criminal jurisprudence of Delaware, it is a vital part of the thinking of many Delawareans.

Another complicating factor has been the effect that the criticism of corporal punishment has had upon some citizens of Delaware. The constant attack against the whipping post has caused these persons to become suspicious and resentful of the opinions of "reformers" and to develop an extreme sensitiveness that quickly bristles at the mere mention of the abolition of the "post." As some wit has remarked, they seem to regard the whipping post as Delaware's totem pole. Be that as it may, in the eyes of such persons the whipping of prisoners is an expression of Delaware's right to punish her prisoners as she thinks best. According to this point of view, then, to surrender this right in the face of attack would be not only a serious blow to the state's program of crime control, but also a shameful capitulation to Delaware's severest critics.

Indifference and cynicism, also, have exercised an obstructing influence. Few persons are vitally concerned over the welfare of prisoners, and many are extremely skeptical about the possibility of effecting their reformation. Usually the majority of citizens, not only in Delaware but in all other states in the United States, do not care how criminals are handled as long as there are not alarming "crime waves," annoying prison scandals, and large expenditures of public funds in the operation of the penal system. In the face of this attitude, it has always been difficult to arouse public opinion in favor of any kind of penal reform.

It is possible that the obstacles that block the movement for the abolition of the whipping post in Delaware may be overcome and the lash eliminated as an instrument of punishment, but it now seems that the process of attrition, by which the use of the "post" has been gradually reduced, will continue until corporal punishment, although still prescribed by law, will no longer be inflicted.

Chapter VII

FORTY-THREE YEARS OF WHIPPINGS IN DELAWARE

BY her insistence upon applying the lash to her criminals, Delaware has attracted a great deal of unfavorable criticism and stirred up a widespread controversy over the value of the whipping post. Both opponents and advocates have argued long and eloquently, but each side remains adamant in its convictions.

Supporters of the "post" have argued: "Society coddles the criminal too much. He doesn't fear imprisonment; he needs to feel the sting of pain. That'll teach him a lesson."

In reply to this, the opponent of the lash has explained: "Cruel and drastic punishments never tend to reform the criminal. They only tend to make him sullen and revengeful."

"But you don't understand," replies the advocate of corporal punishment, "Delaware is a small agricultural state, lying between the large cities of Philadelphia and Baltimore. It is a natural haven for criminals from both these cities and would be overrun with thieves and gangsters if it were not for the whipping post."

"Nonsense!" exclaims his opponent, "other states don't use the lash and they aren't overwhelmed with criminals. The whipping post is a survival of savagery, a blot on the name of Delaware. It ought to be abolished — and quickly."

In this way the argument has moved back and forth, trying the patience of men, ruffling their tempers, and driving them to anger, but rarely uncovering any real facts even though the controversy has been waged for many years. It is the purpose of this chapter, therefore, to make more facts available by presenting a statistical analysis of the use of the whipping post in Delaware for the period 1900 to 1942, inclusive.[1]

During these years, 7,302 prisoners[2] were convicted of crimes in Delaware for which they might have been whipped in accordance with the provisions of the state's criminal laws. Over 75 per cent of these prisoners were convicted in New Castle County, 75.4 per cent were found guilty of larceny, and only 3.1 per cent were convicted of crimes other than larceny, breaking and entering, with intent, or robbery. However, of the total 7,302 prisoners, only 1,604 or 22.0 per cent were actually whipped.[3] The prisoners who received lashes included 58.7 per cent of those convicted of robbery, 22.4 per cent of those convicted of breaking and entering, with intent, and 20.0 per cent of those convicted of larceny.[4] Of those who received lashes, 78.5 per cent had been convicted in New Castle County, 86.5 per cent had been found guilty of either breaking and entering, with intent, or larceny,[5] and 48.3 per cent belonged to the age group 26 to 50, inclusive.[6] A higher percentage of both the whites (68.4 per cent) and the negroes (67.2 per cent) who received lashes were whipped for having committed larceny than for having committed any other crime, but negroes who were whipped tended to be younger than whites who were similarly punished. This is indicated by the fact that 48.0 per cent of the former and only 34.8 per cent of the latter were in the age group under 26.

Although 1,604 prisoners were whipped in Delaware during the period 1900 to 1942, inclusive, this total represented only 1,320 different individuals. Of these, 66.2 per cent were negroes, 65.8 per cent were either unskilled laborers or farm hands, and 86.9 per cent were American. Most of these individuals (83.4 per cent) were whipped only once; but 12.8 per cent were whipped twice; 3.1 per cent, three times; 0.5 per cent, four times; and 0.2 per cent, five times.[7] Among the different individuals whose race was known, a higher percentage of negroes than whites were whipped more than once (18.8 per cent of the negroes as compared with 14.4 per cent of the whites).

Since the beginning of this century there has been a considerable decline in the use of the whipping post in Delaware, so that although in 1900, 70.4 per cent of the prisoners who were convicted of crimes for which they might have been whipped were actually whipped, in 1942 only 6.7 per cent of such prisoners received lashes. However, the lowest point thus far reached in this decline was in 1939, when 4.9 per cent of the prisoners convicted of crimes punishable with whippings were sentenced to be lashed. Chart 1, on the opposite page, shows the decrease in the number of whippings in Delaware during the period 1900 to 1942, inclusive. It will be noted that there was a sharp drop in the number of whippings in 1941 and 1942, and that although 27 prisoners were lashed in 1940, only 10 in 1941 and 8 in 1942 were so punished. While the war undoubtedly was an important factor in this sudden decrease, part of the explanation for it can be found in the law enacted February 14, 1941, which declared that a person convicted of petty larceny (the theft of goods valued at less than $25.00) was not thereafter to be punished with a whipping.[8]

An examination of Chart 2 will reveal how the decline in the percentage of prisoners whipped has taken place in Delaware since 1900. Despite this general trend, however, there was a tendency throughout the period under consideration to whip a large percentage of the prisoners who were convicted of robbery.[9]

So many factors were involved in producing the fluctuations in the downward trend shown in Charts 1 and 2 that it would be exceedingly difficult to interpret their meaning. Such factors as economic conditions, the excitement of the public mind over serious or spectacular crimes,

CHART-1

NUMBER OF PRISONERS WHIPPED, 1900 TO 1944 INCLUSIVE, BY ANNUAL TOTAL AND RACE

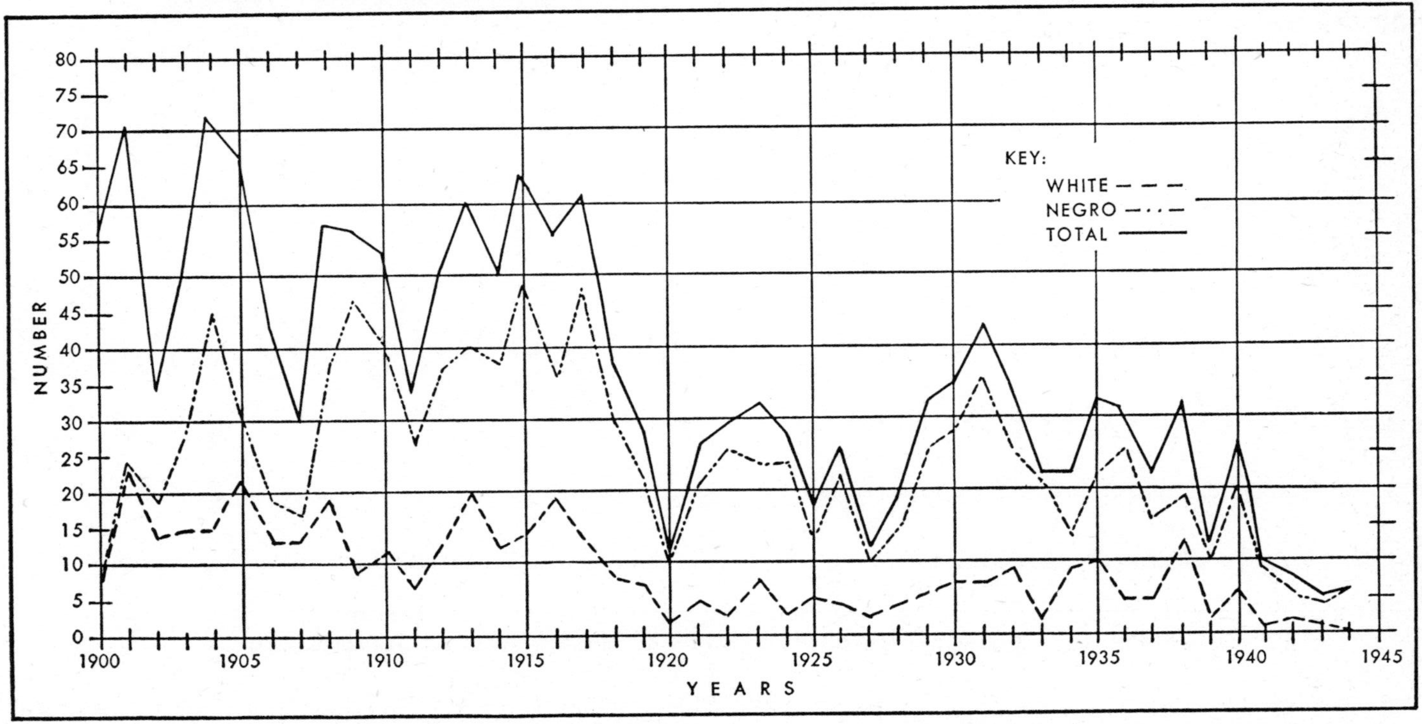

KEY:
WHITE -- --
NEGRO -..-..
TOTAL ———

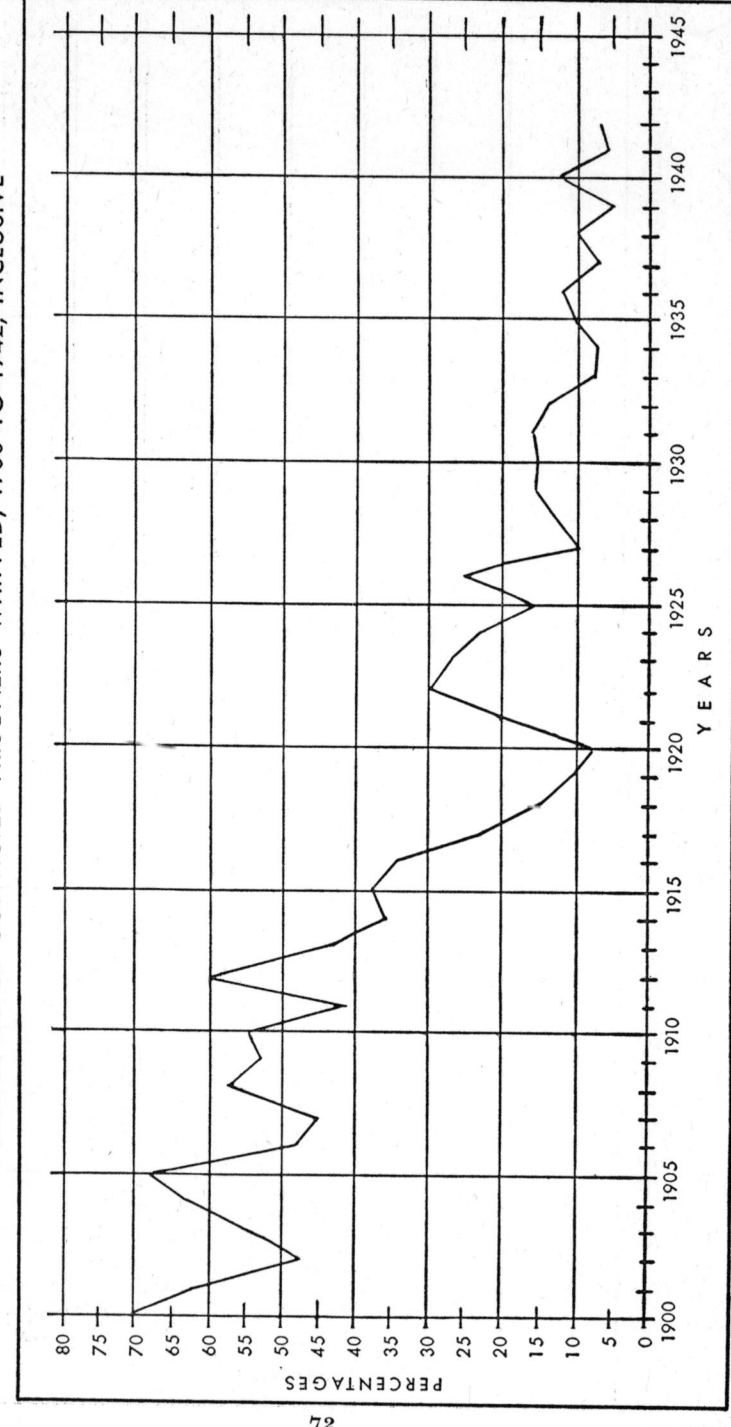

CHART-2

PERCENTAGE OF CONVICTED PRISONERS WHIPPED, 1900 TO 1942, INCLUSIVE

the methods, vigor, and influence of prosecuting attorneys, the procedure used in securing and quashing indictments, the addition of crimes to, or their removal from, the list of offenses punishable with whipping, the philosophy and judgment of the court—all these, and many more, have exercised varying degrees of influence in the use of the whipping post and would therefore have to be taken into consideration in such an interpretation. However, it does seem probable that both the First World War and improved business conditions contributed to the rapid decrease in both the number and percentage of prisoners whipped during the period 1916 to 1920, just as the post-war economic dislocation probably played some part in the sudden rise of these items in 1921 and 1922.

Almost 57 per cent of the 1,604 prisoners who were whipped from 1900 to 1942, inclusive, received ten lashes; 21.1 per cent, twenty lashes; and 7.4 per cent, forty lashes.[10] Among the prisoners whose race was indicated in the records, a slightly higher percentage of negroes than whites received more than ten lashes (36.8 per cent of the negroes as compared with 33.3 per cent of the whites).[11]

Delaware's criminal code prescribes imprisonment for every crime for which whipping may be inflicted, but wife-beaters may be sentenced to pay a fine instead of being sent to prison. Since Delaware does not have an indeterminate sentence law, the court in each case must sentence the prisoner to a definite term. Of the total 1,604 prisoners whipped, 29.7 per cent received definite prison sentences of less than one year; 62.0 per cent, definite sentences ranging from one year to less than five years; and 8.3 per cent, definite sentences of five years or more.

In addition to imprisonment, a fine or restitution also is prescribed as a part of the penalty for almost all the crimes that are punishable with whipping. From 1900 to 1931, inclusive,[12] 44.1 per cent of the restitutions that were to be paid on the 1,013 indictments of larceny (on which 960 prisoners were sentenced to be whipped) were for less than $10, while 77.8 per cent were for less than $50, and only 2.1 per cent were for $500 or more. There was no record of the amount of restitution to be paid on 6.0 per cent of these 1,013 larceny indictments.[13] Since Delaware's criminal code during the period 1900 to 1931, inclusive, stipulated that prisoners convicted of larceny should forfeit as restitution to the owner an amount equal to twice the value of the stolen property, unless it was restored, and then in that case an amount equal to the full value of such property, it will be clearly seen from the foregoing amounts of restitution that many of the crimes of larceny for which prisoners were whipped involved the theft of property of very little value.

From time to time it has been contended that Delaware's courts have discriminated against the poor and the negro in the use of the whipping post. In order to determine whether this charge has had any basis in fact during the past few years in Delaware,[14] the records of all prisoners convicted during 1940, 1941, and 1942 of crimes for which they might have been whipped were examined. Within this period, 510 prisoners[15] (255 whites, 249 negroes, and 6 of unknown race) were convicted of crimes punishable with whipping, but of these only 45 prisoners (9 whites and 36 negroes), or 8.8 per cent (3.5 per cent of the whites and 14.5 per cent of the negroes), were whipped. According to these figures, therefore, among the prisoners whose race was known, a much higher percentage of the negroes than the whites were whipped.

However, since it was recognized that the courts may have found some reason in the past records of the prisoners for whipping a higher proportion of the negroes than the whites, an effort was made to study the earlier criminal careers of all these prisoners. Unfortunately, only in New Castle County were the police, court, and prison records sufficiently complete to make possible such an analysis. In this county, of the 359 prisoners convicted during 1940, 1941, and 1942 of crimes punishable with whipping, 66.3 per cent (59.3 per cent of the whites and 78.5 per cent of the negroes) had been previously convicted of some crime, and 51.5 per cent (46.6 per cent of the whites and 60.4 per cent of the negroes) had been previously convicted of some major crime.[16] Thus a higher percentage of the negroes than the whites had previous criminal careers. This fact may well have influenced the courts of New Castle County in sentencing a greater proportion of the negroes than the whites (18.1 per cent of the negroes as compared with 3.4 per cent of the whites) to corporal punishment. That the courts did take the preceding criminal careers of the prisoners into consideration seems to be indicated by the fact that all except 1 (a negro) of the 34 (7 whites and 27 negroes) who were whipped had previously been convicted of some crime. In fact, 32 (7 whites and 25 negroes) had formerly been convicted of at least one major crime. It may rightly be pointed out, of course, that one reason why more negroes than whites had previous criminal careers is because negroes in general are discriminated against in all phases of our society, including the whole process of law enforcement, prosecution, and conviction, and that, therefore, discrimination is indirectly a factor in the whipping of negroes. This no one will deny, but the foregoing analysis does prove that there existed a difference other than race between the whites and the negroes who during the period 1940 to 1942, inclusive, were convicted in New Castle County of crimes punishable with corporal punishment, and that this difference (the fact that a higher percentage of the negroes than the whites had previous criminal careers) could have been utilized by the courts, without discriminating against the negroes, in sentencing a larger proportion of the negroes than whites to public whippings.

Some light was thrown upon the other controversial point mentioned above; i.e., the charge that Delaware's courts have discriminated against the poor in the use of the whipping post, by ascertaining the occupations of the 359 prisoners convicted in New Castle County during

1940, 1941, and 1942 of crimes for which they might have been whipped.[17] An analysis of these occupations showed that all except a few of the prisoners undoubtedly belonged to the lower income groups. As a matter of fact, 258 (or 71.9 per cent) of them (61.3 per cent of the whites and 89.3 per cent of the negroes) were laborers and therefore members of the lowest income group. It is not strange, then, that all of the whipped prisoners who had been convicted in New Castle County during 1940, 1941, and 1942 came from the lower economic strata. The reason for this was not that the courts had discriminated against the poor in the use of the lash, but simply that the judges had very little opportunity to sentence other than poor persons to such punishment.

At this point the question may well be raised why such a condition should exist. Obviously, one reason is that poverty is an important cause of crime in general, and therefore it is quite natural for a high percentage of persons convicted of crimes punishable with whipping in Delaware to belong to the lower income groups. In an attempt to give a more specific answer to this question, some critics of the "post" have said that various legal devices have been used to keep those who have "pull" and "connections" from having to stand trial for crimes punishable with whipping. For such persons, so it has been contended, charges are changed, dropped, retired, or nol-prossed, and "deals" are made in the prosecuting attorney's office. Those who have friends, wealth, or influence have been thus protected from the harsher side of the law in other states, and it would be extraordinary if some of this has not occurred in Delaware.

In further explanation of why members of the so-called better classes seldom stand trial for crimes that are punishable with whipping, it has been asserted that these persons do not tend to commit crimes that carry this penalty. Some opponents of the lash have even argued that Delaware's laws have been deliberately framed to shelter the upper classes from the whipping post. The basis of these expressions of opinion can be found by an examination of Delaware's criminal code. (See Appendix B.) It will be observed that only two of the crimes against property which are punishable with whipping; i.e., embezzlement by a cashier, servant, or clerk, and the fraudulent misapplication or conversion of funds by executors, administrators, guardians, justices, constables, or attorneys-at-law, are of the type that persons of the higher, rather than the lower, income groups might commit. Moreover, whipping for these offenses was not provided for until April 15, 1925,[18] and even then the stipulation was that prisoners found guilty of the latter (a crime that can be more nearly classified as a crime of the upper classes than can embezzlement by a cashier, servant, or clerk) were to be whipped with "not more than ten lashes." In other words, this is the lowest maximum whipping penalty in Delaware's laws. It should also be explained that embezzlement by a bailee or by a public official still does not carry the penalty of whipping. Apparently some crimes of embezzlement were made punishable with lashes in order to refute the charge that whipping is a "poor man's punishment." Later, on February 14, 1941, whipping was abolished for petty larceny (larceny for less than twenty-five dollars), usually a "poor man's crime."[19] It is quite clear, however, that Delaware can best answer the critics of the "post" not by merely changing the list of crimes punishable with whipping, but by shifting the emphasis in its criminal code from the crime to the criminal and the causes of his behavior. The abolition of corporal punishment will then logically recommend itself.

When the study of the whipping post in Delaware was undertaken, it was hoped that the criminal careers of all whipped prisoners could be analyzed in order to determine the extent to which the infliction of lashes acted as a deterrent influence in each case. However, an examination of the existing records made it quite clear that this aspect of the study would have to be restricted to the criminal records of those who had been sentenced to be whipped by the courts of New Castle County between 1920 and 1939, inclusive. The criminal careers of prisoners whipped for the first time after 1939 were not included in this part of the study so that in each case in the analysis, which was extended down to the end of 1942, there would be a minimum of three years between the first whipping and the conclusion of the study, during which time the effects of the lashes could be observed.[20] Of course, for each prisoner involved, all available information regarding his criminal record from the time of his first contact with the court to the end of 1942 was secured. This meant that whippings given to these prisoners before as well as after 1920 were taken into consideration.[21]

In this study of criminal careers, the records of 320 different prisoners,[22] all of whom had been whipped at least once and 73.8 per cent of whom were negroes, were examined. As a result, it was found that 61.9 per cent of them (52.4 per cent of the whites and 65.3 per cent of the negroes) were again convicted of some crime after their first whipping. It was further revealed that after the first whipping, 51.9 per cent of the men (36.9 per cent of the whites and 57.2 per cent of the negroes) were convicted of crimes committed in Delaware, and 48.8 per cent (45.2 per cent of the whites and 50.0 per cent of the negroes) were convicted of major crimes. In addition, it was ascertained that after the first whipping, 41.9 per cent of the total 320 (32.1 per cent of the whites and 45.3 per cent of the negroes) were found guilty of crimes for which whipping was prescribed by the laws of Delaware (some of these did receive lashes), and 30.9 per cent (15.5 per cent of the whites and 36.4 per cent of the negroes) were convicted of crimes that not only were punishable with whipping according to Delaware's laws, but also had been committed in that state. Of the 320 prisoners included in the analysis of criminal records, 19.7 per cent (4.8 per cent of the whites and 25.0 per cent of the negroes) were whipped at least twice, and 65.1 per cent of these (50.0 per cent of the whites and 66.1 per cent of the negroes) were again convicted of some crime after their second whipping. Furthermore, of the ones who were whipped at least twice, 57.1 per cent (50.0 per cent of the whites and 57.6 per cent of the negroes) were convicted of major crimes after their second whipping.

Anyone who has given much thought to the subject of corporal punishment will undoubtedly raise a question regarding the analysis that has thus far been presented. It may well be asked at this point whether the amount of recidivism among those who have been whipped should not be compared with that of some other group, that is, with a group of prisoners who have not been whipped but who have been punished in some other way. For example, it may be contended that even though a large percentage of prisoners are again convicted of some crime after they receive lashes, nevertheless whipping exerts a greater deterrent influence than imprisonment. Obviously, therefore, the amount of recidivism among those who have been whipped must be compared with that among prisoners who have been punished in some other way if the study of the subject is to be complete.

An examination of Delaware's criminal records for those who were not whipped revealed that any analysis of such records could not be a satisfactory one if it were used for any county except New Castle County, or if it were extended back beyond 1928. Therefore, in order to secure an adequate and representative sample for the period 1928 to 1944, inclusive,[23] it was decided that the criminal careers of those who were convicted in New Castle County during the years 1928, 1932, 1936, and 1940 of crimes for which they might have been whipped but were not would be used.

During these four years, there were 516 different persons convicted in New Castle County of crimes for which they might have been whipped but were not. Of these, 97.7 per cent had been found guilty of either breaking and entering, with intent, or larceny,[24] 57.0 per cent were white, 52.5 per cent belonged to the age group less than 26,[25] 95.3 per cent were American, and 62.0 per cent were either unskilled laborers or farm hands.[26] When a comparison was made between the foregoing characteristics of the unwhipped for 1928, 1932, 1936, and 1940, and the same characteristics of the 211 prisoners who were whipped during the period 1928 to 1939, inclusive,[27] after having been convicted in the courts of New Castle County, it was found that a higher percentage of the unwhipped had been convicted of offenses of breaking and entering, with intent, or larceny (97.7 per cent to 83.4 per cent);[28] that a higher percentage of the unwhipped were white (57.0 per cent to 26.5 per cent); that a higher percentage of the unwhipped were in the age group less than 26 (52.5 per cent to 44.6 per cent);[29] that a higher percentage of the whipped were American (96.7 per cent to 95.3 per cent); and that a higher percentage of the whipped were either unskilled laborers or farm hands (74.9 per cent to 62.0 per cent).

A study of the criminal records of the 516 unwhipped prisoners showed that prior to their first conviction for which they were either imprisoned or placed on probation during the years 1928, 1932, 1936, and 1940,[30] 55.4 per cent (46.9 per cent of the whites and 67.3 per cent of the negroes) had already been convicted of some crime, and 37.6 per cent (32.3 per cent of the whites and 45.0 per cent of the negroes) had already been convicted of some major crime. A similar study of the records of the 211 different New Castle County prisoners who were whipped during the period 1928 to 1939, inclusive, revealed that prior to their first whipping during this period,[31] 73.9 per cent (80.4 per cent of the whites and 71.6 per cent of the negroes) had already been convicted of some crime and 65.9 per cent (76.8 per cent of the whites and 61.9 per cent of the negroes) had already been convicted of some major crime. Thus a much higher percentage of the whipped had previous criminal records (73.9 per cent to 55.4 per cent).

Of the 516 prisoners who were convicted in New Castle County during 1928, 1932, 1936, and 1940 of crimes for which they might have been whipped but were not, 192 (158 whites, 33 negroes, and 1 race unknown) were placed on probation, and the remaining 324 (136 whites, 187 negroes, and 1 race unknown) were imprisoned in the New Castle County Workhouse.[32] A study of the subsequent criminal careers of these 516 unwhipped prisoners showed that after their first conviction during the years 1928, 1932, 1936, and 1940, 52.3 per cent (48.3 per cent of the whites and 58.2 per cent of the negroes) were again convicted of some crime before the end of 1944, and 33.5 per cent (26.9 per cent of the whites and 42.7 per cent of the negroes) were again convicted of some major crime before the end of 1944. The subsequent records of the unwhipped prisoners who were placed on probation were better than those of the unwhipped prisoners who were imprisoned, 37.5 per cent of the former and 61.1 per cent of the latter being again convicted of some crime before the end of 1944, and 18.8 per cent of the former and 42.3 per cent of the latter being found guilty of a major crime before the end of 1944.[33]

An analysis of the subsequent criminal careers of the 211 different New Castle County prisoners who were whipped during the period 1928 to 1939, inclusive, revealed that after their first whipping during this period, 66.8 per cent (60.7 per cent of the whites and 69.0 per cent of the negroes) were again convicted of some crime before the end of 1942, and 52.1 per cent (51.8 per cent of the whites and 52.3 per cent of the negroes) were again convicted of some major crime before the end of 1942. It will be seen from this analysis that the percentage of prisoners who were again convicted of some crime was greater for those who were whipped than it was for those who were not whipped (66.8 per cent of the whipped as compared with 52.3 per cent of the total unwhipped, 37.5 per cent of the unwhipped placed on probation, and 61.1 per cent of the unwhipped imprisoned), and that a higher percentage of the whipped than the unwhipped were again convicted of a major crime (52.1 per cent of the whipped as compared with 33.5 per cent of the total unwhipped, 18.8 per cent of the unwhipped placed on probation, and 42.3 per cent of the unwhipped imprisoned).

However, it may be objected that the proper consideration has not been given to the element of time in the preceding comparisons, and that the criminal careers of the prisoners who were convicted in New Castle County during 1928, 1932, 1936, and 1940 of crimes for which they might have been whipped but were not should be compared during the period 1928 to 1944, inclusive, with the criminal careers of those who were sentenced to be whipped in New Castle County during the same four years. Consequently it has been felt advisable to include below this additional comparison.

During 1928, 1932, 1936, and 1940, 73 different prisoners were whipped after having been convicted in New Castle County.[34] By the end of 1944, 68.5 per cent of these 73 prisoners (61.1 per cent of the whites and 70.9 per cent of the negroes) had again been convicted of some crime, and 49.3 per cent (38.9 per cent of the whites and 52.7 per cent of the negroes) had again been convicted of some major crime. If these percentages are compared with the corresponding ones for the 516 unwhipped prisoners who were convicted during the years 1928, 1932, 1936, and 1940, it will be seen in this case, too, that the percentage of prisoners who were again convicted of some crime was greater for those who were whipped than it was for those who were not whipped (68.5 per cent of the whipped as compared with 52.3 per cent of the total unwhipped, 37.5 per cent of the unwhipped placed on probation, and 61.1 per cent of the unwhipped imprisoned) and that a higher percentage of the whipped than the unwhipped were again convicted of a major crime (49.3 per cent of the whipped as compared with 33.5 per cent of the total unwhipped, 18.8 per cent of the unwhipped placed on probation, and 42.3 per cent of the unwhipped imprisoned).

It now seems possible to summarize in the following manner some of the conclusions that may be drawn from the preceding discussion:

1. Most of the prisoners who might have been whipped in Delaware during the period 1900 to 1942, inclusive, did not receive lashes. Only 1,604, or 22.0 per cent of these prisoners, were so punished.

2. Since 1900 there has been considerable decline in the use of the whipping post in Delaware, so that although in that year, 70.4 per cent of the prisoners who might have been whipped were actually whipped, in 1942, only 6.7 per cent of such prisoners received lashes. However, there is still the tendency to whip a large percentage of the prisoners who are convicted of robbery.

3. The prisoners who were whipped tended to have been convicted in New Castle County (78.5 per cent), to have been found guilty of either breaking and entering, with intent, or larceny (86.5 per cent), and to belong to the age group 26 to 50, inclusive (48.3 per cent).

4. Although 1,604 prisoners were whipped in Delaware during the

period 1900 to 1942, inclusive, this total represented only 1,320 different individuals. Of these, 66.2 per cent were negroes, 65.8 per cent were either unskilled laborers or farm hands, and 86.9 per cent were American.

5. Most of the whipped prisoners received ten lashes (56.8 per cent).

6. Among the prisoners whose race was indicated in the records, a slightly higher percentage of negroes than whites received more than ten lashes (36.8 per cent of the negroes as compared with 33.3 per cent of the whites).

7. All the prisoners who were whipped were also imprisoned, the majority (62.0 per cent) receiving definite prison sentences ranging from one year to less than five years.

8. Many of the crimes of larceny for which prisoners were whipped involved the theft of property of very little value. From 1900 to 1931, inclusive, 44.1 per cent of the restitutions to be paid on the indictments of larceny for which prisoners were to be whipped were for less than $10.

9. Most of the individuals who received lashes were whipped only once (83.4 per cent).

10. A higher percentage of the negroes than the whites were whipped more than once (18.8 per cent of the negroes as compared with 14.4 per cent of the whites).

11. Among the prisoners of known race convicted in Delaware during 1940, 1941, and 1942 of crimes for which they might have been whipped, a much higher percentage of the negroes than whites were whipped (14.5 per cent of the negroes as compared with 3.5 per cent of the whites).

12. The available statistics do not indicate that the courts of New Castle County (the only county in which this analysis was possible) during the years 1940, 1941, and 1942 directly discriminated against the poor and the negro in the use of the whipping post. However, economic status and race appear to be important factors in placing more of the poor and the negro race than of any of the other groups in Delaware's population in a position where they might be whipped. In other words, race and economic status seem to be important factors in making persons "candidates" for the "post," but the available statistics do not indicate that the courts discriminate against the poor and the negro in selecting the prisoners who are to be whipped from the group of "candidates."

13. A statistical analysis made to determine the effect of corporal punishment upon prisoners who were whipped in New Castle County (the only county in which such a study was feasible) shows that:

(1) Criminals who were convicted of crimes for which they might have been whipped but were not, tended to be better educated, younger, less hardened in criminal habits, more often white, and more often

found guilty of crimes against property (rather than crimes against the person) than those who were whipped.

(2) The whipping of criminals did not effectively deter them, after their release from prison, from again committing a crime. Not only were many such persons (61.9 per cent) after their first whipping convicted of crimes, but a large number of them (48.8 per cent) were found guilty of major offenses. Moreover, a high percentage (41.9 per cent) after their first whipping were convicted of crimes for which the laws of Delaware prescribed the penalty of whipping, and many (30.9 per cent) after their first whipping were found guilty of having committed such crimes in Delaware.

It is interesting to observe here that although many Delawareans are convinced that whipping is an efficacious punishment, the laws of Delaware, wherever they prescribe the possible penalty of whipping, also in every such case provide for the imprisonment of the convicted person.[35] In the sentencing of wife-beaters, a fine may be imposed instead of a term of imprisonment. Apparently, then, the legislators believe that some penalty in addition to that of whipping is needed to curb criminal tendencies.

(3) The subjection of criminals to more than one whipping was not effective in changing their criminal habits. After having received at least two whippings, many (65.1 per cent) were again convicted of some crime, and a large percentage (57.1 per cent) were found guilty of major crimes.

(4) Negroes who had been whipped showed a greater tendency to continue their criminal careers than did whites who had been similarly punished. After their first whipping, 65.3 per cent of the negroes, as compared with 52.4 per cent of the whites, were again convicted of some crime. Thus the belief held by many in Delaware that the punishment of whipping is especially effective in dealing with negro criminals is not supported by the facts.

(5) The use of imprisonment as a punishment for those who might have been whipped but were not proved ineffective in deterring them, after their release from prison, from again committing a crime. Of such persons who were imprisoned during 1928, 1932, 1936, and 1940, 61.1 per cent were again convicted of some crime.

(6) Probation was used with better results than imprisonment in the handling of some of those who might have been whipped but were not. Of such persons who were placed on probation during 1928, 1932, 1936, and 1940, 37.5 per cent were again convicted of some crime.

(7) The amount of recidivism was greater among those who had been whipped (66.8 per cent of those whipped during the period 1928 to 1939, inclusive, and 68.5 per cent of those whipped during 1928, 1932, 1936, and 1940) than it was among those who might have been whipped but were not (52.3 per cent of those convicted in 1928, 1932, 1936, and

1940), and among those who might have been whipped but instead were only imprisoned (61.1 per cent of those convicted in 1928, 1932, 1936, and 1940); and there was the least amount of recidivism among those who might have been whipped but instead were placed on probation (37.5 per cent of those convicted in 1928, 1932, 1936, and 1940).

It must be recognized, however, that this comparison is somewhat obscured by the combination of a number of factors. There was, in the first place, the element of selection in the processes of apprehension, prosecution, and punishment. Not all persons who committed crimes for which they might have been whipped were apprehended and prosecuted. It may be that the most skillful and hardened in crime eluded the law enforcement agencies, and so their activities were not reflected in the police, court, and prison statistics. Furthermore, there was the tendency, as revealed by the examination of the prisoners' criminal records, of not whipping the better trained, the younger, and the less hardened in crime. This tendency possibly accounts to some extent for the lower rate of recidivism among those who were not whipped.

In addition, it should be remembered that those who were whipped also received terms of imprisonment as part of their sentences, so there is the possibility that both these methods of punishment affected the subsequent behavior of the prisoners. The problem is further complicated by the fact that some of those who were whipped were not only imprisoned but also fined, and that many of those who were whipped had previously been imprisoned.[36]

Finally, there were other more subtle factors, many of which were not involved in the processes of law enforcement, that greatly affected, in varying degrees, both those who were whipped and those who might have been whipped but were not. The love of dear ones, the hatred of enemies, the encouragement of friends and relatives, the security or insecurity of economic and social position, the attitudes of guards and wardens, and many other influences played in an unending stream upon the lives of those whose criminal careers were statistically analyzed in this study.

All this, of course, is just another way of saying that human beings do not live in a statistical vacuum and that each of us is a product of a multiplicity of environmental and hereditary influences. Even a slight insight into these congeries of human relationships could have been achieved only by an intensive case study of each prisoner. Nevertheless, despite the complexity of the problem, the available statistics do seem to indicate that neither whipping nor imprisonment effectively deterred those who had been so punished from again committing crimes. Perhaps it is significant that those who received the greatest amount of personal attention; i.e., those who were placed on probation, subsequently had the lowest rate of recidivism.

Chapter VIII

THE POST IN THE FORUM

THE use of the whipping post is a subject on which many people are apt to have very decided opinions, and there exists, therefore, a tendency for both opponents and advocates to express their views in vigorous and emotional language. In most discussions of the "post," one finds, over and over again, such statements as: "The whipping post is a relic of barbarism," or "You are a rank outsider and have no right to meddle in the affairs of Delaware," or "The lash is a blot upon the name of Delaware," or "You who desire to abolish the whipping post are sentimentalists and want to coddle the criminal." Words like these are saturated with feeling, and although they add much fuel to the controversy, they contribute in no way to an intelligent analysis of the question.

Despite this emotionalism, however, some arguments susceptible of analysis are used to defend the whipping post, and these will be discussed in this chapter.[1] One of the most common arguments is that the criminal ought to be hurt because he has broken the law and hurt someone else. The best and most direct way to do this is to make him feel the cut of the lash on his back. In this way he pays in pain the debt that he owes to society. "If this is not done," say those who reason in this way, "the angry victim of the crime who seeks revenge may take the law into his own hands or refuse to coöperate with society in bringing the offender to justice."

This is an old argument, and although not so openly expressed as it used to be, it still exists by implication at least, in most of the defenses of the "post." The value here claimed for the lashing of criminals has been given such names as retribution, retaliation, and expiation, but by whatever name it is called it represents the resentful desire to inflict injury upon the offender.[2] There is no attempt here to deny that this desire to "get even" is a natural human tendency and that it is to be found in almost everyone, but the question should be raised whether this feeling should be permitted to dominate our actions against the criminal. If the criminal law is to be written to satisfy the blind demands of outraged feelings, one may well ask why we should stop with mere lashing. Why not gouge out eyes, cut out tongues, crop off ears? Why not flay the criminal alive and boil him in oil? If it's pain that is wanted, why not get as much as possible? "But," a defender of the "post" may object, "the punishment must be made to fit the crime." Well, if this is true, how severe in each case should the whipping be?

Should one lash be inflicted for each dollar's worth of property? And how can we translate the pain and anguish of the victim of the crime into lashes? Then, too, if it's retribution we seek, the offender should be punished only in cases where he has caused actual suffering. Unsuccessful attempts to commit crime should therefore go unpunished.[3]

Obviously the passion for revenge cannot be allowed to drive out reason and to control the policy of the state in its treatment of criminals. To do so would be to encourage and strengthen the very motives that might destroy all collective action. It would array man against man and place a premium upon violence. Retaliation is a game at which two can play,[4] and it aligns the criminal against society in a process which tends to brutalize all who participate. The sensibilities of offenders, officials, and spectators are blunted so that, if an impression is to be made, the process must be increasingly severe, and the public, temporarily satisfied, tends to settle back and disregard the causes that produce the criminal. No, our program for dealing with crime cannot be designed in this way. The injury to the victim of the crime must be considered, but far more important are the causes of criminality and the preparation of prisoners for their return to society; and since the abolition of the "post" does not mean that the offender will escape all pain, any desire that the victim might have for the suffering of the offender would still be satisfied even if the criminal were not whipped.

"Nevertheless," contend those who favor the "post," "you must admit that a public whipping is a spectacular demonstration which helps to unify society against crime and criminals." Such an impressive ceremony, they claim, strengthens the ideals and attitudes of the general law-abiding public, giving them renewed determination to carry on the fight against crime and to furnish greater support to law-enforcement officials.[5]

Granting for the moment that the "post" accomplishes this, one may inquire whether there are not better methods of increasing social solidarity. War also helps to unify a people, but there are few who will advocate the beginning of a war for this purpose. Wouldn't it be better to increase social and economic security for all groups in the population so that all might have greater loyalty and respect for the standards we seek to enforce in our nation? Besides, since almost all prisoners return to society, should we try to stigmatize them so that they cannot take up lawful pursuits upon their release? Furthermore, it can be seriously doubted whether public whippings in Delaware unify society against crime and criminals. Few attend them, and little effort is made to give them publicity. In fact, steps have been taken to reduce publicity by prohibiting the photographing of whippings.

There is, too, an increasing impersonality in our complex society. When a crime is committed, unless it is spectacular or of a revolting nature, few know about it and even fewer are directly affected or injured by it. Since there is no widespread and vigorous movement for the punishment of the average criminal, most citizens can hardly be expected to be deeply impressed or excited when he is whipped. Moreover, the shock of crime is often absorbed by insurance, and even when a person has no insurance he is inclined to drop the charges if he can secure his property or adequate restitution.[6] Such abstractions as law and order seem very unreal and remote to the average person. By comparison, the return of a stolen car or an overcoat is very important. When this is accomplished, anger cools and compassion is felt.

Indeed, another point may be made here against public whippings. The humanitarian movement in Western civilization has made many conscious of the suffering of their fellow human beings and filled some with a desire to reduce pain and misery everywhere. Is there not, therefore, among those whose feelings are affected by public whippings, a tendency to reduce rather than solidify opinion against the whipped criminal? Will it not enlist in the ranks of those who spring to his defense many who would otherwise be anxious to have him punished? Do we not in this way drive a wedge into the law-abiding group and divide rather than unify it?

"But you can't deny," assert the advocates of whipping, "that it is cheaper." Cheaper? Why? Delaware's criminal code prescribes imprisonment for every crime for which whipping may be inflicted, although wife-beaters may be sentenced to pay a fine instead of being sent to prison. This means that a prisoner is almost never just whipped and then released, but that in virtually every case he is also imprisoned. Moreover, since at present in Delaware it is the policy of the courts to whip only those who have become hardened in crime or who have committed serious offenses, the chances are that the prison sentences will be longer for such offenders than for those who are not whipped. That there is this tendency is indicated by the fact that a much higher percentage of the prisoners who were whipped in Delaware during the period 1900 to 1942, inclusive, were imprisoned for one year or more (70.3 per cent) than of those convicted in New Castle County who might have been whipped but were not during the years 1928, 1932, 1936, and 1940 (53.7, 29.6, 36.6, and 30.6 per cent respectively).[7] These facts certainly do not indicate that the expense of maintaining prisoners in Delaware is affected in any significant way by the use of the whipping post. Furthermore, there is the cost in the long run. If whipping does not reform the individual but actually coarsens him and intensifies his criminal tendencies, then in the long run it may really cost the state more to maintain him in the future. And money costs are not the only costs that have to be considered.[8] There is also the loss in human energy and character that might have been saved through the use of scientific methods of rehabilitation and crime prevention. This cost cannot be measured in dollars and cents, but it is a cost that can be less easily borne than the taxes that would have to be levied to maintain a modern penal system. The investment in human values is the most important one that any society can make, and it is one that will pay the largest dividends in the long run — dividends in health, loyalty, industry, and respect for law and order.

Much more frequently used than any of the preceding arguments has been the claim that whipping reforms the offender. Defenders of the "post" have been particularly emphatic in their assertion that the lash is very effective in dealing with the ignorant and lazy, and especially the negro, who, it is stated, has no fear of imprisonment. This argument has undoubtedly induced many persons to support corporal punishment, but one can't help thinking how extraordinary it is that so simple a thing as a lash when applied to so complex an organism as a human being, who is striving for adjustment in such an amazingly intricate interplay of geographical, biological, and social forces, can have such profound significance for the welfare of an entire state.

One wonders also why, if the "post" can reform so effectively, all crimes in Delaware are not made punishable with whippings. Why, for example, isn't lashing prescribed for the crimes of assault with intent to murder, arson, forgery, embezzlement by a public official, and embezzlement by a bailee? And why imprison a man after he has been whipped? Surely, if this penalty is as efficacious as its defenders claim that it is, it shouldn't be necessary to burden the public with the expense of maintaining prisoners in penal institutions. Here another point comes to mind. How do the judges decide how many lashes should be inflicted in order to reform the prisoner? It is true that a definite number of lashes are provided by law for some crimes, but for twelve offenses the law merely sets limits within which the court may use its discretion in imposing the number of lashes to be inflicted. During the period 1900 to 1942, inclusive, 1,604 prisoners were sentenced to be whipped. Of these, only twelve were convicted of crimes for which the criminal code prescribed a definite number of lashes,[9] yet 57.2 per cent of the remaining 1,592 prisoners received ten lashes, 21.2 per cent, twenty lashes, and 7.3 per cent, forty lashes. Why were these three numbers chosen in 85.7 per cent of the cases? Why were such numbers as eleven, twenty-one, or thirty-nine never used? Would they have been less effective? And how, in the first place, did the legislators arrive at their decisions regarding the number of lashes for each crime? It is quite clear that these questions cannot be answered. Neither the legislators nor the courts have had any intelligent basis for the choosing of any particular number. Chance, habit, and tradition have dictated the choice of the number of lashes in each case just as they have dictated the retention of the whipping post.

Of course no one will deny that it is possible to influence human behavior through pain and fear, and that whipping may have some reformative value in certain cases. However, the important question is not this at all, but rather whether whipping is the *best method* that can be used to effect the rehabilitation of criminals. The analysis of the criminal careers presented in Chapter VII definitely indicates that this method has not been effective in Delaware. It will be recalled that the amount of recidivism was greater among those who had been whipped than it was among those who might have been whipped but were not. Futhermore, the negroes who had been whipped showed a greater tendency to continue their criminal careers than did the whites who had been similarly punished. Therefore the belief held by many that whipping is an especially efficacious punishment for negro criminals is not supported by the facts.

Fortunately, another study has been made within recent years to determine the effectiveness of whipping as a punishment for criminals. In 1937 a committee was appointed to consider the question of corporal punishment in England, Wales, and Scotland. After a careful study this committee decided that whipping had not been effective, and recommended "the repeal of all the existing powers to impose sentences of corporal punishment on persons convicted on indictment."[10] Thus the lash has failed in Britain just as it has in Delaware.

"But," insist some of the most rabid advocates of whipping in Delaware, "the 'post' has not been given a fair trial." Most of the whippings, they contend, have been administered by men who have not believed in the "post," and the lashes have not been well laid on as the law requires. It will be remembered that in 1937 Warden Wilson, the present executive officer of the New Castle County Workhouse, publicly declared that he favored the retention of the whipping post because he believed that it was an effective deterrent of crime.[11] Warden Wilson has also made it known that he considers it his duty to lay the lashes on well in accordance with the law, and it is agreed among those who have seen him lash prisoners that he does whip "hard." This naturally should not be interpreted as a criticism of Warden Wilson, who in whipping "hard" is merely discharging an obligation imposed upon him by the law, which states that lashes should be well laid on the bare back. An analysis of the criminal careers of prisoners who have been whipped by Warden Wilson should therefore help us to answer the argument that the "post" exerts a reformative influence when the lashes are well laid on. Between April 1, 1935, and December 31, 1942, Warden Wilson whipped 106 prisoners, 74 of whom were negroes. By June 30, 1945, after their first whipping by Warden Wilson, 66.0 per cent of these prisoners (70.3 per cent of the negroes and 56.3 per cent of the whites) had been again convicted of some crime, and 45.3 per cent (48.6 per cent of the negroes and 37.5 per cent of the whites) had been found guilty of a major crime. Moreover, by that date, 30.2 per cent of the prisoners (36.5 per cent of the negroes and 15.6 per cent of the whites), after their first whipping by Warden Wilson, had been convicted of major crimes in Delaware. Consequently it will be seen that even when lashes are admittedly well laid on by one who believes in the "post" they do not effectively deter those who have been so punished from again committing crimes. In fact, a higher percentage of the prisoners whipped by Warden Wilson in the foregoing analysis again committed crimes than of the 320 different whipped prisoners who were sentenced to be so punished by the courts of New Castle County during the period 1920 to 1939, inclusive (66.0 per cent as compared with 61.9 per cent).

"However," the defender of the "post" may claim, "I was whipped when I was a boy and I'm a better man because of it." In order to answer this point thoroughly, it would be necessary to enter into a discussion which would extend beyond the proper limits of this chapter. Still it may be pointed out here that even though pain and fear can be used to control the behavior of children, students of human nature believe that such a method of control should be avoided wherever possible. Furthermore, it is incorrect to assume that the whipping of a child in its home and the flogging of a criminal in a public institution are exactly parallel cases. There are important differences between the two situations that must not be disregarded in any analysis of this argument. In the first place, whippings that are administered in the home are usually inflicted by someone whom the child loves or respects, and the punishment tends to be a part of the pattern of the family in which the personality of the child is deeply rooted. As administered by society, corporal punishment is formal, impersonal, and cold-blooded, and without the supporting elements of family life, it is likely to appear as an arbitrary and cruel act of a stranger who has himself suffered no wrong. Secondly, in the home the child usually remains under the close supervision of the parent or guardian who may adopt certain corrective measures if he thinks that the punishment has not been taken in the proper spirit. In Delaware there is no such supervision of the prisoner after a whipping, and he is returned to his cell in the same impersonal and official way in which the lashes were inflicted. Thirdly, when a whipping is given in the home, it is likely to come within a short time after the offense. A public whipping, like those in Delaware, on the other hand, almost always takes place weeks, or even months, after the offense has been committed, since the offender must first be apprehended, tried, and convicted. If the infliction of pain is to have any effect at all upon the behavior of a person, it must follow soon after the act for which it is given. Delay tends to disconnect the punishment from the offense in the mind of the offender, and the whipping will probably be considered as merely another painful experience in an unjust world. Finally, unless the whipping is inflicted in the home, parents, friends, and neighbors are likely to give their sympathy and support not to the public officials, but to the prisoner, and any beneficial effect that might have been achieved is thereby materially reduced or destroyed.[12]

One more important point remains to be discussed in this analysis of the argument that the "post" reforms. It has already been shown that whipping is ineffective as a method of preventing the repetition of criminal acts. The analysis must now be pressed further. The "post"

THE WHIPPING POST, KENT COUNTY JAIL AT DOVER. THIRTY-FOUR PRISONERS WERE WHIPPED HERE FROM 1933 THROUGH 1944

not only fails to restrain, but it undoubtedly acts in a positive way to produce harmful effects in the prisoners who are whipped. It is true that in Delaware whippings do not appear to endanger the physical well-being of the prisoners. Persons who are defective or ill, either mentally or physically, are not whipped, and the stiff-armed method of applying the lashes greatly reduces the possibility of lacerations. Then, too, any welts and cuts that are caused by the lashes are treated after the whipping. Nevertheless there remains the possibility of serious damage to the personality of the prisoner and the intensification of undesirable tendencies that he might have already had.

Whipping may mark a man mentally just as surely as it does physically. It may label him as a criminal in his own eyes as well as in the eyes of the community. Thus stigmatized, a man may be psychologically isolated from the law-abiding group and again driven into the association of criminals upon his release from prison. This, of course, is the very thing that society should try to prevent. Moreover, a painful experience like a whipping may simply cause a person to develop caution and skill. A prisoner may remember the whipping, but in remembering, he may thus become an even more dangerous criminal — one who is difficult to apprehend and convict. In still other cases a dramatic experience like a whipping may give the prisoner increased status in the law-violating group, the only group whose opinions have meaning for him.[13]

Some men who feel hated by society may in turn hate society. Resentful and revengeful, stinging under the indignity of the lash and with bitterness in their hearts, they may seek an opportunity to strike back at society. Another whipping may merely deepen the grudge that they bear. Other men, broken in spirit by the whipping, and deprived of self-respect, may no longer care how society regards them. Shiftless and inert, they may not again violate the law after they have been whipped, but society has lost the opportunity to help them, as well as the contribution that they might have made. Criminologists have repeatedly stressed the importance of preserving the self-respect of the prisoner. Any act, such as a whipping, which might destroy self-respect is, they agree, extremely unwise.[14] If a prisoner has been deprived of this personality asset, society has lost the only basis it has for building in him renewed loyalties for group standards, for self-respect when expressed in the values of the law-abiding group becomes simply a reflection of what that group expects of the individual.

It should also be recognized that certain psychopathic individuals may actually delight in a public whipping.[15] No one knows how many such individuals there are, although the writer believes that their number has been grossly exaggerated by certain authors. Nevertheless it must be admitted that a whipping may actually satisfy and strengthen the sadistic impulses of those who order it, witness it, or inflict it, and may likewise indulge and encourage the masochistic tendencies of those who suffer from it or see it. Corporal punishment therefore may intensify dangerous and unwholesome traits in the population, and a criminal jurisprudence may thus pander to the worst in society.

A program of rehabilitation must be a constructive one based upon an intensive study of the individual. It must emphasize the preservation of human potentialities and their redirection along socially acceptable lines. Human wishes are satisfied in terms of values that are learned in association with others. The modification of behavior involves the transfer of loyalties from one group of individuals who have one set of values to another group who cherish different standards. Pain and fear may keep a person from acting in a certain way, but they do not give him the materials for acting in another manner. Education in crime depends upon instruction, approval, companionship, and discussion, in which relatives, friends, and companions participate, encourage, stimulate, praise, and blame.[16] Reëducation in non-criminal behavior must involve the same elements, but the entire process must be expressed in terms of a different set of values. The infliction of suffering may be necessary in a program of rehabilitation, but such suffering is incidental, and not the purpose of the program.[17] Indeed, when blindly used for the purpose of control, as in a public whipping, pain and fear may make rehabilitation impossible. Naturally there are certain individuals who understand only force and must therefore be controlled by force, but a person should be so classified only after his personality has been carefully studied over a considerable length of time; and certainly such a prisoner should not be merely whipped and imprisoned for a few years. In all probability, prisoners of this type should be segregated and kept under supervision for the rest of their lives.

Undoubtedly the most persistently advanced and widely accepted argument in favor of the whipping post is that it deters others from committing crimes and keeps many criminals from coming into Delaware. In view of all that has been said up to this point, this argument should not seem impressive. If the actual experience of a whipping is not effective in keeping those who are so punished from again committing some crime, it is difficult to understand how the mere possibility of a whipping can exert a deterrent influence.

Many of those who defend the whipping post on this ground consciously or unconsciously base their contention on the archaic doctrine of freedom of the will, which modern psychology and sociology have shown to be untenable.[18] According to this doctrine, a person is free to do as he pleases, and society must in some way prevail upon him to bring his behavior into conformity with generally accepted standards. When one violates the law, it is assumed that he might have acted otherwise if he had so desired. Therefore he is held not to have disciplined himself sufficiently and deserves to be punished.[19] He must be taught a lesson, and the "post" will do this in such a spectacular and painful way that others will also choose to obey the law. This, of course, is the philosophy that underlies not only much of the defense of the "post," but also the entire traditional criminal code, and it is deeply rooted in Western civilization.

It is quite evident that this doctrine is vitiated by a fundamental inconsistency. Will is considered as isolated from all psychological and social processes and conditions, and as an entity which may function independently of all experiences and teachings. If this is so, how can the individual be reached through any program of education? Furthermore, what is meant by the statement that a man is free to do as he pleases? He is free to do what? Choosing is a process and must operate in terms of the values which man derives from his culture. What pleases a Hottentot may be very disagreeable to an Eskimo. What is right for a Bantu may be an unforgivable sin for an Englishman. How could one behave like a Trobriand Islander if he were not reared as a Trobriand Islander? Right and wrong are relative to time and place, and the plasticity of man's nature makes him susceptible to a wide range of educational programs. Witness the Japanese and the Nazi! All education must rest upon the assumption that one's "choice" is a function of one's antecedent experience and is expressed in terms of the values which one learns in his association with his fellows. To deny this is to place man definitely beyond the influence of education and send him bounding through life like an utterly unpredictable will-o'-the-wisp. How, one may ask, can so fantastic a being be deterred by anything so mundane as a lash? But assuredly this is not what is meant by those who express themselves in favor of the doctrine of freedom of the will, because they also speak of the importance of early training and of children as twigs to be bent and wax to be molded. This, indeed, is confusion confounded! Will is either a function of previous experiences or a grotesque entity that defies education and control and dooms the efforts of science and religion to dismal failure. The modern criminologist definitely rejects the latter. For him the causes of criminal behavior do not lie in a free will but in the interplay of the forces of heredity and environment as they operate in the life of the individual.

On this point, Professor Wood has well said:

> The individual is *responsible* in the sense that a given act is his. It is what might be expected from an analysis of his traits and his entire social situation. . . . It might be well to discard the term responsibility, burdened as it is with the theological and metaphysical implications of the history of thought; and to substitute therefor the term *accountability*. In a positive sense everyone should be held accountable for his acts, as one who has not only committed them, but who is the sort of person who would commit them. The law would thus be given a scientific basis for its procedure; and the object of penal treatment be changed from punishment to the defense of society, by isolating the criminally inclined individual until such a time as he may be safely released.[20]

According to the modern criminological point of view, therefore, it is both futile and unjust to inflict pain upon a criminal on the assumption that he and others, who by means of his punishment are to be made afraid to commit crimes, can be law-abiding citizens or not as they "freely choose" regardless of their heredity and environment.[21] It is just as foolish to do this as it would be to strike a man over the head for having a toothache so that he and others would choose not to have one. Both criminal behavior and physical pain are but symptoms of underlying causes that must be discovered and eliminated. In any particular case it may be impossible to discover the causes, but that does not mean that they do not exist.

One may, however, reject the doctrine of freedom of the will and still favor the whipping of criminals as a means of controlling the behavior of others through the establishment of fear as a cause of behavior, and it is therefore necessary to explore this argument further. Even if we assume that the "post" prevents some crime, it is clear that there are a number of factors that greatly reduce its effectiveness. Man tends to be a creature of habit and emotions, and handicapped, as criminals often are, by poverty, ignorance, and malnutrition, he becomes notoriously short-sighted. The possibility of detection and apprehension is given little thought by many violators of the law, and often the penalty is not even considered. Here one may well raise another important point. Certainly, if a person is to take the "post" into consideration in formulating plans for the future, he should know what crimes are punishable with whipping and how many lashes are prescribed for each offense. And yet it seems safe to assume that only a small number of persons possess even a modicum of such knowledge. Now, as a matter of fact, comparatively few normal persons so order their lives as to balance the pleasure and pain attendant upon their acts, and obviously the mentally deranged, the mentally deficient, and those who commit crimes in the heat of passion are not in any significant way influenced by thoughts of the future.[22]

Moreover, human nature is exceedingly complex. A criminal may fear the "post," but he may fear the scorn of his companions or his family more, and the fear of economic insecurity may drive him to commit the most daring crimes. Man fears exclusion from the group in which he has status far more than he does the penalties prescribed by law.[23] Furthermore, man does not live by fear alone. Love, loyalty to the gang, craving for excitement, ambition, greed, lust, anger, and resentment may steel him to face the greatest dangers in violating the law and stimulate his inventive powers to create skills and techniques that defy our most modern police methods. Everywhere human beings have shown a willingness, even an eagerness, to suffer and die to achieve their goals.[24] Is it sensible, then, to believe that they will be deterred by anything so simple as the cut of a mere lash? It is not surprising that the courts in Delaware seem to have lost faith in the efficacy of the "post" and that today they use it in so few cases.

Besides, the way whippings are administered in Delaware could not possibly strike terror into the hearts of men. The stiff-armed method that is used almost excludes the possibility of lacerations, and although the lashes, when laid on "hard," hurt and leave welts, many of the men undoubtedly have already received far more severe beatings in their lives. As we have indicated, it should not be inferred from this that the solution to the problem can be found in merely increasing the severity of the punishment. If crime could be prevented by subjecting the criminal to severe punishment, it certainly would have been stamped out long ago, for history is filled with the horrible sufferings of convicted criminals. Imprisonment, transportation, flogging, branding, mutilation, hanging, and drawing and quartering — all these and more have been tried and all have failed. In view of this, could anyone really believe that Delaware could reduce crime by doubling or trebling the number of lashes or by inflicting them with greater severity? In fact, part of the explanation of the failure of all forms of corporal punishment is to be found in their demoralizing influence on society. They tend to breed in the minds and hearts of all an insensibility to human suffering which itself produces crime. It is also important to remember that today society is less inclined than ever before to support a program of severe punishment, and public opinion will often side with the criminal who has received a heavy sentence.[25]

The falsity of the claim that the "post" prevents crime becomes even more apparent when it is realized that very few of the criminals who might be whipped are actually so punished. Any deterrent effect that a punishment might have is greatly weakened if it lacks certainty, and yet in Delaware in addition to the uncertainty of detection, apprehension, and conviction, the criminal even after conviction still stands an excellent chance of not being whipped at all. In 1941 only 5.9 per cent of such persons were whipped, and in 1942 the percentage was only 6.7. Under such circumstances, if criminals think of the lash at all, and most of them do not, they will certainly be inclined to take the slight risk of being sent to the whipping post.

If those who advocate whipping really believe in its deterrent value, why shouldn't women and children be whipped, and why shouldn't this punishment be made mandatory for all crimes in Delaware? Why should the courts have any discretion in the matter, and why should some crimes be punishable with whipping and not others? Why, for example, should the law prescribe whipping for robbery but not for assault with intent to murder? Why does the law prescribe lashes for a cashier who embezzles but not for a county treasurer who commits the same offense? And why is it a whipping offense to bring a stolen horse, ass, or mule into Delaware for the purpose of selling it when one can do the same thing with a stolen automobile without the risk of being whipped? And why does the burning of a mill or granary expose the offender to the "post" when the burning of a dwelling does not? It is generally believed in Delaware that the "post" keeps negroes and poor whites from stealing chickens, and yet in 1941 the state legislature removed petty larceny (the theft of goods valued at less than $25) from the list of crimes punishable with whipping. This in effect means that a great many chicken thieves will no longer feel the cut of the lash. It is revealing, also, to analyze the number of lashes that are prescribed for the various offenses. Counterfeiting carries the penalty of 39 lashes; perjury or subornation of perjury, 40 lashes; poisoning with intent to murder, 60 lashes; robbery, not more than 40 lashes; burning a court house, 60 lashes; burning a church or school, not more than 20 lashes; larceny of a horse, ass, or mule, 20 lashes; grand larceny (the theft of goods valued at $25 or more), not more than 20 lashes. How did the lawmakers choose these numbers? And how can these variations be justified? It is quite clear from these examples that there is no logical principle underlying the use of the whipping post in Delaware's criminal jurisprudence. Offenses have been made punishable with whipping and the number of lashes have been chosen entirely on the basis of what seemed expedient from time to time. Consequently the state's criminal code is full of anomalies, and its provisions constitute a strange hodgepodge of amazing incongruities.

It has already been explained that Delaware, by a law approved on April 12, 1935, prohibited under penalty of fine or imprisonment the taking of any pictures of whippings. This was an extraordinary action by a state that has persistently justified the "post" on the ground that it prevents crime. Why should there be this attempt at secrecy? Should Delaware's reluctance to give publicity to whippings be interpreted to mean that she is ashamed of them? Surely, if the lash deters prisoners from violating the law, whippings should be given as much publicity as possible. Moving pictures should be made of the lurid details of floggings and distributed throughout the nation so as to implant fear in the hearts of all who are thinking of going into Delaware to commit crimes there. Radio programs should be arranged to take the message of deterrence right from the "post" into the home so that everyone could hear the sound of the lash and come to dread it. And then, at least once a year, a great exhibition of public whippings should be staged in Rodney Square, in Wilmington, so that the citizens of Delaware's largest community could gather in a great throng to witness a convincing demonstration that crime does not pay. But why stop here? Why not reintroduce the pillory and the rack, mutilations and brandings? If the "post" really deters, perhaps these more severe methods might be even more effective.

The argument that the "post" has a deterrent value is often stated in this way: "Delaware lies in a peculiar geographical position. It is between two large cities, Philadelphia and Baltimore, and is a highway for tramps and crooks of all kinds from these communities. Therefore, we need the whipping post to keep such undesirable persons out of the state." This view has been stubbornly held by many persons in Delaware for a long time, and they have pointed to the fact that since the bank robbers were convicted and sentenced to be whipped in 1873, there has been no serious bank robbery in Delaware. Let us examine this argument. In the first place, the state is not a highway between Philadelphia and Baltimore. The main coastal highways cut across Delaware and through its northern corner in the vicinity of Wilmington, and, until the comparatively recent construction of its new highway system, most of the state was considerably isolated by its peninsular location. Under these circumstances, as the statistics in Chapter VI revealed, only in Wilmington has there been a complex urban development, and most of the state therefore has not held great attraction for professional criminals.

Besides, as Tables 3 and 4[26] indicate, near-by cities and states before the war were not so criminal in some respects as Delaware. Table 3 shows the number of crimes of robbery, burglary — breaking or entering, larceny, and auto theft known to the police per 100,000 inhabitants, for the year 1940 for Delaware and five near-by states. It will be seen by reference to this table that Delaware did not have the lowest rate for any of the included groups of offenses. It is true that only New York had a lower rate than Delaware for robbery, but better records were achieved by New York, Pennsylvania, and Maryland for burglary — breaking or entering, by New York, New Jersey, Pennsylvania, and Maryland for larceny (other than auto theft), and by New York, New Jersey, and Pennsylvania for auto theft.[27]

TABLE 3

The Number of Crimes of Robbery, Burglary — Breaking or Entering, Larceny, and Auto Theft Known to the Police, per 100,000 Inhabitants, for Delaware and Five Near-by States for the Year 1940.*

State	Robbery	Burglary — breaking or entering	Larceny (except auto theft)	Auto theft
Delaware	33.1	319.6	1,083.3	207.5
New York	16.3	179.8	474.9	136.8
New Jersey	37.3	362.1	560.2	157.5
Pennsylvania	41.3	265.9	404.3	158.1
Maryland	46.0	220.0	544.0	263.1
Virginia	64.8	451.7	1,428.3	227.2

*The figures for TABLE 3 were drawn from TABLE 81 on page 175 in the *Uniform Crime Reports* for the fourth quarter of 1940.

Table 4 shows the number of crimes of robbery, burglary — breaking or entering, larceny, and auto theft known to the police, per 100,000 inhabitants, for the year 1940 for Wilmington, Delaware, and nine near-by cities. An analysis of this table will reveal that Wilmington had a higher rate for robbery than New York City, a higher rate for burglary — breaking or entering than New York City, Camden, Philadelphia, and Baltimore, a higher rate for larceny (other than auto theft) than New York City, Newark, Trenton, Camden, Philadelphia, and Baltimore, and a higher rate for auto theft than New York City, Trenton, and Philadelphia. Thus, Wilmington did not have the lowest rate for any of the included groups of offenses. Indeed, it is significant that this city, despite its "protection" by the "post," had more larcenies and

TABLE 4

THE NUMBER OF CRIMES OF ROBBERY, BURGLARY — BREAKING OR ENTERING, LARCENY, AND AUTO THEFT KNOWN TO THE POLICE, PER 100,000 INHABITANTS, FOR WILMINGTON, DELAWARE, AND NINE NEAR-BY CITIES FOR THE YEAR 1940.*

City	Robbery	Burglary — breaking or entering	Larceny (except auto theft)	Auto theft
Wilmington, Delaware	36.3	337.2	1,172.6	222.1
New York, New York	20.1	110.5	250.8	152.0
Newark, New Jersey	77.0	603.7	928.1	304.0
Trenton, New Jersey	52.0	538.4	856.0	195.2
Camden, New Jersey	55.1	238.1	533.1	225.4
Philadelphia, Pennsylvania	49.6	186.0	203.4	170.7
Baltimore, Maryland	48.3	220.6	508.5	283.4
Washington, D.C.	129.1	384.9	1,177.2	318.9
Richmond, Virginia	85.5	547.7	1,992.2	288.1
Norfolk, Virginia	93.8	604.9	1,572.2	368.1

*The figures for TABLE 4 were based upon TABLE 83 on pages 179–85 in the *Uniform Crime Reports* for the fourth quarter of 1940. Jersey City was not included in TABLE 4 as complete data on this city were not available.

auto thefts in 1940 than Trenton, which also is between two large cities — Philadelphia and New York — but does not use the lash. And, as everyone knows, in the United States there are many small cities like Trenton which, even though they are between large cities, do not find it necessary to whip criminals. If for no other reason than this, therefore, the utter childishness of the argument that corporal punishment shields Delaware from her large neighbors should be obvious to even the most obtuse devotee of the "post."

Furthermore, those who claim that the "post" protects the banks of

TABLE 5

BANK BURGLARIES AND HOLDUPS IN THE UNITED STATES FOR THE FISCAL PERIOD AUGUST 31, 1932, TO AUGUST 31, 1944, INCLUSIVE, AS COMPILED FROM THE RECORDS OF THE AMERICAN BANKERS ASSOCIATION.

Year ended	Burglaries	Loss	Holdups	Loss
August 31, 1932	77	$178,254	554	$3,384,117
August 31, 1935	53	157,915	258	1,256,868
August 31, 1938	27	60,732	110	336,670
August 31, 1941	15	39,984	42	150,275
August 31, 1942	12	55,648	37	161,348
August 31, 1943	6	270	20	65,892
August 31, 1944	7	2,641	23	58,454

Delaware should realize that there has been a remarkable decline in bank burglaries and holdups throughout the United States since the years 1932 and 1933, at which time these crimes reached their peak in this country. An examination of Table 5 will show the extent to which this has taken place.[28] Since only Delaware whips prisoners convicted of bank burglaries and holdups, it is quite clear that the whipping post was not a factor in the general reduction of these offenses to the point where they became very unusual even before the war, and that states where spectacular bank robberies had been committed have been virtually freed from this menace without resorting to corporal punishment.

Even though evidence like the foregoing is called to the attention of the chronic defender of the "post," he will relate some story which he has heard as the reason for his continued belief in the deterrent influence of corporal punishment. At times these stories, like the one shown below, are published in Delaware's newspapers and are immediately added to the protective coating of lore that encases the "post" and fortifies the prejudices of those who want to cling to this symbol of medieval criminal jurisprudence:

A very interesting article written by an ex-bank robber recently appeared in the *Saturday Evening Post* entitled "Locksmiths Laugh Last."

The robber states the following in his article: "There are sentimentalists who will tell you that punishment does not deter. I wish they would explain to me why I steered wide of twenty soft banks in Delaware if it wasn't because there was a whipping post at Dover. You couldn't drag a safe-cracker into Delaware. . . ."[29]

Stories like this will always circulate and will always be eagerly seized upon by those who want to reinforce their minds against change. It is not denied, of course, that some criminals may avoid Delaware because of the "post," but this is not the important point. We must ask ourselves whether corporal punishment is the best method for dealing with criminals. Moreover, the authenticity of some of these stories may well be questioned, and it is quite apparent that many others are flimsy, ridiculous fabrications. Still others are based on statements made by prisoners shortly after their whippings. It is to be expected that a criminal who has just been whipped and who remains in the custody of the one who has whipped him will tend to make some statement which he believes will be pleasing to those who still have him in their power. How natural it is that such a person would praise the "post" and say that it had "cured" him or that he would rather have anything else happen to him than another whipping! One must discount such statements and attribute them to the feelings of the moment which will have little influence on the individual in the long run. It is to be seriously doubted that a criminal who has been unable to plan his life prior to a whipping will, because of the pain inflicted upon him, suddenly find resources in his character to control his behavior in the future in accordance with such a statement.

On the basis of the considerations presented above, it must be concluded that any deterrent effect that a public whipping might have is so weak and uncertain as to be virtually worthless. The British Committee on Corporal Punishment, to which reference has already been made, came to the same conclusion in its report in 1938 and declared:

> After examining all the available evidence, we have been unable to find any body of facts or figures showing that the introduction of a power of flogging has produced a decrease in the number of offences for which it may be imposed, or that offences for which flogging may be ordered have tended to increase when little use was made of the power to order flogging or to decrease when the power was exercised more frequently. We are not satisfied that corporal punishment has that exceptionally effective influence as a deterrent which is usually claimed for it by those who advocate its use as a penalty for adult offenders. . . .[30]

In the analysis presented in this chapter, the five most commonly used arguments for the whipping post have been examined. They are: (1) the argument of retribution; (2) the argument of economy; (3) the argument of unification of public opinion against the criminal; (4) the argument of reform of the offenders; and (5) the argument of deterrence. It is now submitted, as a result of this analysis, that the retention of corporal punishment in Delaware cannot be justified by any one of the values that have been claimed for it, or by any combination of them, and that, therefore, the whipping post should be abolished.

Delaware does not stand alone in its inability to cope with the problem of crime. All other states have been similarly unsuccessful and, in fact, some have been far less successful than Delaware.[31] This nationwide record of failure is not surprising since the United States continues to handle its prisoners in accordance with the principles of the philosophy of punishment. Despite the modifications that have been made in this philosophy during the past few decades, its chief aim is still the infliction of suffering upon the convicted criminal. The application of its principles has failed in Delaware just as it has failed in other states, but Delaware's failure has been rendered conspicuous by its persistence in the use of the whipping post, a spectacular method of punishment. To attack the lash and to say nothing in condemnation of the philosophy of punishment, of which the "post" is but an expression, is therefore futile and misleading. There is needed, not some change in the methods of punishment, but rather the elimination of the entire program of punishment itself, and the establishment in its place of a system of scientific treatment, with its emphasis upon the understanding of the causes of crime, the rehabilitation of the individual in terms of such causes, and the modification of the conditions which produce criminality. Under such a system, questions of guilt would continue to be decided by courts of law, but the disposition of the convicted person would be based upon individual case studies made by trained specialists.[32] Modern criminology would thus concentrate attention upon the criminal rather than upon the crime, upon the person in a situation rather than upon legal abstractions, and this, of course, is as it should be.

In our complex culture the deterrent influence exerted upon others by the punishment of criminals is indirect, weak, and uncertain at best, while the return of almost all criminals to society is a real and indisputable fact. It is evident, therefore, that the emphasis should be placed upon the rehabilitation of the prisoner and not upon deterrence, and that society should do everything within its power to understand criminals and to create and encourage in them those tendencies which make for constructive and useful lives. This is not only the most sensible and profitable way of dealing with criminals, but also the most effective method of expanding the knowledge we already have regarding crime causation and crime prevention.

What has been said up to this point should not be interpreted to mean that the criminal would be "coddled" or "pampered" or kept in a "prison palace" if a complete system of scientific treatment were established. We are not in any way confronted with the problem of having to choose between granting leniency to prisoners or inflicting pain upon them. The essential point is that what we do to a prisoner must be based upon a detailed study of what he is physically, mentally, and emotionally as measured by the best knowledge that science can provide. A process of treatment dictated by such a study might involve the infliction of suffering upon a prisoner, but such suffering would be incidental and unavoidable and not the direct aim of the process,[33] just as is the suffering caused by the surgeon when he removes a malignant growth from the body of his patient. It is in this respect that scientific treatment differs fundamentally from the existing program of punishment in which pain is caused by design and justified by some value it is assumed to have,[34] regardless of the facts in the particular case or even in spite of them.

Furthermore, under a system of scientific treatment, prisoners would not be released simply because they had served a specified number of years in accordance with a predetermined sentence, but would be returned to society only after careful study indicated that they were ready to assume their duties again as law-abiding citizens. As a result of the application of such a policy of releasing prisoners, there is the strong possibility that the average term of confinement might be lengthened, and it is to be expected that the number of persons segregated for life would be increased.[35] Moreover, aggressive law enforcement and effective criminal prosecution would not be interfered with in any way, and there would remain all the discomforts, inconvenience, and disgrace that now exist when a person is arrested, tried, and convicted of a crime. Consequently, under a system of scientific treatment, in addition to a sound program of rehabilitation, it would still be possible to satisfy society's desire for revenge and to have whatever deterrence can be secured by exciting fear in others.[36] Then, too, since many persons have lost confidence in our law enforcement agencies and look upon the whole business as a "racket" run for and by the rich and politically powerful, a system of scientific treatment, with its emphasis upon the objective study of each case, would do much to change this point of view and stimulate greater coöperation with public officials. But far more important than this is the fact that there would be created a more realistic attitude toward human behavior and the recognition that it is not the fear of legal penalties that keeps the great majority of persons from violating the law, but rather the desire to find love, respect, and security among relatives, friends, and business associates. This is the principal form of social control, and it will always exist regardless of what methods are used in dealing with criminals.[37] Society, therefore, should be deeply interested in making it possible for men and women to satisfy this desire in a lawful way by providing them with adequate social and economic opportunities.

A system of scientific treatment of criminals can be introduced only if public opinion is educated to accept its principles as superior to those of punishment.[38] It is obvious that a complete and immediate acceptance of such a system is too much to expect of human nature. Much progress has already been made, however, in the modification of the orthodox methods of punishment by the creation of juvenile courts and the establishment and extension of such systems as probation, parole, and the indeterminate sentence.[39] Every effort should now be exerted to accelerate this process of attrition so that eventually not only corporal punishment but all forms of punishment shall be eliminated.

The road to such an accomplishment is a difficult one, for it is obstructed by barriers of ignorance, cynicism, selfishness, and indifference. The search for a way across these is a challenge to the best in human nature. It is a test of man's ability to forego the indulgence of his feelings of anger and revenge in the present, and of his faith in a coöperative endeavor for a more rational basis of action in the future. It is, therefore, part of a much larger movement in which man is struggling away from fear and force and toward the increased use of reason and understanding in all his social relationships, and his progress in this greater venture will determine to an important extent the success that he will achieve in the introduction of a system of scientific treatment of criminals.

NOTES

Chapter I

[1] *Records of the Court of New Castle, 1676–1681*, pp. 322–28.
[2] The whipping post in southern Delaware used to be painted red, and when a prisoner was whipped, the negroes would say that he had hugged Red Hannah.
[3] *The Docket of the New Castle County Court of General Sessions, January Term, 1945*, pp. 16–19.
[4] Contrary to popular opinion, the law does not specify that the person who applies the lashes must keep his elbow stiff during the whipping, although this practice has been followed for a number of years in Delaware.
[5] *Journal Every Evening*, Wilmington, Delaware, January 20, 1945, p. 2, cols. 6, 7.
[6] *Ibid.*, January 27, 1945, p. 2, cols. 5, 6.

Chapter II

[1] Washington Irving, *A History of New York*.
[2] The first permanent white settlement along the Delaware was made by the Swedes in 1638, but in 1655 its few hundred inhabitants were compelled to surrender to a strong Dutch expedition. In 1664 the English conquered the territory and their sovereignty endured, with but a brief interruption in 1673–74 when the Dutch regained control, until the Revolution.
[3] Samuel Hazard, *Annals of Pennsylvania*, pp. 16–20; Leon deValinger, Jr., *The Development of Local Government in Delaware, 1638–1682*, pp. 2, 4, 5, 11; *Charter to William Penn and Laws of the Province of Pennsylvania, 1682–1700*, pp. 420, 424, 427, 428, 435; J. Thomas Scharf, *History of Delaware*, I, 509, 608, 609; Edwin H. Sutherland, *Principles of Criminology*, pp. 333–45.
[4] Harry Elmer Barnes, *The Evolution of Penology in Pennsylvania*, p. 27.
[5] The English criminal code at that time, however, was not as barbarous as it became a century later, when between two hundred fifty and three hundred crimes were branded as capital. (Harry Elmer Barnes, *The Evolution of Penology in Pennsylvania*, p. 27.)
[6] For a description of these punishments, reference may be made to William Andrews, *Old-Time Punishments*; George Ives, *A History of Penal Methods*; Harry Elmer Barnes, *The Story of Punishment*; Alice M. Earle, *Curious Punishments of Bygone Days*.
[7] Harry Elmer Barnes, *The Evolution of Penology in Pennsylvania*, p. 27.
[8] Thorsten Sellin, "Imprisonment," *Encyclopaedia of the Social Sciences*, VII, 617.
[9] Harry Elmer Barnes, *The Evolution of Penology in Pennsylvania*, p. 28.
[10] *The Public Records of the Colony of Connecticut*, I, 509 ff.
[11] The Quaker code of Pennsylvania named only murder as a capital offense, while that of West Jersey included only treason and murder in the category of crimes punishable with death.
[12] Harry Elmer Barnes, *The Evolution of Penology in Pennsylvania*, p. 28; F. H. Wines, *Punishment and Reformation*, pp. 142 ff., 147, 344.
[13] The Swedes, the Dutch, and the Finns were never numerically strong in the territory now Delaware, and their laws and customs gradually disappeared. They and their descendants were completely absorbed into the rest of the population, and there is no social institution in Delaware that bears an important mark of their cultures, even though Swedish and Dutch influences did continue to operate for some time after the coming of the English. (For data regarding the size of the early Swedish and Dutch

settlements in Delaware, see *Records of the Court of New Castle,* I, 159, 160, 161; J. Thomas Scharf, *History of Delaware,* I, 148; II, 612, 613, 1030, 1201.)

14Benjamin M. Nead, "Historical Notes on the Early Government and Legislative Councils and Assemblies of Pennsylvania," Appendix B to *Charter to William Penn and Laws of the Province of Pennsylvania, 1682–1700,* p. 414.

15Leon deValinger, Jr., *The Development of Local Government in Delaware, 1638–1682,* pp. 107–10.

16*Charter to William Penn and Laws of the Province of Pennsylvania, 1682–1700,* Historical Notes, Appendix B, pp. 459–62.

17*Ibid.,* pp. 455–58.

18It is interesting to note that in this enumeration of capital crimes we find a survival of the medieval practice of inflicting punishment on animals, carnal copulation with a beast resulting not only in the execution of the person but also in the burning of the beast.

19*Charter to William Penn and Laws of the Province of Pennsylvania, 1682–1700,* pp. 14, 15.

20*Ibid.,* pp. 27, 28.
21*Ibid.,* p. 10.
22*Ibid.,* pp. 30, 31.
23*Ibid.,* p. 35.
24*Ibid.,* p. 36.
25*Ibid.,* p. 63.
26*Ibid.,* p. 62.
27*Ibid.,* pp. 59, 62, 63.
28*Ibid.,* p. 73.

29J. Thomas Scharf, *History of Delaware,* I, 508–18; II, 613–19, 1037, 1038, 1204–8.

30*Records of the Court of New Castle, 1676–1681,* pp. 128–31.

31*Ibid.,* p. 143.
32*Ibid.,* p. 320.
33*Ibid.,* p. 440.
34*Ibid.,* p. 386.
35*Ibid.,* p. 386.

36*Records of the Court of Kent County,* Record A, p. 7.

37*Charter to William Penn and Laws of the Province of Pennsylvania, 1682–1700,* pp. 81, 82; Anna T. Lincoln, *Three Centuries Under Four Flags,* p. 51; Walter A. Powell, *A History of Delaware,* pp. 84, 85.

38It is important to note that although this transaction gave Penn the ownership of the land comprising Delaware, it did not empower him to govern those living there. This fact later became generally known and undoubtedly strengthened the movement for the separation of Delaware from Pennsylvania. (Richard S. Rodney, *Early Relations of Delaware and Pennsylvania,* pp. 6–10.)

39J. Thomas Scharf, *History of Delaware,* I, 84, 85.

40*Charter to William Penn and Laws of the Province of Pennsylvania, 1682–1700,* p. 112.

41*Ibid.,* pp. 109, 110.
42*Ibid.,* p. 110.
43*Ibid.,* p. 110.
44*Ibid.,* p. 145.
45*Ibid.,* p. 144.
46*Ibid.,* pp. 192–220.
47*Ibid.,* pp. 371–82; *Laws of Delaware,* I, 64–77.

48Penn, to his dismay, soon found that the union of the Province of Pennsylvania and the three Lower Counties, which now form the State of Delaware, was to prove a constant source of friction and agitation. The relations between the two parts of the colony became so strained that he finally consented to a separation and the Lower Counties elected their own assembly in 1704, although all the counties of the colony still had the same governor. For a discussion of the causes of the separation of the Lower Counties from the Province and the significance of this development in the evolution of penology in Delaware, see the author's *The Penitentiary Movement in Delaware, 1776 to 1829*, Chapter I.

[49] *Laws of Delaware*, I, 64–77.

[50] The exemption of the clergy from secular jurisdiction was one of the privileges claimed by the Catholic Church, and during the Middle Ages its leaders acted to remove all members of the clergy from the jurisdiction of lay courts and to make them subject to ecclesiastical courts only. In this the Church was successful and the privilege became known as the benefit of clergy. Trial by an ecclesiastical court was a distinct privilege, as the Church did not use the death penalty and, in general, was more merciful, except in cases of heresy and witchcraft.

Originally, only a few enjoyed the benefit of clergy in England, but gradually not only the clergy, but also members of the laity who could read were entitled to its protection. When learning became more general, laymen who could read were permitted to claim benefit of clergy only once, and then (unless they were peers or peeresses) were burned on the left thumb. Benefit of clergy was abolished in England in 1827 for all except the peers, and for the latter in 1841. (James F. Stephen, *A History of the Criminal Law of England*, I, 456–63.)

[51] An analysis was made of all the existing laws of colonial Delaware in the compilations of 1734, 1741, 1752, 1763, and 1797.

[52] *Laws of Delaware*, I, 105–9; "Compilation of 1741," pp. 61–65; "Compilation of 1752," pp. 74–77.

[53] *Laws of Delaware*, I, 245; "Compilation of 1752," pp. 218, 219.

[54] *Laws of Delaware*, I, 235–38; "Compilation of 1752," pp. 208–11; J. Thomas Scharf, *History of Delaware*, I, 137.

[55] *Laws of Delaware*, I, 225, 226; "Compilation of 1752," p. 193.

Chapter III

[1] O. F. Lewis, *The Development of American Prisons and Prison Customs, 1776–1845*, pp. 8, 9, 14, 15; Harry Elmer Barnes, *The Evolution of Penology in Pennsylvania*, pp. 74–79; Harry Elmer Barnes and J. P. Shalloo, "Modern Theories of Criminology and Penology," *Contemporary Social Theory*, edited by Harry Elmer Barnes, Howard Becker, and Frances B. Becker, pp. 689, 690; Blake McKelvey, *American Prisons*, pp. 1, 2, 4; John Howard, *State of the Prisons* (Everyman's Library), pp. 94–96, 114–18.

[2] This organization later became known as the Pennsylvania Prison Society.

[3] The penitentiary system had its origin in Pennsylvania, where it was founded upon the principles of solitude, or separate confinement and reflection. However, after a time, in the Pennsylvania System, each prisoner was permitted to work in his own cell. The opponents of the principle of separate confinement advocated the silent system, under which prisoners during the day were permitted to work together in complete silence under strict surveillance, but at night were separated in individual cells. This congregate and silent system was championed by penal reformers in New York State and was applied in the Penitentiary at Auburn, New York. It therefore became known as the Auburn System in contradistinction to the Pennsylvania System.

[4] Although the Pennsylvania System cannot be condoned in the light of the principles of modern criminology, those who introduced it were motivated by high ideals. Imprisonment is not the final answer to the problem of crime and criminality, but for the period under consideration it did represent an enlightened departure in the treatment of criminals. (Harry Elmer Barnes and Negley K. Teeters, *New Horizons in Criminology*, p. 467.)

[5] For a more detailed discussion of this movement in Delaware, see the author's *The Penitentiary Movement in Delaware, 1776 to 1829*.

[6] *Minutes of the Council of the Delaware State, 1777*, pp. 89, 90.

[7] *House Journal, 1797*, p. 4.

NOTES

⁸*Ibid.*, p. 7.
⁹*Legislative Papers, 1797, Reports*, in the Hall of Records, Dover, Delaware.
¹⁰*The Docket of the New Castle County Court of General Sessions, 1781–1793*, p. 58.
¹¹*Ibid.*, p. 65.
¹²*Ibid.*, p. 64.
¹³*Ibid.*, p. 224.
¹⁴*Ibid.*, p. 390.
¹⁵*Laws of Delaware*, Volume I, Frontispiece.
¹⁶*Ibid.*, I, 64–77, 225, 226, 235–38.
¹⁷*Ibid.*, I, 121.
¹⁸*Ibid.*, I, 121; II, 599–602, 773–75, 838–40, 1236–39.
¹⁹*Ibid.*, I, 64–77.
²⁰*Ibid.*, I, 296–98.
²¹*Ibid.*
²²*Ibid.*, II, 667–70.
²³*Ibid.*, I, 235–38.
²⁴*Ibid.*, II, 1093–95.
²⁵*Ibid.*, I, 173, 174.
²⁶*Ibid.*, pp. 64–77.
²⁷*Ibid.*, II, 1321–25.
²⁸Harry Elmer Barnes, *The Evolution of Penology in Pennsylvania*, pp. 110, 111.
²⁹*Legislative Papers, 1798, January–February Petitions*, in the Hall of Records, Dover, Delaware; *House Journal, 1798*, pp. 25, 29.
³⁰*House Journal, 1800*, pp. 14, 15; *House Journal, 1801*, pp. 11–15.
³¹*House Journal, 1805*, p. 7.
³²*House Journal, 1800*, p. 25; *House Journal, 1801*, pp. 32, 33; *House Journal, 1805*, pp. 40, 41; *Legislative Papers, 1805, Miscellaneous Petitions*, in the Hall of Records, Dover, Delaware.
³³*Legislative Papers, January, 1810, Reports*, in the Hall of Records, Dover, Delaware; *Senate Journal, 1810*, pp. 10, 11; *House Journal, 1810*, pp. 30, 31.
³⁴*Senate Journal, 1810*, pp. 11, 12, 13, 15, 17, 18, 19; *House Journal, 1810*, p. 39; *Legislative Papers, January, 1810, Petitions*, in the Hall of Records, Dover, Delaware.
³⁵*Senate Journal, 1810*, pp. 33, 42, 43.
³⁶*House Journal, 1810*, pp. 78, 79, 80, 81; *Senate Journal, 1810*, pp. 63, 64, 65, 70.
³⁷*Senate Journal, 1812*, pp. 7, 8; *House Journal, 1812*, pp. 7, 8, 9; *Senate Journal, 1813*, pp. 10–12.
³⁸*House Journal, 1812*, pp. 22, 23, 31, 46, 47; *Senate Journal, 1812*, p. 42; *Legislative Papers, 1813, Bills Not Passed*, in the Hall of Records, Dover, Delaware; *Senate Journal, 1813*, p. 18; *House Journal, 1813*, p. 113.
³⁹*House Journal, 1818*, pp. 14, 15, 38, 39, 40.
⁴⁰*Ibid.*, pp. 47, 89, 90.
⁴¹*Legislative Papers, January, 1819, Miscellaneous Petitions*, in the Hall of Records, Dover, Delaware; *Senate Journal, 1819*, p. 40; *House Journal, 1819*, pp. 34, 35.
⁴²*Legislative Papers, January, 1819, Bills Not Passed*, in the Hall of Records, Dover, Delaware; *Senate Journal, 1819*, p. 64; *House Journal, 1819*, p. 108.
⁴³*Senate Journal, 1822*, p. 59.
⁴⁴*Senate Journal, 1823*, pp. 73, 74, 83, 121, 122.
⁴⁵*Senate Journal, 1824*, pp. 10–13.
⁴⁶*Laws of Delaware*, I, 123–58, 561. See Tables 1 and 2, Appendix A, for the list of crimes punishable with whipping in the code of 1829, together with the number of lashes prescribed for each crime.
⁴⁷The law of February 8, 1826, had abolished benefit of clergy for all crimes in Delaware. (*Laws of Delaware*, "Code of 1829," p. 147.)
⁴⁸Neither negroes nor mulattoes were to be employed to inflict corporal punishment upon prisoners. (*Laws of Delaware*, "Code of 1829," p. 157.)
⁴⁹*The Docket of the Kent County Court of General Sessions, 1804*, p. 52.

50 An act of Delaware's general assembly, passed on June 14, 1793, ordered the whipping post and the pillory moved from Lewes to Georgetown, which a short time before had become the county seat of Sussex.

51 *The Docket of the Sussex County Court of General Sessions, 1811,* p. 10.

52 *The Docket of the New Castle County Court of General Sessions, 1829,* p. 247.

Chapter IV

1 In November 1831, a convention had met to frame a new constitution for Delaware, and in it all three counties were given the same number of representatives that had been provided for in the two previous constitutions; that is, seven in the House and three in the Senate from each county. In the debates of this convention is to be found further evidence of the antagonism that existed among the counties and tended to prevent united action on social problems. (*Debates of the Delaware Convention of 1831,* pp. 97–102; *The Delaware State Constitution of 1831,* Article II, Sections 2, 3.)

2 *House Journal, 1835,* pp. 11–13.

3 *Legislative Papers, 1835, Committee Reports,* in the Hall of Records, Dover, Delaware; *House Journal, 1835,* pp. 52, 53.

4 *House Journal, 1837,* pp. 79, 80; *House Journal, 1839,* p. 8; *Legislative Papers, 1839, Reports,* in the Hall of Records, Dover, Delaware; *Senate Journal, 1841,* pp. 8, 9, 16, 17.

5 *Legislative Papers, 1841, Petitions,* in the Hall of Records, Dover, Delaware; *House Journal, 1841,* pp. 326, 372, 411, 420, 463; *Senate Journal, 1841,* p. 307.

6 *Delaware Gazette,* November 26, 1841, p. 3, col. 1.

7 *Senate Journal, 1843,* pp. 8, 9.

8 Blake McKelvey, *American Prisons,* pp. 16, 23; O. F. Lewis, *The Development of American Prisons and Prison Customs, 1776–1845,* pp. 325–27.

9 *Legislative Papers, 1843, Bills Not Passed,* in the Hall of Records, Dover, Delaware; *House Journal, 1843,* pp. 440, 472, 473.

10 Despite the fact that years of criticism on the part of many persons had produced little change in the fundamentals of the criminal code, an important modification was quickly effected in one of its provisions by an event which occurred on February 8, 1849. On that day Perry Bailey, a negro, who had been convicted of rape upon a white woman, was publicly executed in the Town of New Castle amid such a turmoil of drunken brawling and outrageous violence that enlightened and progressive citizens organized to prohibit public executions. The legislature was not insensible to this evidence of public resentment and indignation, and on February 24, 1849, abolished public executions in Delaware. Thereafter all executions were to be as private as possible, witnessed only by a jury of twelve men and such other persons as the sheriff might deem it proper to invite. (*Delaware Gazette,* February 13, 1849, p. 2, col. 4; *Delaware State Journal,* February 13, 1849, p. 3, col. 2, February 16, 1849, p. 3, col. 1; *Legislative Papers, 1849, Petitions,* in the Hall of Records, Dover, Delaware; *Laws of Delaware,* X, 367.)

11 *Delaware Laws,* "Revised Code of 1852," pp. 256–59, 471–94. See Tables 1 and 2, Appendix A, for the list of crimes punishable with whipping in the code of 1852, together with the number of lashes prescribed for each crime.

12 The Code of 1852 contained no penalty of servitude for white criminals. The sale of white convicts had been abolished by the law of February 15, 1839, and the provisions of this law were made part of the new code. (*Laws of Delaware,* IX, 256, 257.)

13 A convict's jacket was prescribed for some crimes. This was a badge of crime and was to be given to the convict at the time of his release from prison. The jacket was dark in color and plainly marked on the back with a large, conspicuous "C." Any person who neglected or refused to wear this garment was to be fined twenty dollars and whipped with ten lashes. (*Laws of Delaware,* "Revised Code of 1852," pp. 478, 483.)

14 *Laws of Delaware,* "Revised Code of 1852," p. 489.

NOTES

¹⁵*Ibid.*, "Revised Code of 1852," pp. 493, 494. The requirement that the whipping post and the pillory be in or near the jail yard of each county resulted in their removal from the public green of New Castle, where they had stood "for so many years," to the jail yard in that town, according to the *Delaware Gazette* of May 20, 1853 (p. 3, col. 3).

¹⁶A constitutional convention, scheduled to meet in December 1852, entered into the actual performance of its duties on March 10, 1853. As in the case of the constitutional convention of 1831, the antagonism and divergence of interests between the northern and southern parts of Delaware again became clearly apparent in the debates and proceedings. The constitution finally adopted by this convention was later rejected by the voters of the state, and New Castle County therefore did not receive increased representation in the legislature until the adoption of the constitution of 1897. (*Debates and Proceedings of the Constitutional Convention of 1853*, pp. 180, 181, 187, 196, 197, 199; J. Thomas Scharf, *History of Delaware*, I, 315.)

¹⁷*Ibid.*, XI, 161, 162.

¹⁸*Delaware Gazette*, November 11, 1853, p. 2, col. 4.

¹⁹*Ibid.*, November 11, 1853, p. 3, col. 3.

²⁰This tendency appeared throughout the country during this period. The following may be listed as some of the most important factors that contributed to this change: the success already achieved in eliminating medieval punishments from the criminal codes, the general loss of faith in the efficacy of solitary confinement, the struggle to maintain prosperous prison industries in order to ward off effective opposition to established prison systems, the lack of any widespread vital interest in the prisoner as a reclaimable human being, the conviction held by many that prisoners should have work inflicted upon them as an additional penalty, and the general belief that regular work in prison exerted a reformative influence. (Blake McKelvey, *American Prisons*, pp. 38–46; O. F. Lewis, *The Development of American Prisons and Prison Customs, 1776–1845*, pp. 325–40; Enoch Wines and Theodore Dwight, *Prisons in the United States and Canada*, pp. 287, 288.)

²¹*Senate Journal, 1859*, pp. 15–17.

²²*Senate Journal, 1861*, p. 19.

²³*Senate Journal, 1866*, p. 32; *Senate Journal, 1867*, pp. 22–24; *Senate Journal, 1869*, p. 21; *House Journal, 1871*, pp. 21, 22.

²⁴*Delaware Republican*, March 14, 1861, p. 3, col. 1; *Delawarean*, June 18, 1859, p. 3, col. 3; *Senate Journal, 1867*, pp. 258–60, 319, 437, 452; *House Journal, 1837*, pp. 490, 573, 608, 611, 619; *House Journal, 1869*, pp. 159, 160; *Wilmington Daily Commercial*, January 6, 1871, p. 2, col. 1.

²⁵There was a tendency by the general public to use the terms "prison," "penitentiary," and "workhouse" interchangeably in referring to an institution where prisoners might be kept at work, the original meanings of these terms being unknown or disregarded.

²⁶*Wilmington Daily Commercial*, April 13, 1867, p. 2, col. 1.

²⁷*Ibid.*, November 7, 1867, p. 4, col. 1.

²⁸*Delawarean*, January 4, 1868, p. 1, col. 5. (This was quoted from the *Delaware Gazette*.)

²⁹*Wilmington Daily Commercial*, November 21, 1868, p. 4, col. 3.

³⁰*Ibid.*, November 24, 1868, p. 1, col. 2.

³¹*Delawarean*, December 7, 1872, p. 1, col. 2.

³²*Wilmington Daily Commercial*, November 22, 1873, p. 1, col. 6.

³³*Every Evening*, Wilmington, Delaware, May 20, 1873, p. 4, col. 2. (This criticism had appeared in the editorial columns of the *Philadelphia Press* of May 20, 1873, and was reprinted in the *Every Evening*, of Wilmington, on the same day.)

³⁴*The Docket of the New Castle County Court of Oyer and Terminer, May Term, 1873*, pp. 190, 191.

³⁵*Every Evening*, Wilmington, Delaware, June 14, 1873, p. 1, col. 6.

³⁶*The Docket of the New Castle County Court of General Sessions, November Term, 1865*, p. 54.

37*The Docket of the Kent County Court of Quarter Sessions, October Term, 1861,* pp. 3, 4.
38*The Docket of the Sussex County Court of General Sessions, October Term, 1865,* p. 348.
39*Delawarean,* May 27, 1876, p. 3, col. 2.
40*Ibid.,* December 2, 1876, p. 3, col. 2.
41*Wilmington Daily Commercial,* November 8, 1873, p. 4, col. 2; *Every Evening,* Wilmington, Delaware, November 8, 1873, p. 3, col. 1. The facts of the attempted robbery here presented have been derived from the issues of these newspapers published during November and December of 1873.
42*Wilmington Daily Commercial,* November 8, 1873, p. 1, col. 7.
43*Ibid.,* November 10, 1873, p. 1, cols. 2, 3, 4.
44*The Docket of the New Castle County Court of General Sessions, November Term, 1873,* pp. 485–87; *Wilmington Daily Commercial,* December 10, 1873, p. 2, col. 1.
45*Wilmington Daily Commercial,* December 9, 1873, p. 1, col. 1.
46*Ibid.,* December 10, 1873, p. 1, col. 4; *Every Evening,* Wilmington, Delaware, December 10, 1873, p. 3, cols. 4, 5.
47*Wilmington Daily Commercial,* December 11, 1873, p. 1, col. 2.
48*Ibid.,* December 10, 1873, p. 2, col. 1.
49*Every Evening,* Wilmington, Delaware, December 12, 1873, p. 4, col. 2. A summary of editorial comment by leading newspapers in New York, Pennsylvania, and Maryland, regarding the whipping of the bank burglars, was printed in this issue of the *Every Evening.*
50*Ibid.,* December 13, 1873, p. 2, col. 1.
51*Every Evening,* Wilmington, Delaware, January 3, 1874, p. 1, col. 4. (In an introductory paragraph, it was explained that this poem was from John Hill Martin's manuscript history of Chester and its vicinity.)
52*Laws of Delaware,* "Revised Code of 1852 As Amended in 1874," pp. 764–800. See Tables 1 and 2, Appendix A, for the list of crimes punishable with whipping in the code of 1874, together with the number of lashes prescribed for each crime.
53This had been accomplished by a law enacted on March 12, 1867. (*Laws of Delaware,* XIII, 160, 161.)
54This had been effected by the law of January 27, 1855, which had abolished whipping for white women convicted of larceny, and the law of March 12, 1867, which had made the punishment of all negro and mulatto criminals the same as that prescribed for white offenders. (*Laws of Delaware,* XI, 161, 162; XIII, 160, 161.)
55*House Journal, 1875,* pp. 285, 311, 427, 625, 649; *Senate Journal, 1875,* pp. 526, 629, 646, 712; *House Journal, 1877,* pp. 273, 334, 470, 550, 564, 565; *Senate Journal, 1877,* pp. 544, 545.
56*Senate Journal, 1877,* p. 19; *Senate Journal, 1879,* pp. 16, 17, 123, 124.
57*Senate Journal, 1881,* p. 20; *Every Evening,* Wilmington, Delaware, January 5, 1881, p. 2, col. 2. (A board of pardons was eventually provided for in Article VII of the Constitution of 1897. See "Journal of the Constitutional Convention of the State of Delaware," p. 563.)
58Blake McKelvey, *American Prisons,* pp. 8, 13, 14, 15, 16, 37.
59On February 26, 1879, the Delaware Society for the Prevention of Cruelty to Children was incorporated. Later this society, by an act approved on March 19, 1925, became the Children's Bureau of Delaware. (*Laws of Delaware,* XVI, 114–16; XXXIV, 394–99.)
60*Laws of Delaware,* XVII, 527.
61*Ibid.,* pp. 713–18; J. Thomas Scharf, *History of Delaware,* II, 893; C. Spencer Richardson, *Dependent, Delinquent and Defective Children of Delaware,* p. 4; *Laws of Delaware,* "Revised Code of 1852 As Amended in 1893," pp. 260, 261; *First Annual Report of the Delaware Industrial School for Girls, 1894,* pp. 2–6; *Report of the Delaware Woman's Christian Temperance Union, 1891,* p. 34.
62Delaware's Industrial School for Colored Girls was not opened until June 1920,

NOTES

and its establishment was made possible through the efforts of the Federation of Colored Women's Clubs of Delaware. It became a state-owned and operated institution by a law passed on April 7, 1921. (*Report of the Industrial School for Colored Girls of Delaware, December 1928*, p. 3; *Laws of Delaware*, XXXII, 465–72.)

63Howard M. Jenkins, "Live Wood in Our Whipping Post," *Lippincott Magazine*, XXIII, 364–74, March 1879.

64*Laws of Delaware*, XVIII, 948.

65The *House* and *Senate Journals* do not show how many votes were cast for and against this measure, but simply that the bill was passed.

66*Laws of Delaware*, "Revised Code of 1852 As Amended in 1874," p. 799.

67J. Thomas Scharf, *History of Delaware*, I, 609.

68*Ibid.*, p. 610.

69This penalty was abolished on February 13, 1883 (*Laws of Delaware*, XVII, 527).

70*Laws of Delaware*, "Revised Code of 1852 As Amended in 1893," pp. 922–88. See Tables 1 and 2, Appendix A, for a list of crimes punishable with whipping in the code of 1893, together with the number of lashes prescribed for each crime.

71*Ibid.*, p. 943; in the act of February 9, 1875, XV, 314.

72*Ibid.*, p. 939; in the act of March 25, 1879, XVI, 220, 221.

73*Ibid.*, p. 974; in the act of May 13, 1891, XIX, 513, 514.

74For a discussion of the movement to establish the New Castle County Workhouse and the history of this institution, see the author's *The New Castle County Workhouse*.

Chapter V

1*Delawarean*, July 19, 1899, p. 2, col. 2.

2*Delawarean*, May 19, 1900, p. 1, col. 3.

3*Morning News*, Wilmington, Delaware, January 21, 1901, p. 1, col. 5; *Delaware Gazette and State Journal*, January 24, 1901, p. 1, cols. 5, 6; *Every Evening*, Wilmington, Delaware, January 21, 1901, p. 4, cols. 1, 2.

4*Judge Lore's Scrapbooks*, in the Delaware Historical Society, Wilmington, Delaware.

5*Senate Journal, 1901*, p. 206.

6*Senate Journal, 1897*, p. 114.

7*House Journal, 1899*, p. 1138.

8*Senate Journal, 1901*, p. 206.

9Walter A. Powell, *A History of Delaware*, p. 327.

10*Senate Journal, 1901*, p. 206; *Every Evening*, Wilmington, Delaware, November 9, 1898, p. 1, col. 4; *Every Evening*, November 7, 1900, p. 3, cols. 3–7.

11*House Journal, 1901*, p. 533.

12*Delawarean*, February 2, 1901, p. 1, col. 6; February 9, 1901, p. 1, cols. 5, 6.

13*Laws of Delaware*, XXII, 493.

14*Delawarean*, February 2, 1901 (p. 1, col. 6), stated that this was the first time in fifty years that a bill providing for the whipping of women had been placed before the legislature.

15*Delawarean*, February 2, 1901, p. 1, col. 6.

16*Ibid.*

17*Ibid.*

18*Ibid.*

19*Delaware Gazette and State Journal*, June 13, 1901, p. 5, col. 4.

20*Ibid.*, November 28, 1901, p. 3, col. 7.

21*The Docket of the New Castle County Court of General Sessions, November Term, 1901*, pp. 467, 486, 493; *Delaware Gazette and State Journal*, November 28, 1901, p. 3, col. 7.

22*Delaware Gazette and State Journal*, November 28, 1901, p. 3, col. 7.

23David Ferris, *An Appeal to the Citizens of Delaware for the Abolishment of the Whipping Post*.

[24] *Senate Journal, 1905,* p. 383.
[25] *Delawarean,* March 18, 1905, p. 1, col. 5.
[26] *Morning News,* Wilmington, Delaware, March 17, 1905, p. 1, col. 3, p. 2, col. 1. In thus advocating the retention of the whipping post, Justice Lore was merely repeating an argument that had been advanced for many years by the newspapers of the state. See, for example, the *Delaware Gazette,* June 8, 1847, p. 2, col. 1.
[27] *House Journal, 1905,* p. 746.
[28] *Laws of Delaware,* XXIII, 458.
[29] Walter A. Powell, *A History of Delaware,* p. 331.
[30] *The Docket of the Court of General Sessions of New Castle County, February Term, 1905,* pp. 140, 148.
[31] *The Docket of the Court of General Sessions of Kent County, October Term, 1904,* p. 184.
[32] *The Docket of the Court of General Sessions of Sussex County, April and October Terms, 1904,* pp. 492, 493, 497, 502.
[33] *The Docket of the New Castle County Court of General Sessions, February Term, 1905,* pp. 140, 148.
[34] *The Docket of the New Castle County Court of General Sessions, May Term, 1904,* p. 478.
[35] *The Docket of the Kent County Court of General Sessions, October Term, 1904,* p. 184.
[36] *The Docket of the Sussex County Court of General Sessions, October Term, 1904,* p. 502.
[37] *Judge Lore's Scrapbooks,* in the Delaware Historical Society, Wilmington, Delaware.

Although deeply disappointed, David Ferris nevertheless continued his work for penal reform, and not long after the pillory had been eliminated from Delaware's penal code he published an appeal to the citizens of Delaware in which he urged them to abolish the whipping post. (See "An Appeal to the Citizens of Delaware for the Abolishment of the Whipping Post," by David Ferris.)

[38] *Laws of Delaware,* XXIII, 219, 220.
[39] Robert Graham Caldwell, *The New Castle County Workhouse,* pp. 82, 83, 214.
[40] *House Journal, 1907,* p. 138.
[41] *Senate Journal, 1907,* p. 211. In joint session, the Republicans had thirty-five members; and the Democrats, seventeen in the 1907 legislature. (Walter A. Powell, *A History of Delaware,* p. 334.)
[42] *Ninth Annual Report of the New Castle County Workhouse, 1907,* p. 5; *Every Evening,* Wilmington, Delaware, August 20, 1907, p. 2, col. 1.
[43] *Every Evening,* Wilmington, Delaware, August 19, 1907, p. 4, col. 2.
[44] *Every Evening,* Wilmington, Delaware, August 22, 1907, p. 4, cols. 1, 2.
[45] *Delawarean,* January 2, 1909, p. 3, col. 2.
[46] During its conference in 1909, the Delaware Woman's Christian Temperance Union, which for many years had worked for penal reform in the state, passed a resolution condemning the whipping post and calling for its abolition. (*Report of the Delaware Woman's Christian Temperance Union, 1909,* p. 128.)
[47] *The Docket of the Kent County Court of General Sessions, February Term, 1912,* pp. 439, 440, 441; *Sunday Star,* Wilmington, Delaware, March 3, 1912. It should be noted here that the sentence of seventy lashes given to Wright was ten lashes in excess of the number permitted by Delaware's criminal code. (*Laws of Delaware,* "Revised Code of 1852," p. 489.)
[48] *Sunday Star,* Wilmington, Delaware, March 3, 1912.
[49] *Ibid.*
[50] *Ibid.,* March 17, 1912.
[51] *Senate Journal, 1913,* p. 34.
[52] *Speech of the Honorable Franklin Brockson on Corporal Punishment in the State of Delaware,* made in the House of Representatives on November 14, 1913 (United States Printing Office).

NOTES

⁵³*Ibid.*, p. 16; *Every Evening*, Wilmington, Delaware, November 14, 1913, p. 1, col. 3.

⁵⁴*Congressional Record*, L, 5983-85.

⁵⁵While this controversy was being waged, Governor Miller of Delaware expressed himself in favor of the whipping post and declared that it kept crime at a minimum in the state. (*Literary Digest*, Vol. 47, December 6, 1913, p. 11, col. 2.)

⁵⁶Louis N. Robinson, *The Whipping Post in Delaware*, Friends' Social Service Series, Bulletin No. 5, Third Month, 1914, pp. 5-13.

⁵⁷*Ibid.*, pp. 13-39.

⁵⁸*Every Evening*, Wilmington, Delaware, January 28, 1915, p. 2, col. 3.

⁵⁹*Ibid.*, March 3, 1915, p. 2, col. 2.

⁶⁰*Ibid.*, March 4, 1915, p. 4, col. 2.

⁶¹*Ibid.*

⁶²*Report of the Organizing Committee of the General Service Board of Delaware Civic and Social Welfare*, p. 67.

⁶³*Laws of Delaware*, "Code of 1915," pp. 2057-2118. See Tables 1 and 2, Appendix A, for a list of crimes punishable with whipping in the code of 1915, together with the number of lashes prescribed for each crime.

⁶⁴*Ibid.*, "Code of 1915," p. 2070, in the act of April 3, 1905, XXXIII, 450.

⁶⁵*Ibid.*, p. 2062, in the act of February 22, 1901, XXII, 493.

⁶⁶*Ibid.*, p. 2089, in the act of April 7, 1903, XXII, 980.

⁶⁷*Every Evening*, Wilmington, Delaware, January 22, 1917, p. 2, col. 3.

⁶⁸*Ibid.*

⁶⁹*Ibid.*, January 23, 1917, p. 4, col. 2.

⁷⁰*Ibid.*, January 26, 1917, p. 4, col. 4.

⁷¹*Ibid.*, February 19, 1917, p. 1, col. 3.

⁷²*Ibid.*, February 26, 1917, p. 4, col. 1.

⁷³*House Journal, 1917*, pp. 151, 460, 516.

⁷⁴*Senate Journal, 1919*, p. 417. Two Republicans, Robertson of New Castle County and Short of Sussex County, supported the bill, and ten Republicans and five Democrats (five of whom were from Kent, four from Sussex, and six from New Castle County) voted against the measure. (*Every Evening*, Wilmington, Delaware, November 8, 1916, p. 9, col. 5; *Every Evening*, November 6, 1918, p. 3, cols. 2, 3.)

⁷⁵*Every Evening*, Wilmington, Delaware, March 3, 1919, p. 4, col. 1.

⁷⁶*Ibid.*, May 24, 1921, p. 13, cols. 1, 2, 3.

⁷⁷In this the warden was mistaken, because the law specifically required that the lashes be well laid on the bare back.

⁷⁸O. F. Lewis, "Delaware's Prison — A Paradox," *The Survey*, July 2, 1921, pp. 465-7.

⁷⁹Bailey Millard, "The Bloody Lash Versus Reform," *Technical World Magazine*, Volume XXI, April 1914, pp. 168-78.

⁸⁰*Sunday Star*, Wilmington, Delaware, February 18, 1923.

⁸¹*Ibid.*, January 5, 1923, p. 6, col. 5.

⁸²*Senate Journal, 1923*, pp. 115, 523, 545; *Every Evening*, Wilmington, Delaware, March 29, 1923, p. 11, col. 2. Three Republicans and two Democrats cast their ballots for the bill, while eight Democrats and three Republicans opposed its passage. (*Every Evening*, Wilmington, Delaware, November 13, 1922, p. 1, col. 2.)

⁸³*House Journal, 1925*, pp. 465, 466.

⁸⁴*Every Evening*, Wilmington, Delaware, March 26, 1925, p. 2, col. 3.

⁸⁵*House Journal, 1925*, p. 495. There were twenty-one Republicans and fourteen Democrats in the House at the 1925 legislative session. (*Every Evening*, Wilmington, Delaware, November 6, 1924, p. 1, col. 1, p. 16, col. 3.)

⁸⁶*Boston Evening Transcript*, April 8, 1925.

⁸⁷*New York Times*, March 26, 1925, p. 1, col. 4.

⁸⁸*Every Evening*, Wilmington, Delaware, October 10, 1925, p. 6, cols. 4, 5.

⁸⁹*Laws of Delaware*, XXXIV, 504.

⁹⁰*Ibid.*, XVII, 527.

⁹¹*Ibid.*, XXXIV, 540, 541, in the law approved on April 15, 1925.

92*Ibid.*, XXXIV, 542, in the law approved on April 15, 1925.
93*House Journal, 1931*, pp. 213, 512, 523, 525, 565.
94*Ibid.*, p. 678.
95*Ibid.*
96*Philadelphia Inquirer*, March 19, 1931.
97*Ibid.*, April 4, 1932.
98*Evening Journal*, Wilmington, Delaware, September 1, 1931.
99*Laws of Delaware*, XXXVIII, 670, 671; Robert Graham Caldwell, *The New Castle County Workhouse*, pp. 170, 171.
100*Journal Every Evening*, Wilmington, Delaware, January 16, 1935, p. 8, col. 3.
101*Philadelphia Record*, January 20, 1935, p. 1, cols. 3, 4, p. 4, col. 1.
102*Ibid.*
103*Journal Every Evening*, Wilmington, Delaware, February 16, 1935, p. 2, cols. 2, 3.
104*Laws of Delaware*, XL, 858.
105*Journal Every Evening*, Wilmington, Delaware, January 26, 1935, p. 1, col. 3, p. 6, cols. 6, 7.
106*Laws of Delaware*, "Code of 1935," pp. 1047–80. (Burglary is defined by Delaware's law as breaking and entering into the dwelling of another in the nighttime, with intent to commit murder, rape, or arson of the first degree.) According to the law of March 15, 1917, life imprisonment instead of death may be given by the court, if it seems proper to do so, in all cases upon the recommendation of mercy by the jury when they render the verdict. See Tables 1 and 2, Appendix A, for the list of crimes punishable with whipping in the code of 1935, together with the number of lashes prescribed for each crime. See Appendix B for an enumeration of all penalties that, at the present time (December 31, 1945), may be imposed upon persons convicted of committing crimes punishable with whippings.
107By the law of April 18, 1935. (*Laws of Delaware*, "Code of 1935," p. 1050; XL, 855, 856.)
108By the law of April 15, 1925. (*Laws of Delaware*, "Code of 1935," p. 1056; XXXIV, 540, 541.)
109*Ibid.*, p. 542.
110By the law of April 7, 1925. (*Laws of Delaware*, "Code of 1935," p. 913; XXXIV, 504.)
111*Laws of Delaware*, "Code of 1935," p. 1077; XLIII, 963–66. (By the law of May 14, 1941, when the jail of Kent County was placed under the supervision of a warden instead of the sheriff, it became the duty of the warden to administer the whippings.)
112*Ibid.*, "Code of 1935," pp. 1073, 1074.
113*Journal Every Evening*, Wilmington, Delaware, April 16, 1937, p. 8, col. 2.
114*Ibid.*
115*Journal Every Evening*, Wilmington, Delaware, August 2, 1938, p. 8, col. 1.
116*Laws of Delaware*, XLII, 318, 319.
117The one exception to this was in that part of the law which referred to the breaking and entering into a dwelling house of another at night. Here the wording was changed from "with intent to commit any felony other than murder, rape, or arson of the first degree" to "with intent to commit any crime or misdemeanor other than murder, rape, or arson of the first degree."
118*Laws of Delaware*, XLIII, 1008–11.
119*Journal Every Evening*, Wilmington, Delaware, December 4, 1942, p. 1, col. 3.
120*The Docket of the New Castle County Court of General Sessions, May Term, 1943*, p. 349, *September Term, 1943*, p. 443, *November Term, 1943*, p. 49, *May Term, 1944*, pp. 228, 276, *November Term, 1944*, pp. 425, 427; *The Docket of the Kent County Court of General Sessions, February Term, 1943*, p. 18, *April Term, 1944*, p. 120; *The Docket of the Sussex County Court of General Sessions, June Term, 1943*, p. 279.
121*Journal Every Evening*, Wilmington, Delaware, February 9, 1945, p. 4, col. 1.
122William A. Vrooman, *Why Abolish the Whipping-Post?* (Reprinted from the *Sunday Star*, Wilmington, Delaware, March 4, 1945.)

NOTES

Chapter VI

[1] For a more complete discussion of these factors, see the author's *The Penitentiary Movement in Delaware, 1776 to 1829*, Chapter VI.

[2] Whipping was reintroduced into Maryland's criminal code as a penalty for wife-beating, but it has been seldom used.

[3] For an interpretative summary of the workhouse movement, see the author's *The New Castle County Workhouse*, pp. 225–42.

[4] Robert Graham Caldwell, *The New Castle County Workhouse*, p. 228.

[5] *Ibid.*, pp. 1, 2.

[6] *Ibid.*, p. 228.

[7] New Castle County was the home of almost all of the early Swedes, Dutch, and Finns in Delaware, and the great majority of the Quakers in the state settled there.

[8] The parentage statistics in the census of 1930 are shown here because these figures for Delaware's counties are not available in the census of 1940. However, the census of 1940 does contain an estimate, based on a five-percent sample, of the number of native whites of mixed or foreign parentage in the city of Wilmington. According to this estimate, Wilmington had about 70 per cent of the native whites of foreign or mixed parentage residing in Delaware. This indicates that there had not been any important shift in the distribution of this segment of the state's population since 1930, when about 74 per cent of Delaware's native whites of foreign or mixed parentage lived in Wilmington.

[9] Of the 26,974 persons classified as rural in Kent County, 12,978 lived on farms and 13,996 did not.

[10] Of the 44,550 persons classified as rural in Sussex County, 23,137 lived on farms and 21,413 did not.

[11] In 1940, New Castle County had 55,549, or 30.9 per cent of its total population of 179,562, classified as rural by the United States Census Bureau. Of the 55,549 persons classified as rural in New Castle County, 9,558 lived on farms and 45,991 did not.

[12] For a similar analysis of the 1930 census for Delaware, see the author's *The New Castle County Workhouse*, pp. 225–31.

[13] See the author's *The Penitentiary Movement in Delaware, 1776 to 1829* and *The New Castle County Workhouse*.

Chapter VII

[1] The data for this chapter were secured by a study of the police, court, and prison records of Delaware for this period.

[2] This does not represent 7,302 different individuals since some persons during this period were convicted more than once of crimes punishable with whipping.

[3] See Table 1, Appendix C.

[4] See Table 2, Appendix C.

[5] See Table 3, Appendix C.

[6] Of the 1,604 prisoners who were whipped in Delaware for the period 1900 to 1942, inclusive, 41.3 per cent were in the age group less than 26; 48.3 per cent, in the age group 26 to 50; and 2.5 per cent, in the age group over 50. The records did not show the ages of 7.9 per cent of these prisoners.

[7] See Table 4, Appendix C.

[8] *Laws of Delaware*, XLIII, 1008–11.

[9] See Table 2, Appendix C.

[10] All except 21 of the total 1,604 prisoners received all of their lashes at one time. Of these 21, 5 had been sentenced to twenty lashes; 4, to thirty lashes; and 12, to forty lashes. In each of these 21 cases, the whippings were divided into two parts, which were usually separated by one week.

[11] See Table 5, Appendix C.

[12] The penalty of restitution was eliminated from the punishment for larceny by the

law of February 14th, 1941 (*Laws of Delaware*, XLIII, 1008–11). However, from the beginning of 1932 until the passage of this law, the court records of Delaware (except in three cases tried in Sussex County) do not show the amounts of restitution to be paid by prisoners convicted of larceny. Inquiry brought the explanation that although the law still prescribed the payment of restitution in cases of larceny during these years, experience had shown that few prisoners could pay the amounts of money involved. It became customary, therefore, to omit the penalty of restitution from the sentence.

[13] The largest amount of restitution included in any sentence for larceny was $2,368, which was part of the penalty imposed upon a white man on two indictments ($278 on one and $2,090 on the other) in 1919 in New Castle County.

[14] In the analysis of these figures, it should be remembered that the use of the whipping post has been entirely within the discretionary powers of the courts of Delaware since April 1925.

[15] Of these 510 prisoners, 359 (204 whites, 149 negroes, and 6 of unknown race) were convicted in New Castle County; 66 (20 white and 46 negroes), in Kent County; and 85 (31 whites and 54 negroes), in Sussex County. Convictions among the 510 prisoners were divided as follows: 1 (a negro) was convicted of wife-beating; 2 (2 negroes), of assault to ravish; 1 (a white), of burning; 3 (2 whites and 1 negro), of assault to rob; 50 (12 whites and 38 negroes), of robbery; 113 (71 whites, 41 negroes and 1 of unknown race), of breaking and entering, with intent; 339 (169 whites, 165 negroes, and 5 of unknown race), of larceny; and 1 (a negro), of unlawfully obstructing railroad tracks. The age range in the total of 510 prisoners is indicated by the fact that 59.0 per cent were in the age group 17 to 25, inclusive; 23.5 per cent, in the age group 26 to 35, inclusive; 16.3 per cent, over 35; and 1.2 per cent, of unknown age. Of the 465 prisoners who were convicted of crimes for which they might have been whipped but were not, 64.5 per cent (52.8 per cent of the whites and 79.8 per cent of the negroes) were imprisoned, and 35.5 per cent (47.2 per cent of the whites and 20.2 per cent of the negroes) were placed on probation.

[16] The classification into major and minor crimes used in this chapter is the same as that used by the Bureau of Census in the compilation of its judicial statistics. Such crimes as murder, manslaughter, robbery, aggravated assault, burglary, larceny, embezzlement, receiving stolen property, forgery, counterfeiting, rape, commercialized vice, violation of the drug laws, bigamy, blackmail, kidnapping, and perjury are classified as major offenses; and such crimes as minor assault, nonsupport, violation of liquor laws, driving while intoxicated, disorderly conduct, vagrancy, and gambling, as minor offenses.

[17] Here again the incompleteness of the records of Kent and Sussex counties made it impossible to include the prisoners convicted in these counties of crimes for which they might have been whipped.

[18] *Laws of Delaware*, XXXIV, 540–42.

[19] *Ibid.*, XLIII, 1008–11.

[20] A total of 29 prisoners, of whom 22 were negroes, received their first whipping during the period 1940 to 1942, inclusive.

[21] Twenty-one of these prisoners had received their first lashes before 1920.

[22] During the period 1920 to 1942, inclusive, 349 different prisoners were whipped in New Castle County. Of these, 26.1 per cent were white, 47.0 per cent were in the age group less than 26 at the time of their first whipping, 96.8 per cent were American, and 73.9 per cent were either unskilled laborers or farm hands. The 349 different prisoners received 403 different sentences to whippings during the years 1920 to 1942, inclusive, and 81.1 per cent of these sentences were either for breaking and entering, with intent, or for larceny. Of the 403 sentences to whippings, 219 were for larceny; 108, for breaking and entering, with intent; 63, for robbery; 5, for wife-beating; 2, for assault to rape; 3, for assault to rob; 2, for unlawfully obstructing a railroad; and 1, for embezzlement.

[23] This part of the study was completed after the war, and the period analyzed was extended down to 1944 so as to include the more recent years.

NOTES

[24] Of these 516 prisoners, 73.7 per cent had been convicted of larceny; and 24.0 per cent, of breaking and entering, with intent.

[25] Of the 516 prisoners, 52.5 per cent were in the age group 17 to 25, inclusive; 27.3 per cent, in the age group 26 to 35, inclusive; 19.8 per cent, over 35; and .4 per cent, of unknown age.

[26] Of the 516 prisoners, 2 were of unknown race; 2, of unknown age; 6, of unknown nationality; and 14, of unknown occupation.

[27] When this part of the study was completed, data on the subsequent criminal careers of the whipped prisoners were available only to the end of 1942. The criminal careers of prisoners whipped for the first time after 1939 were not included so that in each case in the analysis, which was extended down to the end of 1942, there would be a minimum of three years between the first whipping and the conclusion of the study, during which time the effects of the lashes could be observed.

[28] This comparison was based upon an analysis of the types of offenses committed for which each whipped prisoner received his first whipping during the period 1928 to 1939, inclusive, and for which each unwhipped prisoner received his first punishment during the years 1928, 1932, 1936, and 1940.

[29] Here the comparison was based upon an analysis of the ages of the whipped prisoners at the time of their first whipping during the period 1928 to 1939, inclusive, and the ages of the unwhipped prisoners at the time of their first conviction during the years 1928, 1932, 1936, and 1940.

[30] If one of the 516 different unwhipped persons was convicted more than once during the years 1928, 1932, 1936, and 1940 of crimes for which he might have been whipped but instead was either imprisoned or placed on probation, all calculations regarding his characteristics and criminal career were computed as of the date of his first conviction during these four years.

[31] If a prisoner was whipped more than once during the period 1928 to 1939, inclusive, all calculations regarding his characteristics and criminal career were computed as of the date of his first whipping during this period.

[32] If one of the 516 different unwhipped prisoners was convicted more than once during the years 1928, 1932, 1936, and 1940, and after one conviction was placed on probation and after another was imprisoned, his classification as having been placed on probation or imprisoned depended upon which of these punishments was imposed first during these four years.

[33] Of the unwhipped prisoners who were placed on probation, 35.4 per cent of the whites and 48.5 per cent of the negroes were subsequently convicted of some crime, and 18.4 per cent of the whites and 21.2 per cent of the negroes were subsequently convicted of a major crime.

Of the unwhipped prisoners who were imprisoned, 63.2 per cent of the whites and 59.9 per cent of the negroes were subsequently convicted of some crime, and 36.8 per cent of the whites and 46.5 per cent of the negroes were subsequently convicted of some major crime.

[34] Of these, 71.2 per cent received their first whipping during the years 1928, 1932, 1936, and 1940 after having been found guilty of either breaking and entering, with intent, or larceny, 24.7 per cent were white, 39.7 per cent belonged to the age group less than 26 at the time of their first whipping during 1928, 1932, 1936, and 1940, 95.9 per cent were American, and 79.5 per cent were either unskilled laborers or farm hands. Prior to their first whipping during these four years, 82.2 per cent of these 73 prisoners (83.3 per cent of the whites and 81.8 per cent of the negroes) had already been convicted of some crime and 76.7 per cent (83.3 per cent of the whites and 74.5 per cent of the negroes) had already been convicted of some major crime.

[35] The payment of a fine and/or a forfeit, as well as the penalties of whipping and imprisonment, is prescribed by law for some crimes, but in many cases the fines and forfeits are never paid.

[36] It should be explained here, however, that only fourteen of the 516 different persons who were imprisoned during 1928, 1932, 1936, and 1940 had been whipped before their conviction and imprisonment during these four years.

Chapter VIII

[1] For a discussion of the values claimed for punishment in general, the reader is referred to such texts as the following: *New Horizons in Criminology*, by Harry Elmer Barnes and Negley K. Teeters, *Crime and Society*, by Nathaniel F. Cantor, *Criminology and Penology*, by John L. Gillin, *Criminology*, by Fred E. Haynes, *Principles of Criminology*, by Edwin H. Sutherland, and *Crime and Its Treatment*, by Arthur Evans Wood and John Barker Waite.

[2] Louis N. Robinson, "The Whipping Post in Delaware," *Friends' Social Service Series*, Bulletin No. 5, Third Month, 1914, pp. 6, 7; Harry Elmer Barnes and Negley K. Teeters, *New Horizons in Criminology*, pp. 391, 392; Edwin H. Sutherland, *Principles of Criminology*, pp. 356, 357, 375, 376, 377; Arthur Evans Wood and John Barker Waite, *Crime and Its Treatment*, pp. 346, 349, 350, 435, 454.

[3] Arthur Evans Wood and John Barker Waite, *Crime and Its Treatment*, pp. 346, 347.

[4] *Ibid.*, p. 454.

[5] Edwin H. Sutherland, *Principles of Criminology*, pp. 358, 359, 365, 366, 377.

[6] *Ibid.*, pp. 365, 366.

[7] Of the 1,604 prisoners whipped in Delaware during the period 1900 to 1942, inclusive, 29.7 per cent received sentences of less than one year; 62.0 per cent, sentences ranging from one year to less than five years; and 8.3 per cent, sentences of five years or more.

Of the 67 prisoners convicted in New Castle County in 1928 who might have been whipped but instead were imprisoned, 46.3 per cent were sentenced for less than one year; 52.2 per cent, for terms ranging from one year to less than five years; and 1.5 per cent, for five years or more.

Of the 62 prisoners convicted in New Castle County in 1940 who might have been whipped but instead were imprisoned, 69.4 per cent were sentenced for less than one year; 27.4 per cent, for terms ranging from one year to less than five years; and 3.2 per cent, for five years or more.

[8] Louis N. Robinson, "The Whipping Post in Delaware," *Friends' Social Service Series*, Bulletin No. 5, Third Month, 1914, pp. 7, 8.

[9] These crimes were: poisoning to murder, 60 lashes (1 prisoner); assault to ravish, 30 lashes (7 prisoners); perjury or subornation of perjury, 40 lashes (2 prisoners); and unlawfully and feloniously obstructing a railroad track, 20 lashes (2 prisoners).

[10] *Report of the Departmental Committee on Corporal Punishment*, p. 94. (This report was presented by the Secretary for the Home Department to the British Parliament, by command of the King, in March 1938.)

[11] *Journal Every Evening*, Wilmington, Delaware, April 16, 1937, p. 8, col. 2.

[12] *Report of the Departmental Committee on Corporal Punishment*, pp. 35–45.

[13] Edwin H. Sutherland, *Principles of Criminology*, pp. 360–63.

[14] *Ibid.*, pp. 362, 363.

[15] Harry Elmer Barnes and Negley K. Teeters, *New Horizons in Criminology*, p. 407; Edwin H. Sutherland, *Principles of Criminology*, pp. 364, 365.

[16] Edwin H. Sutherland, *Principles of Criminology*, pp. 363–65; Frank Tannenbaum, *Crime and the Community*, pp. 51–56.

[17] Edwin H. Sutherland, *Principles of Criminology*, p. 355.

[18] Harry Elmer Barnes and Negley K. Teeters, *New Horizons in Criminology*, pp. 173, 174, 392, 393, 394, 426, 427, 952, 957; Nathaniel F. Cantor, *Crime and Society*, pp. 183–87; Edwin H. Sutherland, *Principles of Criminology*, pp. 364–67; Arthur Evans Wood and John Barker Waite, *Crime and Its Treatment*, pp. 480, 484–86.

[19] Harry Elmer Barnes and Negley K. Teeters, *New Horizons in Criminology*, pp. 392, 393.

[20] Arthur Evans Wood and John Barker Waite, *Crime and Its Treatment*, p. 484.

[21] Harry Elmer Barnes and Negley K. Teeters, *New Horizons in Criminology*, p. 952.

[22] Arthur Evans Wood and John Barker Waite, *Crime and Its Treatment*, pp. 452,

453; Louis N. Robinson, "The Whipping Post in Delaware," *Friends' Social Service Series,* Bulletin No. 5, Third Month, 1914, p. 10; Edwin H. Sutherland, *Principles of Criminology,* pp. 364, 365.

[23] Edwin H. Sutherland, *Principles of Criminology,* p. 374.

[24] Arthur Evans Wood and John Barker Waite, *Crime and Its Treatment,* pp. 353, 354.

[25] Edwin H. Sutherland, *Principles of Criminology,* p. 371.

[26] These tables are based on statistics secured from the *Uniform Crime Reports* for the last quarter of 1940, published by the United States Department of Justice. The year 1940 was chosen because it was the last complete year during which the crime rates of the United States were free from the influence of our participation in the war.

[27] Certain crimes which are not punishable with whippings in Delaware, namely, burglary, attempted burglary, attempted robbery, some forms of breaking and entering, and some forms of larceny, are included in the four groups of offenses shown in Tables 3 and 4. The reader therefore should bear this in mind when trying to use them as a basis for comparing the deterrent influence of corporal punishment in Delaware with that of other forms of punishment employed in the other five states. However, even when allowance is made for this, the figures are still quite revealing.

[28] The figures for Table 5 were drawn from a report especially prepared for the author by the American Bankers Association.

[29] *Delaware Coast News,* February 17, 1933.

[30] *Report of the Departmental Committee on Corporal Punishment,* pp. 90, 91.

[31] Thorsten Sellin, Statistician for American Law Institute; *Uniform Crime Reports,* Issued by the Federal Bureau of Investigation, Washington, D.C.; Edwin H. Sutherland, *Principles of Criminology,* p. 585; Arthur E. Wood and John B. Waite, *Crime and Its Treatment,* pp. 353, 354; Harry Elmer Barnes and Negley K. Teeters, *New Horizons in Criminology,* pp. 77–120.

[32] Harry Elmer Barnes and Negley K. Teeters, *New Horizons in Criminology,* pp. 957–64; Edwin H. Sutherland, *Principles of Criminology,* pp. 371–73; Arthur Evans Wood and John Barker Waite, *Crime and Its Treatment,* pp. 439–42.

[33] Edwin H. Sutherland, *Principles of Criminology,* p. 355.

[34] *Ibid.,* p. 328.

[35] On the other hand, under a system of scientific treatment, a large number of criminals would not be imprisoned at all but would be kept under careful supervision in the community where, as a matter of fact, the ultimate adjustment of almost all criminals must take place.

[36] Edwin H. Sutherland, *Principles of Criminology,* pp. 375–77.

[37] *Ibid.,* pp. 374, 375.

[38] *Ibid.,* p. 378.

[39] Harry Elmer Barnes and Negley K. Teeters, *New Horizons in Criminology,* pp. 952, 953; Edwin H. Sutherland, *Principles of Criminology,* pp. 371–78; Arthur E. Wood and John B. Waite, *Crime and Its Treatment,* pp. 484–86.

Appendix A

TABLES SHOWING THE CRIMES PUNISHABLE WITH PUBLIC WHIPPINGS

In the Codes of the State of Delaware for 1829, 1852, 1874, 1893, 1915, and 1935

Table 1 — Crimes Punishable with Whipping in the Codes of the State of Delaware[a]

Crimes	1829[b] Number of lashes prescribed	1852[b] Number of lashes prescribed	1874 Number of lashes prescribed	1893 Number of lashes prescribed	1915 Number of lashes prescribed	1935[c] Number of lashes prescribed
Murder of the second degree	None	60	60	None	None	None
Malicious poisoning	60	60	60	60	60	60
Mayhem by lying in wait	60	30	30	30	30	30
Assault to ravish	60	30	30	30	30	30
Sodomy	60	None	None	None	None	None
Wife-beating	None	None	None	None	5 to 30 (At the discretion of the court)	5 to 30
Robbery	(1) Highway robbery or robbery in dwelling by force: 60 (2) Other robbery: 39	(1) Highway robbery or robbery in dwelling by force: 40 (2) Other robbery: 20	(1) Highway robbery or robbery in dwelling by force: 40 (2) Other robbery: 20	(1) Highway robbery or robbery in dwelling by force: 40 (2) Other robbery: 20	(1) Highway robbery or robbery in dwelling by force: 40 (2) Other robbery: 20	(1) First offense: Not more than 40 (2) Second offense: 40
Assault to rob	39	None	None	None	None	Not more than 20
Kidnapping	(Any free negro and carrying him into another state— first offense) 60	(Any free negro and carrying him into another state) 39	None	None	None	None
Burglary with explosives at night, no one in bldg.	None	None	None	None	15 to 25	15 to 25
Burglary with explosives at night, person in the bldg.	None	None	None	None	20 to 40	20 to 40

[a] The edition of laws published in 1797 was only a compilation.
[b] These were the lashes prescribed for whites and free negroes.
[c] The use of the whipping post was placed entirely within the discretionary powers of the court.

TABLE 1 (continued).—CRIMES PUNISHABLE WITH WHIPPING IN THE CODES OF THE STATE OF DELAWARE[a]

Crimes	1829[b] Number of lashes prescribed	1852[b] Number of lashes prescribed	1874 Number of lashes prescribed	1893 Number of lashes prescribed	1915 Number of lashes prescribed	1935[c] Number of lashes prescribed
Breaking and entering with felonious intent	(1) Where public records were kept: 39 (2) Other breaking and entering with felonious intent: 39	(1) A dwelling at night: 20 to 40 (2) Other breaking and entering with felonious intent: 20	(1) A dwelling at night: 20 to 40 (2) Other breaking and entering with felonious intent: 20	(1) A dwelling at night: 20 to 40 (2) Other breaking and entering with felonious intent: 20	(1) A dwelling at night: 20 to 40 (2) Other breaking and entering with felonious intent: 20	(1) A dwelling at night: 20 to 40 (2) Other breaking and entering with felonious intent: 20
Larceny of slave, horse, ass, or mule, or larceny by breaking a lock	39	20	20	20	20	20
Knowingly receiving a stolen slave, horse, ass, or mule	39	20	20	20	20	20
Bringing stolen horse, ass, or mule into state to sell it	39	20	20	20	20	20
Larceny of goods other than slave, horse, ass, or mule, or other than breaking a lock	(1) By whites: First offense — 21 Second offense — 39 (2) By free negroes: 21	(1) By whites: Not more than 20 (2) By free negroes: First offense — 12 to 39 Second offense — None	Not more than 20	Not more than 20	Not more than 20	Not more than 20
Knowingly receiving stolen goods other than slave, horse, ass, or mule	(1) By whites: First offense — 21 Second offense — 39 (2) By free negroes: 21	(1) By whites: None (2) By free negroes: First offense — 12 to 39 Second offense — None	None	None	None	None
Embezzlement by carrier or porter	None	None	None	Not more than 20	Not more than 20	Not more than 20

[a] The edition of laws published in 1797 was only a compilation.
[b] These were the lashes prescribed for whites and free negroes.
[c] The use of the whipping post was placed entirely within the discretionary powers of the court.

Crimes	1829[b] Number of lashes prescribed	1852[b] Number of lashes prescribed	1874 Number of lashes prescribed	1893 Number of lashes prescribed	1915 Number of lashes prescribed	1935[a] Number of lashes prescribed
Embezzlement by cashier, servant, or clerk	None	None	None	None	None	Not more than 20
Fraudulent misapplication of funds by executors, etc.	None	None	None	None	None	Not more than 10
Unlawfully obstructing railway	None	None	None	20	20	20
Burning other than arson	(1) Church, school, ship, mill, court house, or other bldg: Not more than 60 (2) Grain, wheat, lumber, coal, etc.: Not more than 39 (3) Attempted burning of any kind: Not more than 39	(1) Court house or other place where public records were kept: 60 (2) Another's vessel or building, or church, or school: Not more than 20	(1) Court house or other place where public records were kept: 60 (2) Another's vessel or building, or church, or school: Not more than 20	(1) Court house or other place where public records were kept: 60 (2) Another's vessel or building, or church, or school: Not more than 20	(1) Court house or other place where public records were kept: 60 (2) Another's vessel or building, or church, or school: Not more than 20	(1) Court house or other place where public records were kept: 60 (2) Another's vessel or building, or church, or school: Not more than 20
Showing false lights to wreck vessel	The same number of lashes as prescribed for grand larceny	39	39	39	39	39
Counterfeiting	39	39	39	39	39	39
Altering or destroying legislative bills or acts	None	None	None	10 to 30	10 to 30	10 to 30
Witchcraft or fortune telling	21	None	None	None	None	None
Perjury or subornation of perjury	None	None	None	None	40 (At the discretion of the court)	40
Not wearing convict's badge or jacket	10	10	10	None	None	None

[a] The edition of laws published in 1797 was only a compilation.
[b] These were the lashes prescribed for whites and free negroes.
[c] The use of the whipping post was placed entirely within the discretionary powers of the court.

TABLE 2 — CRIMES COMMITTED BY SLAVES PUNISHABLE WITH WHIPPING IN THE CODES OF THE STATE OF DELAWARE[a]

Crimes	1829 Number of lashes prescribed	1852 Number of lashes prescribed
Assault to murder	60	60
Malicious poisoning	60	60
Manslaughter	(1) Of the first degree: 40 to 60 (2) Of the second degree: 20 to 40	39
Assaulting a white woman with intent to rape	60	60
Mayhem by lying in wait	60	60
Robbery	60	60
Assault to rob	60	60
Breaking and entering with felonious intent	60	60
Burning other than arson	60	60
Larceny	20 to 40	30
Riot or unlawful assembly	10 to 40	20
Assault and battery	(1) Upon a white person: 10 to 40 (2) Upon a negro (if fine not paid): not more than 30	(1) Upon a white person: 20 (2) Upon a negro (at the discretion of court): 10
Carrying dangerous weapons without permission	10 to 40	20
All other felonies	30 to 60	30 to 60

[a] The edition of laws published in 1797 was only a compilation.

Appendix B

AN ENUMERATION OF CRIMES PUNISHABLE WITH PUBLIC WHIPPINGS

As of December 31, 1945, Together with Their Prescribed Penalties

PUBLIC whippings may be inflicted as a part of the punishment for male prisoners convicted of the following crimes, here listed with their prescribed penalties:

1. *Poisoning with intent to murder,* a felony, a fine of from $500 to $5,000, *60 lashes,* and imprisonment for not more than 4 years;[1]
2. *Maiming by lying in wait,* a felony, a fine of from $200 to $1,000, *30 lashes,* and imprisonment for not more than 4 years;[2]
3. *Assault with intent to ravish,* a felony, a fine of from $200 to $500, *30 lashes,* and imprisonment for not more than 10 years;[3]
4. *Wife-beating,* a misdemeanor, *not less than 5 nor more than 30 lashes,* and a fine or imprisonment;[4]
5. *Robbery,* a felony, a fine of not less than $500, imprisonment for from 3 to 25 years, and, for the first offense, *not more than 40 lashes,* and, for an offense other than the first, *40 lashes;*[5]
6. *Assault with intent to rob,* a felony, a fine of not less than $300, imprisonment for not less than 1 year and not more than 10 years, and *not more than 20 lashes;*[6]
7. *Burning a court house or office where public records are kept,* a felony, a fine of $1,000, *60 lashes,* and imprisonment for not more than 20 years;[7]
8. *Burning a vessel, mill, granary, church, school, etc.,* a felony, a fine of from $100 to $500, and in the case of destruction of private property, *not more than 20 lashes,* and imprisonment for not more than 10 years;[8]
9. *Burglary with explosives, in a building in which there is a human being, in the nighttime,* a felony, a fine of from $1,000 to $5,000, *not less than 20 nor more than 40 lashes,* and imprisonment for from 25 to 40 years;[9]
10. *Burglary with explosives, in a building in which there is no human being, in the nighttime,* a felony, a fine of from $500 to $2,000, *not less than 15 nor more than 25 lashes,* and imprisonment for from 10 to 20 years;[10]
11. *Breaking and entering a dwelling in the nighttime with intent to commit a crime other than murder, rape or arson of the first degree,* a felony, a fine of from $100 to $500, *not less than 20 nor more than 40 lashes,* and imprisonment for not more than 20 years;[11]
12. *Breaking and entering a dwelling in the daytime, with intent; entering by day or night without breaking, with intent; committing a crime in, and breaking out at night; breaking and entering warehouse, store, office, etc.,*

by night, with intent to commit larceny, a felony, *20 lashes,* imprisonment for not more than 3 years, and in the case of larceny, restitution to the owner of twice the value of the property stolen, unless restored, and then in that case, the full value thereof;[12]

13. *Larceny of horse, ass, or mule, or larceny by breaking a lock,* a felony, a forfeit as restitution to the owner of twice the value of the property stolen, unless restored, and in that case the full value thereof, a fine of not more than $200, *20 lashes,* and imprisonment for not more than 5 years;[13]

14. *Bringing a stolen horse, ass, or mule into the state, and selling or attempting to sell it,* a fine of not more than $200, a forfeit as restitution of twice the value received to the buyer of the stolen property, *20 lashes,* and imprisonment for a term not exceeding 2 years;[14]

15. *Knowingly buying, receiving or concealing a stolen horse, ass, or mule,* a felony, a forfeit as restitution to the owner of twice the value of the stolen property, unless restored, and in that case the full value thereof, *20 lashes,* and imprisonment for not more than 1 year;[15]

16. *Grand larceny, other than that of a horse, ass, or mule, or by picking a lock,* a felony, *not more than 20 lashes,* and imprisonment for not more than 3 years;[16]

17. *Embezzlement by carrier or porter,* a felony, a forfeit as restitution to the owner of twice the value of the amount embezzled, unless restored, and in that case the full value thereof, *not more than 20 lashes,* and imprisonment for not more than 3 years;[17]

18. *Embezzlement by a cashier, servant or clerk,* a felony, *not more than 20 lashes,* and imprisonment for not more than 10 years;[18]

19. *Fraudulent misapplication or conversion of funds by executors, administrators, guardians, justices, constables or attorneys-at-law,* a felony, *not more than 10 lashes,* and imprisonment for from 1 to 5 years;[19]

20. *Making, or having in one's possession, plates, etc., for counterfeiting, or having unfinished counterfeit notes with the intention of completing them,* a felony, a fine of from $500 to $4,000, *39 lashes,* and imprisonment for not more than 2 years;[20]

21. *Willfully and feloniously showing false lights to cause a vessel to be wrecked,* a felony, a fine of not more than $500, imprisonment for 6 months, and *39 lashes;*[21]

22. *Unlawfully obstructing railway tracks so as to make them unsafe,* a felony, imprisonment for not more than 15 years, *20 lashes,* and in the discretion of the court, a fine of not more than $1,000;[22]

23. *Perjury or subornation of perjury,* a felony, a fine of from $500 to $2,000, imprisonment for from 1 to 10 years, and *40 lashes;*[23]

24. *Tampering with, altering or destroying legislative bills or acts,* a felony, a fine of from $100 to $5,000, costs of prosecution, *not less than 10 nor more than 30 lashes,* and imprisonment for from 1 to 10 years.[24]

The penalty of whipping must be inflicted publicly with strokes well laid on the bare back. In New Castle County, the whippings must be administered by the board of trustees of the New Castle County Workhouse through their keepers, officers, agents, and servants. In Kent and Sussex counties, the lashes must be applied by the warden of the jail. The law requires that the whipping post be located in or near the yard of the jail or workhouse of each of the three counties.[25]

APPENDIX B

Whenever corporal punishment is a part of the sentence, the day of its execution must be fixed by the court. If a person is convicted at the same term of the court on several indictments for crimes punishable with whipping, the court must so graduate the sentences of such a person that he will not be whipped with more than a combined total of sixty lashes under all sentences.[26]

NOTES

[1] *Laws of Delaware*, "Code of 1935," p. 1048.
[2] *Ibid.*
[3] *Ibid.*
[4] *Ibid.*, p. 1049.
[5] *Ibid.*, p. 1050.
[6] *Ibid.*
[7] *Ibid.*, p. 1052.
[8] *Ibid.*
[9] *Ibid.*, p. 1053.
[10] *Ibid.*
[11] *Ibid.*, XLII, 318, 319.
[12] *Ibid.*, XLII, 318, 319.
[13] *Ibid.*, p. 1054.
[14] *Ibid.*
[15] *Ibid.*
[16] *Ibid.*, pp. 1054, 1055. By a law enacted on February 14, 1941, larceny was divided into grand larceny (the theft of goods valued at $25 or upwards) and petty larceny, and the latter was no longer to be punishable with whipping. (*Laws of Delaware*, XLIII, 1008–11.)
[17] *Ibid.*, p. 1056.
[18] *Ibid.*
[19] *Ibid.*
[20] *Ibid.*, p. 1061.
[21] *Ibid.*, p. 897. If the death of any person is caused by the showing of such lights, the offender is to be deemed guilty of murder.
[22] *Ibid.*, pp. 846, 847. If any personal injury is caused by such an act, the offender is to be answerable as for like injury maliciously inflicted by any other means.
[23] *Ibid.*, p. 1062.
[24] *Ibid.*, p. 94.
[25] *Ibid.*, p. 1077; XLIII, 963–66. (By the law of May 14, 1941, when the jail of Kent County was placed under the supervision of a warden instead of the sheriff, it became the duty of the warden to administer the whippings.)
[26] *Ibid.*, "Code of 1935," pp. 1073, 1074.

Appendix C

TABLES ON WHIPPINGS IN DELAWARE

For the Period 1900 to 1942, Inclusive

TABLE I. PERCENTAGE OF CONVICTED PRISONERS WHIPPED — 1900 TO 1942, INCLUSIVE, BY YEAR, COUNTY, AND STATE

Years	New Castle County Prisoners convicted	New Castle County Prisoners whipped	%[a]	Kent County Prisoners convicted	Kent County Prisoners whipped	%[a]	Sussex County Prisoners convicted	Sussex County Prisoners whipped	%[a]	State of Delaware Prisoners convicted	State of Delaware Prisoners whipped	%[a]
1900	65	42	64.6	14	14	100.0	2	1	50.0	81	57	70.4
1901	94	57	60.6	15	11	73.3	6	3	50.0	115	71	61.7
1902	62	33	53.2	8	0	0.0	4	2	50.0	74	35	47.3
1903	80	43	53.8	11	6	54.5	6	3	50.0	97	52	53.6
1904	94	57	60.6	12	9	75.0	9	6	66.7	115	72	62.6
1905	79	51	64.6	9	7	77.8	11	9	81.8	99	67	67.7
1906	68	29	42.6	12	9	75.0	9	5	55.6	89	43	48.3
1907	51	24	47.1	12	4	33.3	4	2	50.0	67	30	44.8
1908	75	43	57.3	13	5	38.5	12	9	75.0	100	57	57.0
1909	81	43	53.1	13	9	69.2	12	4	33.3	106	56	52.8
1910	78	41	52.6	10	7	70.0	9	5	55.6	97	53	54.6
1911	65	27	41.5	10	5	50.0	10	3	30.0	85	35	41.2
1912	62	37	59.7	12	10	83.3	9	3	33.3	83	50	60.2
1913	119	58	48.7	6	0	0.0	15	2	13.3	140	60	42.9
1914	126	47	37.3	7	2	28.6	16	1	6.2 (16.7?)	139	50	36.0
1915	136	52	38.2	18	7	38.9	16	5	31.3	170	64	37.6
1916	128	49	38.3	14	3	21.4	22	4	18.2	164	56	34.1
1917	220	59	26.8	19	1	5.3	27	1	3.7	266	61	22.9
1918	223	38	17.0	9	0	0.0	21	0	0.0	253	38	15.0
1919	227	26	11.5	22	3	13.6	20	0	0.0	269	29	10.8
1920	114	8	7.0	24	2	8.3	19	2	10.5	157	12	7.6
1921	111	19	17.1	8	2	25.0	16	5	31.3	135	26	19.3
1922	80	25	31.3	9	3	33.3	8	1	12.5	97	29	29.9
1923	84	23	27.4	22	7	31.8	13	2	15.4	119	32	26.9
1924	105	23	21.9	16	5	31.3	3	0	0.0	124	28	22.6
1925	89	15	16.9	13	2	15.4	15	1	6.7	117	18	15.4
1926	66	14	21.2	15	2	13.3	23	10	43.5	104	26	25.0
1927	95	11	11.6	13	0	0.0	26	2	7.7	134	13	9.7
1928	104	11	10.6	19	6	31.6	26	2	7.7	149	19	12.8
1929	147	24	16.3	27	7	25.9	31	1	3.2	205	32	15.6
1930	178	23	12.9	17	6	35.3	37	6	16.2	232	35	15.1
1931	202	28	13.9	27	6	22.2	45	9	20.0	274	43	15.7
1932	179	23	12.8	25	4	16.0	54	8	14.8	258	35	13.6
1933	227	18	7.9	28	3	10.7	38	2	5.3	293	23	7.8
1934	228	14	6.1	35	4	11.4	50	5	10.0	313	23	7.3
1935	195	21	10.8	43	9	20.9	74	2	2.7	312	32	10.3
1936	183	21	11.5	21	5	23.8	56	5	8.9	260	31	11.9
1937	225	15	6.7	36	5	13.9	68	2	2.9	329	22	6.7
1938	233	23	9.9	40	3	7.5	51	6	11.8	324	32	9.9
1939	161	10	6.2	41	0	0.0	45	2	4.4	247	12	4.9
1940	141	21	14.9	38	1	2.6	41	5	12.2	220	27	12.3
1941	127	8	6.3	13	0	0.0	30	2	6.7	170	10	5.9
1942	91	5	5.5	15	2	13.3	14	1	7.1	120	8	6.7
Totals	5498	1259	22.9	791	196	24.8	1013	149	14.7	7302	1604	22.0

[a] Percentage of Convicted Prisoners Whipped.

TABLE 2. PERCENTAGE OF CONVICTED PRISONERS WHIPPED — 1900 TO 1942, INCLUSIVE, BY YEAR AND OFFENSE PUNISHABLE WITH WHIPPING

Years	Robbery			Breaking and entering for crime			Larceny			Other offenses			Total offenses punishable with whipping		
	Prisoners convicted	Prisoners whipped	%[a]	Prisoners convicted	Prisoners whipped	%[a]	Prisoners convicted	Prisoners whipped	%[a]	Prisoners convicted	Prisoners whipped	%[a]	Prisoners convicted	Prisoners whipped	%[a]
1900	2	2	100.0	6	5	83.3	73	50	68.5	0	0	0.0	81	57	70.4
1901	1	1	100.0	18	14	77.8	95	55	57.9	1	1	100.0	115	71	61.7
1902	1	1	100.0	8	4	50.0	60	29	48.3	5	1	20.0	74	35	47.3
1903	6	5	83.3	11	6	54.5	77	38	49.4	3	3	100.0	97	52	53.6
1904	5	4	80.0	20	12	60.0	86	54	62.8	4	2	50.0	115	72	62.6
1905	10	8	80.0	11	10	90.9	71	49	69.0	7	0	0.0	99	67	67.7
1906	3	1	33.3	3	2	66.7	77	38	49.4	6	2	33.3	89	43	48.3
1907	3	3	100.0	3	3	100.0	61	25	41.0	1	0	0.0	67	30	44.8
1908	5	5	100.0	13	8	61.5	79	44	55.7	3	0	0.0	100	57	57.0
1909	3	2	66.7	29	13	44.8	71	39	54.9	3	1	33.3	106	56	52.8
1910	3	3	100.0	21	11	52.4	72	40	55.6	3	0	0.0	97	53	54.6
1911	1	1	100.0	12	8	66.7	68	26	38.2	4	0	0.0	85	35	41.2
1912	4	3	75.0	18	12	66.7	56	32	57.1	5	3	60.0	83	50	60.2
1913	4	4	100.0	25	13	52.0	100	41	41.0	11	2	18.2	140	60	42.9
1914	7	3	42.9	11	5	45.5	107	39	36.4	14	3	21.4	139	50	36.0
1915	14	12	85.7	30	10	33.3	120	40	33.3	6	2	33.3	170	64	37.6
1916	9	7	77.8	29	9	31.0	121	39	32.2	5	1	20.0	164	56	34.1
1917	22	14	63.6	25	6	24.0	207	39	16.9	12	6	50.0	266	61	22.9
1918	13	6	46.2	21	4	19.0	205	26	12.7	14	2	14.3	253	38	15.0
1919	23	12	52.2	28	2	7.1	208	15	7.2	10	0	0.0	269	29	10.8
1920	2	2	100.0	24	2	8.3	125	8	6.4	6	0	0.0	157	12	7.6
1921	9	5	55.6	34	5	14.7	90	15	16.7	2	1	50.0	135	26	19.3
1922	6	3	50.0	20	11	55.0	73	16	21.9	2	0	0.0	97	29	29.9
1923	3	1	33.3	22	5	22.7	89	24	27.0	3	0	0.0	119	32	26.9
1924	3	1	33.3	35	8	22.9	83	18	21.7	3	1	33.3	124	28	22.6
1925	3	3	100.0	22	5	22.7	87	10	11.5	5	0	0.0	117	18	15.4
1926	8	4	50.0	18	6	33.3	74	14	18.9	4	2	50.0	104	26	25.0
1927	2	2	100.0	27	3	11.1	102	8	7.8	3	0	0.0	134	13	9.7
1928	3	3	100.0	23	2	8.7	119	12	10.1	4	2	50.0	149	19	12.8
1929	11	6	54.5	35	6	17.1	148	18	12.2	11	2	18.2	205	32	15.6
1930	3	3	100.0	50	3	6.0	174	29	16.7	5	0	0.0	232	35	15.1
1931	2	2	100.0	52	6	11.5	212	34	16.0	8	1	12.5	274	43	15.7
1932	9	7	77.8	69	3	4.3	178	24	13.5	2	1	50.0	258	35	13.6
1933	4	4	100.0	62	6	9.7	218	13	6.0	9	0	0.0	293	23	7.8
1934	7	3	42.9	39	5	12.8	257	14	5.4	10	1	10.0	313	23	7.3
1935	1	0	0.0	64	17	26.6	239	15	6.3	8	0	0.0	312	32	10.3
1936	6	3	50.0	63	12	19.0	186	15	8.1	5	1	20.0	260	31	11.9
1937	8	2	25.0	66	4	6.1	249	14	5.6	6	2	33.3	329	22	6.7
1938	9	2	22.2	59	7	11.9	253	23	9.1	3	0	0.0	324	32	9.9
1939	7	0	0.0	40	5	12.5	196	7	3.6	4	0	0.0	247	12	4.9
1940	10	7	70.0	34	7	20.6	175	12	6.3	1	1	100.0	220	27	12.3
1941	21	6	28.6	47	2	4.3	99	1	1.0	3	1	33.3	170	10	5.9
1942	19	6	31.6	32	0	0.0	65	2	3.1	4	0	0.0	120	8	6.7
Totals	293	172	58.7	1279	287	22.4	5505	1100	20.0	225	45[b]	20.0	7302	1604	22.0

[a] Percentage of Convicted Prisoners Whipped.
[b] Poisoning to Murder, 1; Assault to Ravish, 7; Wife-beating, 9; Assault to Rob, 4; Perjury and Subornation of Perjury, 2; Burning or Embezzlement, 2; Unlawfully Ob...

128

Years	Robbery			Breaking and entering for crime			Larceny			Other offenses			Totals			
	White	Negro	Race unknown	Total	White	Negro	Race unknown	Total	White	Negro	Race unknown	Total	White	Negro	Race unknown	Total
	White	Negro	Race unknown	Total	White	Negro	Race unknown	Total	White	Negro	Race unknown	Total	White	Negro	Race unknown	Total
1900	2	0	0	2	1	0	4	5	4	8	38	50	0	0	0	0	7	8	42	57
1901	0	1	0	1	4	5	5	14	19	17	19	55	0	1	0	1	23	24	24	71
1902	0	1	0	1	1	5	--	4	14	14	1	29	0	1	0	1	14	19	2	35
1903	2	3	0	5	2	3	1	6	11	19	8	38	3	3	0	3	15	29	8	52
1904	0	4	1	5	1	4	4	12	14	33	7	54	0	3	0	3	15	45	12	72
1905	0	7	1	8	1	7	3	10	21	18	10	49	0	2	0	2	22	31	14	67
1906	1	1	0	2	0	6	1	3	13	16	9	38	0	0	0	0	13	19	11	43
1907	0	5	0	5	1	2	0	3	11	14	0	25	1	1	0	2	13	17	0	30
1908	3	5	0	8	4	4	0	8	15	29	0	44	1	0	0	1	19	38	0	57
1909	0	2	0	2	4	12	0	13	8	31	0	39	0	0	0	0	9	47	0	56
1910	1	2	0	3	2	9	0	11	10	30	0	40	0	0	0	0	12	41	0	53
1911	0	1	0	1	1	7	0	8	6	19	1	26	0	0	0	0	7	27	1	35
1912	1	3	0	3	2	8	0	12	10	22	0	32	0	2	1	3	13	37	0	50
1913	1	3	0	4	5	8	0	13	13	28	0	41	2	1	0	3	20	40	0	60
1914	1	8	0	3	0	5	0	5	10	29	0	39	1	2	0	3	12	38	0	50
1915	4	4	0	12	2	8	0	10	8	32	0	40	0	2	0	2	14	50	0	64
1916	3	4	0	7	5	4	0	9	11	27	1	39	1	1	0	1	19	36	1	56
1917	1	13	0	14	2	4	0	6	7	28	0	35	3	3	0	6	13	48	0	61
1918	1	5	0	6	0	4	0	4	6	20	0	26	1	3	0	2	8	30	0	38
1919	3	9	0	12	0	2	0	2	4	11	0	15	0	0	0	0	7	22	0	29
1920	0	2	0	2	1	1	0	2	1	7	0	8	0	0	0	0	2	10	0	12
1921	0	5	0	5	3	2	0	5	2	14	0	15	0	0	0	0	5	21	0	26
1922	0	2	0	2	1	10	0	11	4	14	0	16	0	0	0	0	5	26	0	29
1923	3	0	0	3	3	4	0	5	2	20	0	24	0	0	0	0	8	24	0	32
1924	1	2	0	3	1	6	0	8	0	17	1	18	2	0	0	2	3	24	1	28
1925	0	2	0	2	1	6	0	6	3	7	0	10	2	0	0	2	5	13	0	18
1926	0	4	0	4	0	6	0	6	2	12	0	14	0	0	0	0	4	22	0	26
1927	0	2	0	2	0	1	0	3	1	7	0	8	0	0	0	0	3	10	0	13
1928	0	3	0	3	2	2	0	6	2	10	0	12	2	0	0	2	4	15	0	19
1929	1	5	0	6	0	4	0	6	1	16	0	18	2	1	0	2	4	26	0	32
1930	0	3	0	3	3	2	0	3	6	23	0	29	0	0	0	0	7	28	0	35
1931	5	2	0	7	3	3	0	6	4	30	0	34	1	1	0	1	7	36	0	43
1932	0	4	0	4	0	6	0	6	3	21	0	24	0	0	0	0	9	26	0	35
1933	3	0	0	3	0	4	0	5	4	10	0	14	1	0	0	1	2	21	0	23
1934	0	0	0	0	1	9	0	17	4	13	0	15	1	0	0	1	9	14	0	23
1935	0	3	0	3	8	4	0	12	3	12	0	15	0	0	0	0	10	22	0	32
1936	0	2	0	2	1	11	0	4	3	12	0	15	1	1	0	1	5	26	0	31
1937	1	1	0	3	1	3	0	4	3	15	0	14	0	1	0	2	5	17	0	22
1938	1	0	0	2	4	3	0	7	8	6	0	23	0	0	0	0	13	19	0	32
1939	0	0	0	0	1	4	0	5	1	15	0	7	0	0	0	0	5	10	0	12
1940	2	5	0	7	3	4	0	7	1	6	0	12	0	0	0	1	6	21	0	27
1941	0	6	0	6	0	2	0	2	1	0	0	1	0	0	0	0	1	9	0	10
1942	1	5	0	6	0	0	0	0	1	0	0	2	0	0	0	0	2	6	0	8
Totals	38	133	1	172	71	198	18	287	271	734	95	1100	16	27	2	45[b]	396	1092	116	1604
%[a]				10.7				17.9				68.6				2.8	24.7	68.1	7.2	100.0

[a] Percentage of Total Whippings for Delaware.
[b] Poisoning to Murder, 1 Negro; Assault to Ravish, 2 Whites, 5 Negroes; Wife-beating, 9 Whites, 15 Negroes; Assault to Rob, 2 Whites, 2 Negroes; Perjury and Subornation of Perjury, 1 White, 1 Negro; Burning, 1 White, 2 Race Unknown; Embezzlement, 1 White, 1 Negro; Unlawfully Obstructing Railroad Tracks, 2 Negroes.

TABLE 4. INDIVIDUALS WHIPPED — 1900 TO 1942, INCLUSIVE, CLASSIFIED BY RACE AND THE NUMBER OF WHIPPINGS RECEIVED

Number of whippings	White		Negro		Race unknown		Total	
	No.	% of total whites	No.	% of total negroes	No.	% of total race unknown	No.	% of total persons whipped
1	292	85.6	710	81.2	98	93.3	1100	83.4
2	44	12.9	121	13.9	4	3.8	169	12.8
3	4	1.2	35	4.0	2	1.9	41	3.1
4	1	0.3	5	0.6	1	1.0	7	0.5
5	0	0.0	3	0.3	0	0.0	3	0.2
Totals	341	100.0	874	100.0	105	100.0	1320	100.0
% of total persons whipped	25.8		66.2		8.0		100.0	

TABLE 5. NEW CASTLE, KENT, AND SUSSEX COUNTY WHIPPINGS – 1900 TO 1942, INCLUSIVE, CLASSIFIED BY RACE OF THE PRISONERS WHIPPED AND THE NUMBER OF LASHES INFLICTED

Number of Lashes Inflicted	New Castle County					Kent County					Sussex County					Totals for Delaware						
	White	Negro	Race Unknown	Total		White	Negro	Race Unknown	Total		White	Negro	Race Unknown	Total		%[a]	Negro	%[a]	Race Unknown[b]	%	Total	%[d]
1	1	0	0	1		0	0	0	0		0	0	0	0		0.3	0	0.0	0	0.0	1	0.1
2	0	0	0	0		0	0	0	0		0	0	0	0		0.0	0	0.0	0	0.0	0	0.0
3	0	0	0	0		0	1	0	1		0	0	0	0		0.0	1	0.1	0	0.0	1	0.1
4	0	0	0	0		0	0	0	0		0	0	1	1		0.0	0	0.0	1	0.0	1	0.0
5	27	37	0	64		4	21	4	29		5	8	1	14		9.1	66	6.0	5	4.3	107	6.7
6	0	0	0	0		0	1	0	1		0	0	0	0		0.0	1	0.1	0	0.0	1	0.1
7	0	0	0	0		0	0	0	0		0	0	0	0		0.0	0	0.0	0	0.0	0	0.0
8	0	0	0	0		0	1	0	1		0	0	0	0		0.0	1	0.1	0	0.0	1	0.1
9	0	0	0	0		0	0	0	0		0	0	0	0		0.0	0	0.0	0	0.0	0	0.0
10	204	492	25	721		9	69	24	102		14	60	14	88		57.3	621	56.9	63	54.3	911	56.8
15	21	52	9	82		1	5	7	13		0	1	2	3		5.6	58	5.3	18	15.5	98	6.1
20	64	199	5	268		7	18	15	40		4	19	8	31		18.9	236	21.6	28	24.1	339	21.1
25	4	2	0	6		0	0	0	0		0	0	0	0		1.0	2	0.2	0	0.0	6	0.3
30	2	15	0	17		0	0	0	0		0	0	1	1		0.5	15	1.4	1	0.9	18	1.1
35	0	0	0	0		0	0	0	0		0	0	0	0		0.0	0	0.0	0	0.0	0	0.0
40	25	74	0	99		2	7	0	9		2	8	1	11		7.3	89	8.1	1	0.9	119	7.4
45	0	0	0	0		0	0	0	0		0	0	0	0		0.0	0	0.0	0	0.0	0	0.0
50	0	0	0	0		0	0	0	0		0	0	0	0		0.0	0	0.0	0	0.0	0	0.0
55	0	0	0	0		0	0	0	0		0	0	0	0		0.0	0	0.0	0	0.0	0	0.0
60	0	1	0	1		0	0	0	0		0	1	0	1		0.0	2	0.2	0	0.0	2	0.1
Total	348	872	39	1,259		23	123	50	196		25	97	27	149		100.0	1,092	100.0	116	100.0	1,604[e]	100.0

[a] Percentage of Total Whites Whipped.
[b] Percentage of Total Negroes Whipped.
[c] Percentage of Total Prisoners Whipped Whose Race Was Unknown.
[d] Percentage of Total Prisoners Whipped.
[e] All except 21 of the total 1,604 prisoners received all of their lashes at one time. Of these 21, 5 had been sentenced to twenty lashes; 4, to thirty lashes; and 12, to forty lashes. In each of these 21 cases, the whippings were divided into two parts, which were usually separated by one week.

BIBLIOGRAPHY

I. GENERAL REFERENCES AND GUIDES

Beers, D. G., *Atlas of the State of Delaware.* Philadelphia, 1868.
"Bibliography on Criminology and Penology," pp. 1056–70, Vol. 1, Appendix V of the Osborne Association, *Handbook of American Prisons and Reformatories.* New York, 1933.
Check List of Legislative Journals of States of the United States of America. Compiled by Grace E. Macdonald for the Public Document Clearing House Committee of the National Association of State Libraries, Oxford Press, Providence, Rhode Island, 1938. Delaware section, pp. 24–31, inc.
Culver, Dorothy C., *Bibliography of Crime and Criminal Justice, 1927–31.* New York, 1934.
Encyclopaedia of the Social Sciences. New York, 1930.
Harper's Book of Facts. "A Chronological List of the Events in the History of the State of Delaware," p. 223. Edited by C. T. Lewis, New York, 1895.
Hasse, Adelaide R., "Materials for a Bibliography of the Public Archives of the Thirteen Original States, Covering the Colonial Period and the State Period to 1789," *Annual Report of the American Historical Association for the Year 1906,* Vol. 2, for New York, pp. 354–89; New Jersey, pp. 390–412; Pennsylvania, pp. 412–44; Delaware, pp. 440–48; Maryland, pp. 448–68. Government Printing Office, Washington, D.C., 1908.
——*Index of Economic Material in Documents of the United States,* "Delaware, 1789–1904." Carnegie Institute of Washington, April, 1910.
Index to Legal Periodicals. 1908–, New York.
International Index to Periodicals. 1907–, New York.
Johnson, Amandus, "A Detailed Bibliography of Sources, Contemporary Accounts and Secondary Works," pp. 767–809 in Vol. 2, *Swedish Settlements on the Delaware.* Philadelphia, 1911.
Kuhlman, A. F. (Editor), *A Guide to Material on Crime and Criminal Justice.* New York, 1929.
New York Times Index. 1913–, New York.
Poole's Index to Periodical Literature. 1802–1906, 7 vols., Boston.
Public Affairs Information Service, Bulletin. 1915–, New York.
Reader's Guide to Periodical Literature. 1900–, New York.
Ryden, George H., *Bibliography of Delaware History.* University of Delaware, Newark, Delaware, 1927.
Sellin, Thorsten, "A Brief Guide to Penological Literature." *Annals of the American Academy of Political and Social Science,* 157:225–32, September, 1931.
——"Bibliography," *Journal of the American Institute of Criminal Law and Criminology,* Vol. 18, pp. 147–58, 295–318, 451–84, 629–39; Vol. 19, pp. 118–58, 290–320, 450–508, 656–91, May, 1927–February, 1929.
——and Shalloo, J. P., *A Bibliographical Manual for the Student of Criminology.* Philadelphia, 1935.
Social Science Abstracts. March, 1929–January, 1934.

BIBLIOGRAPHY 133

Union List of American Newspapers in the United States and Canada, 1821–1936. Edited by Winfred Gregory, New York, 1943.
United States Census Reports.
U.S. Attorney General's Advisory Committee on Crime, *Annotated Bibliography on Jails,* Washington, D.C., 1937, mimeographed.
U.S. Investigation Bureau, *Bibliography of Crime and Kindred Subjects,* Washington, D.C., 1937, mimeographed.
U.S. Library of Congress, Division of Bibliography, *List of Bibliographies on Crime and Criminals,* Washington, D.C., 1922, mimeographed.
U.S. Library of Congress, Division of Bibliography, *Select List of References on the Whipping Post,* Washington, D.C., 1914, typewritten.

II. PRIMARY SOURCES

A. LAWS AND PRINTED DOCUMENTS

Bayard, *Papers of James A., 1796–1815, Annual Reports,* American Historical Association, 1913, Vol. II, Washington, 1915, Elizabeth Donnan, Editor.
Congressional Record, House of Representatives, Vol. 50, pp. 5920–25, Speech of Representative Franklin Brockson of Delaware on "Corporal Punishment in the State of Delaware."
Congressional Record, House of Representatives, Vol. 50, pp. 5983–85, "Speech of Representative Evans, Montana, against the Whipping Post."
Debates and Proceedings of the Constitutional Convention of the State of Delaware, 1853. Reported by Richard Sutton, Dover, 1853.
Debates of the Delaware Convention for Revising the Constitution of the State, held at Dover, November, *1831.* Reported by William M. Gouge, Wilmington, 1831.[1]
"Delaware," *Colony and State Legislative Journals* (1739–1945).
Delaware State Constitutions, 1776, 1792, 1831, 1897.
Fernow, Berthold, *Documents Relating to the Colonial History of New York,* Vol. 12, *Documents Relating to the History of the Dutch and Swedish Settlements on the Delaware.* Albany, N.Y., 1877.
Governors' Register, "State of Delaware, 1674–1851." Compiled by H. C. Conrad. Published by the Public Archives Commission of Delaware, Wilmington, 1926.
Laws of Delaware, "Colony and State," 1700–1945.
Minutes of the Constitutional Convention of the Delaware State, November 29, 1791. Wilmington, 1792.
Minutes of the Council of the Delaware State, 1776–92, Historical Society of Delaware, Wilmington, 1887.
Minutes of the Council of the Delaware State, 1776–92; Corrections and Addenda, by H. C. Conrad, Public Archives Commission, Dover, 1928.
Minutes of the Delaware State Constitutional Convention, August, September, 1776 (original printed edition in the possession of Judge Richard Rodney, New Castle, Delaware).
Pennsylvania Archives, Second Series, Vol. 5 (1877) contains papers relating to the Colonies on the Delaware from 1614 to 1682; Vol. 7 (1878) contains papers relating to the Dutch and Swedish Settlements on the Delaware River; Vol. 8 (1878) and Vol. 9 (1880) contains list of officers of the colonies

on the Delaware and the Province of Pennsylvania, 1614–1776. Edited by J. B. Linn and W. H. Eglo, Harrisburg, 1874–93.
Records of the Court of New Castle on Delaware, 1676–81, published by the Colonial Society of Pennsylvania, Lancaster, Pa., 1904.
The Record of the Court of Upland in Pennsylvania, 1676–81, Historical Society of Pennsylvania, Philadelphia, 1860.
United States Revised Statutes, 1873–84, 2nd ed., Sec. 5327, p. 1035, "Special Act of 1839 Abolishing Pillory and the Whipping Post."

B. MANUSCRIPT DOCUMENTS

Deeds (Three) of Feoffment from the Duke of York to William Penn, August, 1682, for New Castle Town and Circle and Kent and Sussex Counties (in possession of the Delaware State Archives).
Grant of Three Lower Counties from Charles II to Duke of York, March, 1683 (in possession of the Delaware State Archives).
Legislative Papers, Bills Not Passed, from 1775 to 1850, Hall of Records, Dover.
Legislative Papers, Resolutions, from 1795 to 1850, Hall of Records, Dover.
Legislative Petitions, from 1775 to 1850, Hall of Records, Dover.
Legislative Reports, from 1775 to 1850, Hall of Records, Dover.
Levy Court Petitions; for New Castle County, Kent County, and Sussex County, Hall of Records, Dover.
Levy Court Proceedings; for New Castle County, Kent County, and Sussex County, Hall of Records, Dover.
Minutes of the Annual Meetings of the Prisoners' Aid Society, 1920–38 (in possession of the Prisoners' Aid Society of Delaware).
Minutes of the Convention at New Castle of the Delegates from the Three Lower Counties of Delaware. August 1, 2, 1774; Caesar Rodney, Chairman, to choose delegates to the first Continental Congress in Philadelphia, September 5, 1774. (Manuscript in the possession of the Archives Commission of Delaware.)
Minutes of the Council, 1776–92; published by the State of Delaware, 1886, and by the Historical Society of Delaware. (Original manuscript in the possession of the Archives Commission of Delaware.)
Minutes of the Proceedings of the Burgesses and Assistants of the Borough of Wilmington, Relating to the Public Affairs of the Corporation, September 8, 1771 to September 8, 1783, Hall of Records, Dover.
Treasurers' Accounts; for New Castle County, Kent County, Sussex County. Hall of Records, Dover.
Votes and Proceedings of the House of Assembly, 1738–39 and 1739–40. (Manuscript in the possession of the Archives Commission, Dover.)
Votes and Proceedings of the House of Assembly, 1740–41 and 1741–42. (Manuscript in the possession of the Archives Commission, Dover.)
Votes and Proceedings of the Legislative Council, 1788–89, October. (Manuscript in the possession of the Archives Commission, Dover.)

C. REPORTS

Delaware; Ferris Industrial School for Boys Reports (1886–1945).
Delaware; Industrial School for Colored Girls Reports (1922–45).
Delaware; Industrial School for Girls Reports (1894–1945).
Delaware; New Castle County Workhouse Reports (1899–1945).

BIBLIOGRAPHY

Delaware State Board of Charities Reports (1920–45).
Delaware State Board of Health Reports (1879–1945).
Delaware Woman's Christian Temperance Union Reports (1880–1929).
Judicial Criminal Statistics, United States Department of Commerce, Bureau of the Census, Washington, D.C.
Uniform Crime Reports for the United States and Its Possessions, Issued by the Federal Bureau of Investigation, United States Department of Justice, Washington, D.C.

D. NEWSPAPERS, PAMPHLETS, AND PERIODICALS

Delaware Register and Farmers' Magazine, 1838–39, Dover.
Newspapers:
American Watchman (semi-weekly), Wilmington (1814–21).
American Watchman and Delaware Advertiser (semi-weekly), Wilmington (1822–28).
American Watchman and Delaware Republican (semi-weekly), Wilmington (1809–12).
Baltimore Sun, Baltimore, Md. (1925).
Blue Hen's Chicken (weekly), Wilmington (1847–62).
Constitutionalist; The Defender of the Peoples' Rights (weekly) (1804).
Delawarean (weekly) (semi-weekly 1898, August 1900), Dover (1859–1906).
Delaware Abolitionist, Wilmington (1848).
Delaware and Eastern Shore Advertiser (semi-weekly), Wilmington (1796–99).
Delaware Gazette (weekly, February, 1820, semi-weekly after 1820), Wilmington (1815–31).
Delaware Sentinel (weekly), Dover (1855).
Delaware State Reporter (weekly), Dover (1854–56).
Delaware Statesman (weekly), Wilmington (1812).
Evening Journal, Wilmington (1889–1933).
Every Evening, Wilmington (1895–1933).
Journal Every Evening, Wilmington (1932–45).
Mirror of the Times (semi-weekly), Wilmington (1805–79).
Morning News (daily), Wilmington (1897–1945).
New York Times, New York (1925).
Philadelphia Inquirer, Philadelphia (1931).
Political Primer, a norm book for the Jacksonites (weekly), Dover (1828).
State Sentinel (weekly), Dover (1876–94).
Sunday Star, Wilmington (1904–45).
Sussex Journal (weekly), Georgetown, Delaware (1874).
Sussex News (weekly) (1853).
Wilmington Daily Commercial, Wilmington (1866–74).
Wilmington Daily Gazette (daily), Wilmington (1872–82).
Old Sussex Day (pamphlets), Wilmington Public Library, Wilmington (no date).
Plummer, Mordecai S., *The Last Public Address of*. Address was made to the New Century Club of New Castle, Delaware, on November 21, 1922. Board of Trustees, New Castle County Workhouse (no date).
Prison Leaflets, New Castle County Workhouse, Delaware. National Committee on Prisons and Prison Labor, New York, 1920.

E. MISCELLANEOUS

Judge Charles B. Lore, *Scrap Book,* Historical Society, Wilmington, Delaware. (His original scrapbook.)

III. SECONDARY SOURCES

A. GENERAL HISTORIES AND HISTORICAL ACCOUNTS RELATING TO DELAWARE

Bevan, Wilson L., *History of Delaware Past and Present.* New York, 1929.
Biographical and Genealogical History of Delaware. Chambersburg, Pa., 1899.
Bolles, A. S., *Pennsylvania Province and State.* Philadelphia and New York, 1899.
Conrad, Henry C., *History of the State of Delaware.* Wilmington, 1908.
Cooper, Alex B., *Fort Casimir,* the starting point in the history of New Castle in Delaware. Its location and history, 1651–71. Historical Society of Delaware, Wilmington, 1905.
deValinger, Jr., Leon, *The Development of Local Government in Delaware, 1638–82.* Wilmington, 1935.
Duke of York Record, 1646–79, printed by order of the general assembly of the State of Delaware, Wilmington, 1903.
Duke of York's Book of Laws, included in charter to William Penn and Laws of the Province of Pennsylvania, 1682–1700, published by the State of Pennsylvania. Harrisburg, Pa., 1879.
Fernow, Berthold, "New Netherland, or the Dutch in North America," Vol. IV, Chapter 8 of Justin Winsor's *Narrative and Critical History of America.* Boston and New York, 1884–89.
Ferris, Benjamin, *Original Settlements on the Delaware.* Wilmington, 1846.
Fisher, George P., *Recollections of Dover in 1824.* Edited by the Rev. Joseph Brown Turner, the Historical Society of Delaware, Wilmington, 1896.
Fisher, Sydney G., *The Making of Pennsylvania.* Philadelphia, 1896.
——*Pennsylvania Colony and Commonwealth.* Philadelphia, 1897.
——*The Quaker Colonies.* New Haven, Yale University Press, 1919.
Fiske, John, *The Dutch and Quaker Colonies in America.* New York, 1899.
Friends in Wilmington, 1738–1938. Compiled by Bicentennial Celebration Committee of Wilmington Friends Meeting, Wilmington, 1938.
Garber, John P., *Valley of the Delaware.* Philadelphia, 1934.
Hazard, Samuel, *Annals of Pennsylvania* (1609–82). Philadelphia, 1850.
Historical and Biographical Encyclopaedia of Delaware. Wilmington, 1882.
Historical and Biographical Papers of Delaware. Historical Society of Delaware, Wilmington, 1879.
History of Wilmington. Compiled by *Every Evening,* Wilmington, 1894.
Holcomb, Thomas, *Sketch of Early Ecclesiastical Affairs of New Castle, Delaware.* Wilmington, 1890.
Ingersoll, Robert, "Capital Punishment and the Whipping Post," *Interviews.* Dresden Edition, New York, 1907.
Janvier, Anne R. (Compiler), *Stories of Old New Castle.* New Castle, Delaware, 1930.
Johnson, Amandus, *The Swedes on the Delaware* (1638–64). The Swedish Colonial Society, Philadelphia, 1915.

——— *Swedish Settlements on the Delaware.* Reprint by the Swedish Colonial Society, Philadelphia, 1911.
Jones, Lester M., *Quakers in Action.* New York, 1929.
Jones, Rufus M., *The Quakers in America.* London, 1923.
Lincoln, Anna T., *Wilmington, Delaware, Three Centuries Under Four Flags* (1609–1937). Rutland, Vermont, 1937.
Montgomery, Elizabeth, *Reminiscence of Wilmington.* Philadelphia, 1851.
Myres, Albert C. (Editor), *Narratives of Early Pennsylvania, West Jersey and Delaware* (1630–1707). New York, 1912.
Osgood, H. L., *American Colonies in the 17th Century.* New York, 1904–07.
Powell, Walter A., *A History of Delaware.* Boston, 1928.
Root, Winfred T., *The Relations of Pennsylvania with the British Government* (1696–1765). Philadelphia, 1912.
Ryden, George H. (Editor), *Letters to and from Caesar Rodney.* Philadelphia, 1933.
Scharf, J. Thomas, *History of Delaware.* Philadelphia, 1888.
——— *History of Philadelphia.* Philadelphia, 1884.
Shepherd, William R., "A History of the Proprietary Government in Pennsylvania," Vol. VI, *Studies in Historical Economics and Public Law.* Columbia University, 1896, Chapter VI of Part II, pp. 322–50, relates to the Three Lower Counties; Chapter VII of Part I, pp. 117–46, is a very good account of the boundary dispute with Maryland.
Tanner, Edwin P., "The Province of New Jersey, 1664–1738," *Studies in History, Economics and Public Law,* Vol. 30. Columbia University, New York, 1908.
Turner, C. H. B., *Some Records of Sussex County.* Philadelphia, 1909.
Vincent, Francis, *A History of the State of Delaware.* Philadelphia, 1870.
Watson, John F., *Annals of Philadelphia and Pennsylvania.* Philadelphia, 1844.

B. CRIMINOLOGICAL AND PENOLOGICAL SOURCES

1. *Historical*

Andrews, William, *Old-Time Punishments.* London, 1899.
Barnes, Harry E., *The Evolution of Penology in Pennsylvania; A Study in American Social History.* Indianapolis, 1927.
——— "A History of the Penal, Reformatory, and Correctional Institutions of the State of New Jersey, Analytical and Documentary." Trenton, N.J., 1918. (Vol. 2 of the *Report of the Prison Inquiry Commission of the State of New Jersey,* 1917.)
——— *The Story of Punishment.* Boston, 1930.
Caldwell, Robert Graham, *The New Castle County Workhouse,* Greenbank, Delaware. Delaware Notes, Thirteenth Series, 1940.
——— *The Penitentiary Movement in Delaware, 1776 to 1829.* Delaware Historical Society, Wilmington, 1946.
Dickens, Charles, *American Notes* (1842). (Available from several American publishers.)
Dix, Dorothea, *Remarks on Prisons and Prison Discipline.* London, 1845.
Earle, Alice M., *Curious Punishments of Bygone Days.* New York, 1929.
Howard, John, *The State of the Prisons* (1777). New York, 1929.
Ives, George, *A History of Penal Methods.* New York, 1914.

Lewis, O. F., *The Development of American Prisons and Prison Customs* (1776–1845). The Prison Association of New York, 1922.
McKelvey, Blake, *American Prisons; a Study in American Social History Prior to 1915*. University of Chicago Press, Chicago, 1936.
Pike, L. O., *History of Crime in England*. London, 1873.
Robinson, Louis N., *Penology in the United States*. Philadelphia, 1932.
Sellin, Thorsten, "Imprisonment," *Encyclopaedia of the Social Sciences*, Vol. 7, pp. 616–19.
——"Penal Institutions," *Encyclopedia of Social Sciences*, Vol. 12, pp. 57–65.
Stephen, James F., *A History of the Criminal Law of England*. London, 1883.
Teeters, Negley K., *They Were in Prison*. Philadelphia, 1937.
Webb, Sidney and Beatrice, *English Prisons Under Local Government*. With a Preface by Bernard Shaw. New York, 1922.
Wilson, Margaret, *Crime of Punishment*. New York, 1931.
Wines, Frederick H., *Punishment and Reformation*. New York, 1919.
Wines, E. C. and Dwight, T. W., "Report on the Prisons and Reformatories of the United States and Canada." New York, *Assembly Doc. No. 5, 1867*, II, 314–36.

2. General

Barnes, Harry Elmer, and Shalloo, J. P., "Modern Theories of Criminology and Penology," in *Contemporary Social Theory* (edited by Harry E. Barnes, Howard Becker, and Frances Becker), pp. 688–753. New York, 1940.
——and Teeters, Negley K., *New Horizons in Criminology*. New York, 1943.
Cantor, Nathaniel, *Crime and Society*. New York, 1939.
Falk, Herbert A., *Corporal Punishment*. Bureau of Publications, Columbia University, New York, 1941.
Gault, Robert H., *Criminology*. New York, 1932.
Gillin, John L., *Criminology and Penology*. New York, 1945.
Glover, Edward, *The Psychopathology of Flogging*. Howard League, London (no date).
Haynes, Fred E., *Criminology*. New York, 1935.
Hentig, Hans von, *Punishment, Its Origin, Purpose and Psychology*. London, 1937.
——"The Limits of Deterrence," *The Howard Journal*, Volume V, No. 2, Autumn, 1938. Published by the Howard League for Penal Reform.
Lea, H. C., *Superstition and Force, Essays on the Wager of Law, the Wager of Battle, the Ordeal, Torture* (third edition). Philadelphia, 1878.
Lunden, Walter A., *Statistics on Crime*. Pittsburgh, Pa., 1942.
Morris, Albert, *Criminology*. New York, 1934.
Oppenheimer, Heinrich, *The Rationale of Punishment*. London, 1913.
Reckless, Walter C., *Criminal Behavior*. New York, 1940.
Rusche, Georg, and Kirchheimer, Otto, *Punishment and Social Structure*. Columbia University Press, New York, 1939.
Sellin, Thorsten, *Culture Conflict and Crime*. Social Science Research Council, New York, 1938.
Sutherland, Edwin H., *Principles of Criminology*. Philadelphia, 1939.
Taft, Donald, *Criminology*. New York, 1942.
Tannenbaum, Frank, *Crime and the Community*. Boston, 1938.

BIBLIOGRAPHY

Waller, Willard, "A Deterministic View of Criminal Responsibility," *Journal of Criminal Law and Criminology*, May, 1929, pp. 88–101.
Weber, C. O., "Pseudo-Science and the Problem of Criminal Responsibility," *Journal of Criminal Law and Criminology*, August, 1928, pp. 181–95.
Wood, Arthur E., and Waite, John Barker, *Crime and Its Treatment*. New York, 1941.

3. Periodicals and Society Publications

American Prison Associations, *Proceedings*. 135 East 15th Street, New York.
Journal of Criminal Law and Criminology. Northwestern University Press, Chicago, Ill.
Mental Hygiene (quarterly), and *Mental Hygiene Bulletin* (monthly). Published by the National Committee for Mental Hygiene, 1790 Broadway, New York City.
National Committee on Prisons and Prison Labor (irregular and miscellaneous publications and reports). 1108 Sixteenth St., N.W., Washington, D.C.
National Conference of Social Work, *Proceedings*. 82 North High Street, Columbus, Ohio.
National Probation Association, *Yearbook*. (Contains the Proceedings of the Annual Conference.) 1790 Broadway, New York City.
Pennsylvania Committee on Penal Affairs (irregular publications). 311 South Juniper Street, Philadelphia.
Probation, the official bulletin of the National Probation Association (five issues yearly). 1790 Broadway, New York City.
The Howard Journal. Published by The Howard League for Penal Reform, London.
The Prison Journal. Published quarterly by the Pennsylvania Prison Society, 311 South Juniper Street, Philadelphia.
The Social Work Yearbook, 1929 and 1933. Russell Sage Foundation, 130 E. 22nd Street, New York City.
The Survey. The Survey Associates, Inc., 112 East 19th Street, New York City.

4. Surveys and Reports — Delaware

Maxey, Chester C., *County Administration in the State of Delaware*. New York, 1919.
Report of the Organizing Committee of the General Service Board of Delaware; Civic and Social Welfare, 1915–16. Wilmington.

5. List of Selected Articles and Reports on Whipping

Baldwin, S. E., "The Restoration of Whipping as a Punishment for Crime," *The Green Bag*, 13:65 (1901).
Caldwell, Robert Graham, "The Deterrent Influence of Corporal Punishment upon Prisoners Who Have Been Whipped," *American Sociological Review*, Volume IX, No. 2, April, 1944.
"Corporal Punishment in the State of Delaware," speech of the Hon. Franklin Brockson of Delaware in the House of Representatives, November 14, 1913. Government Printing Office, Washington, D.C., 1913.
"Delaware Whipping Post," *The Literary Digest*, Vol. 47, p. 11, December 6, 1913.
Elliott, Byron K., "Philosophy of Punishment — Flogging," *Indiana Law Magazine*, 4:129.

Ferris, David, *An Appeal to the Citizens of Delaware for the Abolishment of the Whipping Post.* Wilmington, circa 1903.

Gerry, E. T., "Must We Have the Cat-o'-nine-tails?" *North American Review*, Vol. 160, March, 1895, pp. 318–24. New York (edited by Lloyd Bryce).

Gould, S. B., "Advantages of Whipping," *Once a Week*, 16:398.

Griffith, G. S., "Views on the Penal System of Delaware," Baltimore, 1892; 8 pages, No. 13, of a volume of pamphlets. Columbia University Library, N.Y.

Hochheimer, L., "The Whipping Post," *Popular Science Monthly*, 28:830.

Jenkins, H. M., "Live Wood in Our Whipping Post," *Lippincott Magazine*, Vol. 23, pp. 364–74, March, 1879.

Lee, Francis B., "The Whipping Post and Some of Its Uses," *New Jersey Law Journal*, 15:356.

Leonard, Priscilla, "Whipping Post in Delaware," *Outlook*, Vol. 53, pp. 55–6, January 11, 1896.

Lewis, O. F., "Delaware Prison a Paradox," *Survey*, Vol. 46, pp. 465–7, 1921.

Millard, Bailey, "Bloody Lash Versus Reform," *Technical World*, Vol. 21, pp. 168–78, April, 1914.

Miller, Bianca A., "Delaware's Abolition of the Whipping Post," *The Cosmopolitan*, Vol. 22, April, 1897, p. 661.

Monch, W. H. S., "Corporal Punishment and Crime," 17 *Medical Legal Journal*, 267 (1899).

Mowry, Duane, "Whipping, A Punishment for Crime," 13 *The Green Bag*, 553 (1901).

Powell, E. N., former President of the Kansas City Bar Association. "The Whip of Justice." Reprint from Kansas City Quill Club *Yearbook*, December, 1924.

Ralph, Julian, "Whipping Post," in *The Making of a Journalist*, p. 126. New York, 1903.

Report of the Departmental Committee on Corporal Punishment. Presented by the Secretary of State for the Home Department to Parliament by Command of His Majesty, March, 1938. Printed and Published by His Majesty's Stationery Office, London.

Sharp, F. C., "Study of the Popular Attitude Towards Retributive Punishment," *International Journal of Ethics*, 1910, pp. 341–57.

Smith, M. Hamblin, "Corporal Punishment for Cruelty," *The Howard Journal*, Volume IV, No. 1, 1934. Published by the Howard League for Penal Reform.

"The Whipping Post," *Public Opinion*, Vol. 26, p. 718 (June 8).

"The Whipping Post and the Pillory" (F. Watt), *New Republic*, Vol. 14, p. 687.

The Whipping Post in Delaware, Committee on Philanthropic Labor of Philadelphia Yearly Meeting of Friends, Friends' Social Service Series, Bulletin No. 5, Third Month, 1914.

"Whipping, Not a Cruel and Unusual Punishment," Annotated Case, *Criminal Law Magazine*, 4:401.

"Whipping Post and Pillory," Georgetown, Delaware, *Harper's Weekly*, Vol. 20, pp. 937–8, November 18, 1876.

"Workhouse vs. Whipping Post," *Outlook*, Vol. 61, p. 665 (March 25).

[1]Unless otherwise stated, Dover and Wilmington refer to Dover, Delaware and Wilmington, Delaware.

INDEX

A

Adultery, 7, 8
Altering, defacing, or destroying legislative bills or acts, 31, 121, 124
Andros, Sir Edward (Colonial Governor), 4
Arson, 4, 7, 8, 11, 14, 86
Assault and battery, 4, 5, 122
Assault to murder, 86, 93, 122
Assault to rape, 14, 119, 122, 123
Assault to rob, 54, 119, 122, 123

B

Badge of crime, 12, 14; see also Convict's jacket
Bank burglaries and holdups, 94–97
Bank robbers of 1873, Wilmington, 24–28, 33, 46, 47, 94, 95
Barnes, Harry Elmer, cited, 102, 104, 105, 116, 117
Bassett, Richard (Governor of Delaware), 13
Bastardy, 8, 9
Becker, Howard, cited, 104
Bedford, Gunning (Governor of Delaware), 11
Benefit of clergy, 8, 9, 12, 13, 104 (note 50), 105 (note 47)
Bennett, Caleb (Governor of Delaware), 16
Bestiality, 4, 9, 103 (note 18)
Bigamy, 5, 9
Billop, Captain Christopher, 6
Blasphemy, 4, 12
Branding, 5, 8, 9, 12, 14
Breaking and entering, 9, 14, 56, 95, 96, 112 (note 117), 120, 122–124
Bringing stolen horse, ass, or mule into state to sell it, 120, 124
British Committee on Corporal Punishment, 87, 98
Brockson, Franklin (U. S. Representative from Delaware), 43
Buck, Clayton D. (Governor of Delaware), 51
Buggery, 4, 8, 11
Burglary, 5, 8, 11, 14, 46, 54, 95, 96, 112 (note 106), 119, 123
Burton, William (Governor of Delaware), 19

C

Caldwell, Robert G., cited, 104, 109, 110, 112, 113
Cantor, Nathaniel F., cited, 116
Capital crimes:
 in Delaware's laws, 8, 9, 11, 12, 14, 54, 112 (note 106)
 in English laws, 4, 103 (note 18)
 in Quaker laws, 7
Carrying dangerous weapons, 122
Cat-o'-nine-tails, 2, 21, 30, 31
Causey, Peter F. (Governor of Delaware), 19
Charles II, King of England, 6
Comegys, Cornelius P. (Governor of Delaware), 16
Convict's jacket, 18, 31, 106 (Ch. IV, note 13), 109 (Ch. IV, note 69), 121
Cooper, William B. (Governor of Delaware), 17
Corporal punishment, 3–5, 7, 9–11, 13, 15–17, 29–33, 35, 36, 39, 42, 43, 50, 52, 55, 57, 59–61, 66–68, 76, 90, 97, 98, 100, 105 (note 48), 125; see also Branding, Mutilation, Pillory, Whipping
Counterfeiting, 11, 94, 121, 124
Crawford, Leonard (Warden of the New Castle County Workhouse), 41, 48, 55
Criminal codes, see Criminal legislation
Criminal legislation:
 in Delaware, 3–5, 7–9, 11–14, 17, 18, 29–31, 35, 37, 39, 46, 50–57, 67, 75, 76
 in Pennsylvania, 3–5, 7, 8, 13
Cross, Captain Richard F. (Warden of the New Castle County Workhouse), 46–48, 55

D

Delaware:
 divergence between Delaware and Pennsylvania in criminal legislation, 13, 59, 60
 first assembly in, 7
 geography of, 63, 64
 population of, 61–64
 union with Pennsylvania, 6, 7
 see also Criminal legislation, Jails, Workhouses
deValinger, Leon, cited, 102, 103
Dover, 5, 30, 63, 65
Drunkenness, 5, 12
Duke of York, 4–6, 9, 59
Dutch, 3, 102 (Ch. II, notes 2, 13), 113 (Ch. VI, note 7)

E

Embezzlement by carrier or porter, 31, 120, 124
Embezzlement by cashier, servant, or clerk, 51, 54, 75, 93, 121, 124
English, 3–9, 102 (Ch. II, notes 2, 5, 13)
Evans, John M. (U. S. Representative from Montana), 42, 43

F

Felonious burning, 93, 94, 121–123
Ferris, David, 33, 34, 38, 39, 110 (note 37)
Finns, 102 (Ch. II, note 13), 113 (Ch. VI, note 7)
Forgery, 4, 11, 86
Fornication, 4, 7–9

INDEX

Fort Casimir, 3
Fraudulent misapplication of funds by executors, etc., 51, 54, 75, 121, 124
Freedom of will, 90–92

G

Georgetown, 30, 106 (Ch. III, note 50)
Gillin, John L., cited, 116
"Great Law" of Penn, 7

H

Hall, David (Governor of Delaware), 13
Hall, John W. (Governor of Delaware), 29
Haslet, Joseph (Governor of Delaware), 13
Haynes, Fred E., cited, 116
Hazard, Samuel, cited, 102
Hendriks, Agnieta, 6
House of correction, 7, 13
Howard, John, cited, 104

I

Imprisonment, 3, 7, 11–13, 17; see also Criminal legislation
Incest, 9
Incorporated places in Delaware with population over 1,000 in 1940, 63
Irving, Washington, cited, 102
Ives, George, cited, 102

J

Jails, 3, 11, 26, 27, 30, 31, 39, 52, 60; see also Kent County jail, New Castle County jail, Sussex County jail

K

Kent County:
  conditions in, 59, 63–66
  conflict with New Castle County on penal reform, 13, 14, 31, 35, 37, 38, 59–61, 66, 67, 106 (Ch. IV, note 1), 107 (note 16)
  population of, 61, 62, 65, 67, 113 (Ch. VI, note 9)
Kent County court, 6, 15, 23, 38, 52
Kent County jail, 11, 30, 39, 52, 112 (note 111); see also Jails
Kidnapping, 4, 12, 14, 54, 119

L

Larceny, 5, 9, 12, 14, 56, 57, 67, 76, 93–96, 113 (Ch. VII, note 12), 120, 122, 124
Leach, Elmer J. (Warden of the New Castle County Workhouse), 49, 50, 52–55
Lewes, 5, 106 (Ch. III, note 50)
Lewis, O. F., cited, 104, 111
Lincoln, Anna T., cited, 103
Long Finn (Marcus Jacobson), 4
Lore, Charles B., 33, 34, 37–39, 67

M

Malicious poisoning, 14, 94, 119, 122, 123
Manslaughter, 8, 9, 11, 122
Mayhem, 8, 11, 14, 119, 122, 123
McKelvey, Blake, cited, 106, 108

Meserve, A. S. (Warden of the New Castle County Workhouse), 36, 40, 48, 55
Murder, 4, 7–9, 11, 12, 14, 54, 119
Mutilation, 5, 8, 9, 12–14

N

Nead, Benjamin M., cited, 103
Negro slaves, punishment prescribed for, 8, 9, 13, 122
New Castle, see Town of New Castle
New Castle County:
  conditions in, 59, 63–66
  conflict with Kent and Sussex on penal reform, 13, 14, 31, 35, 37–39, 60, 61, 66, 67, 106 (Ch. IV, note 1), 107 (note 16)
  population of, 61, 62, 64, 65, 113 (Ch. VI, note 11)
New Castle County court, 1, 6, 11, 15, 23, 38
New Castle County jail, 26, 27, 30, 31; see also Jails
New Castle County Workhouse, 1, 2, 31–33, 36, 39, 41, 46–50, 52–54, 61, 87

P

Pardoning power, 17, 29, 61, 108 (note 57)
Penitentiary movement, 10, 11, 13–19, 59, 60
Penitentiary system, 10, 11, 13–19, 59, 60, 104 (Ch. III, notes 3, 4); see also Penitentiary movement
Penn, William, 6, 7, 103 (notes 38, 48)
Pennewill, Simeon S. (Governor of Delaware), 41, 42
Perjury, 4, 46, 94, 121, 124
Philadelphia, 10, 15, 64, 95, 96
Philadelphia Society for Alleviating the Miseries of Public Prisons, 10, 60
Philosophy of punishment, 98–100
Pillory:
  abolishment of, 30, 37, 39, 46, 67
  abolishment of for women, 30
  county alignment on in legislature, 35, 37, 38
  crimes punishable with in laws of Delaware, 12–14, 17, 30, 50, 51, 61
  description of, 31, 36, 56
  emerges as a separate issue, 19, 29
  last prisoners punished with in Delaware, 38
  legislative bills to abolish, 34, 35, 37
  location of in Delaware, 5, 17, 30, 31, 36, 106 (Ch. III, note 50), 107 (note 15)
  party alignment on in legislature, 35, 38
  use of in colonial Delaware, 4, 5, 8
Plummer, Mordecai S. (Warden of the New Castle County Workhouse), 47, 48, 55, 111 (note 77)
Political parties in Delaware, 35, 38, 110 (note 41)
Powell, Walter A., cited, 103, 109, 110
Prisoners' Aid Society of Delaware, 57, 58
Public executions abolished, 106 (Ch. IV, note 10)

INDEX 143

Q

Quakers:
  criminal codes of, 4, 7, 59, 102 (Ch. II, note 11)
  influence on use of corporal punishment in Delaware, 4, 7, 10, 13, 33, 39, 43, 44, 46, 47, 49, 59–61, 66

R

Rape, 7, 8, 11, 13, 14, 54
Rationalism, 10
Receiving stolen property, 12, 14, 120, 124
Red Hannah, 1, 56, 102 (Ch. I, note 2)
Rehabilitation of prisoners, 90, 99
Riot or unlawful assembly, 122
Risingh, Johan, 3
Robbery, 5, 8, 11, 14, 93–96, 119, 122, 123
Robinson, Louis N., 43, 44, 46; cited, 111, 116, 117
Rodney, Richards, cited, 103

S

Saulsbury, Gove (Governor of Delaware), 19
Scharf, J. Thomas, cited, 102–104, 108, 109
Scientific treatment of criminals, 99–101
Sellin, Thorsten, cited, 102, 117
Servitude, 5, 8, 9, 12, 17, 106 (Ch. IV, note 12)
Shalloo, J. P., cited, 104
Shaw, George Bernard, 51, 52
Showing false lights to wreck a vessel, 121, 124
Sodomy, 8, 11, 14, 119
Stephen, James F., cited, 104
Stocks, 5, 12, 14
Subornation of perjury, 46, 94, 121, 124
Sussex County:
  conditions in, 59, 63–66
  conflict with New Castle County on penal reform, 13, 14, 31, 35, 37, 38, 59–61, 66, 67, 106 (Ch. IV, note 1), 107 (note 16)
  population of, 61, 62, 65, 67, 113 (Ch. VI, note 10)
Sussex County court, 15, 23, 38, 52
Sussex County jail, 30, 39, 52; *see also* Jails
Sutherland, Edwin H., cited, 102, 116, 117
Swedes, 3, 102 (Ch. II, notes 2, 13), 113 (Ch. VI, note 7)

T

Tannenbaum, Frank, cited, 116
Teeters, Negley K., cited, 104, 116, 117
Thomas, Charles (Governor of Delaware), 14
Town of New Castle, 1, 3, 5, 26, 27, 30, 63
Treadmill, 14
Treason, 4, 8, 9, 11, 14, 54

U

Unlawfully and feloniously obstructing railroad, 31, 121, 124

V

Vroman, William A., cited, 112

W

Waite, John Barker, cited, 116, 117
Wheatley, Thomas J. (Deputy Warden of the New Castle County Workhouse), 2
Whipping in Delaware:
  abolishment of for women, 17, 18, 29, 30, 57, 67, 108 (note 54)
  ages of prisoners punished with, 70, 77, 113 (Ch. VII, note 6), 114 (note 22), 115 (note 34)
  by whom administered, 55, 112 (note 111), 124
  cases of cited, 1–4, 6, 11, 15–27, 36, 37, 40–42, 53, 54, 57, 110 (note 47)
  county where sentence of imposed, 69, 70, 74–81, 87, 88, 127, 131
  crimes for which administered, 69, 70, 77, 79, 80, 114 (note 22), 115 (note 34), 128, 129
  crimes punishable with in laws of Delaware, 11–14, 17, 29, 31, 46, 51, 54, 56, 60, 67, 119–125
  criminal careers of prisoners punished with, 76–82, 87, 88, 115 (note 34)
  deterrent value of, 90–99
  economy of as a punishment, 85, 86
  first administered at the New Castle County Workhouse, 36
  instrument used in, 2, 30, 31
  last women punished with in Delaware, 22, 23
  law prohibiting photographing of, 53, 57, 67, 94
  length of sentence of prisoners punished with, 73, 80, 116 (note 7)
  maximum lashes allowed in one sentence, 17, 55, 125
  must be administered publicly, 55, 124
  nationalities of prisoners punished with, 70, 77, 80, 114 (note 22), 115 (note 34)
  negro's and poorman's punishment, 48, 49, 73–76, 80
  number of criminals punished with, 57, 69–71, 79, 86, 113 (Ch. VII, note 6), 114 (note 22), 127, 128
  number of criminals receiving more than one, 70, 80, 130
  number of lashes inflicted in, 73, 80, 86, 113 (Ch. VII, note 10), 131
  number of persons convicted of crimes punishable with, 69, 70, 79, 113 (Ch. VII, note 2), 114 (note 15), 127–131
  occupations of prisoners punished with, 70, 77, 80, 114 (note 22), 115 (note 34)
  placed within discretionary powers of court, 30, 50, 51, 57, 67
  procedure used in, 2
  race of prisoners punished with, 57, 70, 71, 73–81, 87, 114 (note 22), 115 (note 34), 129–131
  reformative value of, 86–90

INDEX

restitution on larceny indictments of prisoners punished with, 73, 80, 113 (Ch. VII, note 12), 114 (note 13)
retributive value of, 83, 84
social solidarity produced by, 84, 85
use of in colonial Delaware, 3–9
use of stiff arm in administering, 2, 55, 92, 93, 102 (Ch. I, note 4)
women punished with, 17, 18, 22, 23
youthful offenders punished with, 21, 22, 29, 30, 50, 51, 57

Whipping in England, Scotland, and Wales, 87, 98
Whipping in Maryland, 113 (Ch. VI, note 2)
Whipping post:
agitation against as part of penitentiary movement, 10, 13, 14, 59, 60
agitation by Quakers against, 33, 39, 43, 44, 46, 47, 49, 59, 61, 66
arguments for and against, 83–101
county alignment on in legislature, 40, 45, 49, 50
declining use of, 56, 57, 67
description of, 31, 36, 56
emerges as a separate issue, 19, 29, 60
fight against reaches U. S. Congress, 40, 42, 43
governors' statements on, 41, 51, 111 (note 55); *see also* Penitentiary movement
legislative bills to abolish, 34, 39, 40, 44, 45, 47, 49, 50, 57, 58, 61
legislative petitions on, 39, 40
legislative votes on bills to abolish, 40, 45, 49, 50
location of in Delaware, 5, 17, 30, 31, 36, 55, 106 (Ch. III, note 50), 107 (note 15), 124
newspaper and magazine criticism of, 16–22, 30, 32, 33, 40, 41, 45–51, 53, 55, 56, 61, 97
obstacles to abolishment of, 65–68
origins of in Delaware, 3
party alignment on in legislature, 110 (note 41), 111 (notes 74, 82, 85)
poem on, 28, 29
wardens' statements on, 40, 46–50, 52, 53, 55, 56; *see also* Whipping

Wife-beating, 35, 36, 46, 119, 123
Wilmington, 1, 24, 26, 33, 37, 39, 43–46, 66
population of, 61–65, 67, 95, 96, 113 (Ch. VI, note 8)
Wilson, Elwood H. (Warden of the New Castle County Workhouse), 2, 55, 56, 87, 88
Wines, Frederic H., 37; cited, 102
Witchcraft, 8, 14, 121
Wood, Arthur Evans, cited, 116, 117
Workhouse, 13, 19, 29, 31, 60, 107 (notes 20, 25)
Wright, Dick, 40–42, 110 (note 47)

"The Shortest Culprit"